Living a Motivated Life

Living a Motivated Life

A Memoir and Activities

By

Raymond J. Wlodkowski

BRILL SENSE

LEIDEN | BOSTON

Cover art: Painting by Daniel Phill

All chapters in this book have undergone peer review.

The Library of Congress Cataloging-in-Publication Data is available online at http://catalog.loc.gov

Typeface for the Latin, Greek, and Cyrillic scripts: "Brill". See and download: brill.com/brill-typeface.

ISBN 978-90-04-38832-1 (paperback)
ISBN 978-90-04-38833-8 (hardback)
ISBN 978-90-04-38834-5 (e-book)

Copyright 2019 by Koninklijke Brill NV, Leiden, The Netherlands.
Koninklijke Brill NV incorporates the imprints Brill, Brill Hes & De Graaf, Brill Nijhoff, Brill Rodopi, Brill Sense, Hotei Publishing, mentis Verlag, Verlag Ferdinand Schöningh and Wilhelm Fink Verlag.
All rights reserved. No part of this publication may be reproduced, translated, stored in a retrieval system, or transmitted in any form or by any means, electronic, mechanical, photocopying, recording or otherwise, without prior written permission from the publisher.
Authorization to photocopy items for internal or personal use is granted by Koninklijke Brill NV provided that the appropriate fees are paid directly to The Copyright Clearance Center, 222 Rosewood Drive, Suite 910, Danvers, MA 01923, USA. Fees are subject to change.

This book is printed on acid-free paper and produced in a sustainable manner.

For Margery

The most important motive for work in the school and in life is the pleasure in work, pleasure in its results, and the knowledge of the value of the result to the community.
    ALBERT EINSTEIN

Contents

Acknowledgements IX
About the Author X
Introduction XI

Prologue 1

PART 1
Memoir

1 Real Life Education 5

2 Sister Mary Desiderata 11

3 Having a Ball 16

4 Doing Duty 27

5 Lucking Out 35

6 Learning to Flow 43

7 Transformative Friendship 51

8 Teacher Newbie 58

9 Teaching Troubles 67

10 There Are Ways 81

11 Entering a Life of Study 94

12 Human Relations 102

13 Therapy Lessons 119

14 Adult Learning 130

15 Perspectives and Connections   139

16 Conversations of Respect   148

PART 2
Activities

17 An Overview of Intrinsic Motivation, Flow, and Vital Engagement   159

18 Transformative Learning: A Partner to Intrinsic Motivation throughout Life   165

19 Learning to Evoke and Sustain Intrinsic Motivation with Transformative Learning   171

Notes and References   179

Acknowledgements

When learning is vital, when teachers and learners create knowledge together, it exceeds craft and becomes a dimension in which people live and breathe as one. I want to gratefully acknowledge the colleagues, the learners, and the friends with whom I've had this experience. It has been life giving.

There is at least a touch of fanaticism and narcissism in writing a memoir. It involves taking your ideas seriously, using events from your own life to disclose them, and often years to write about them with emotions bordering on clinical anxiety. Friends showing serious interest in such a project gave me the confidence to consider making the idea of this memoir a reality. David Oliensis, Paul Krajniak, David Gardner, and Matthew Ginsberg-Jaeckle were among the first. It was a beginning I will always appreciate.

Once I believed there was merit in the conception of this book, I had to learn how to write a memoir. A result of more chance than wisdom, I went to StoryStudio and found an exceptional teacher, Nadine Kenney Johnstone, a memoirist and the author of *Of This Much I'm Sure: A Memoir*, her inspirational account of the risks she faced and overcame during in vitro fertilization. Thank you for your committed and vital mentoring and for being an example of what it is to be a writer.

I had consummate good fortune: finding a writing group with imagination, skill, honesty, and deep and sensitive caring. Every person a gift—Rob Constantine, Janie Gabbett, Julie Lambert, and Paula Mikrut. We assembled ourselves from Nadine's writing course and three years later we're still together. The insights, transitions, selections of characters and anecdotes, cohesion, humor, and genuineness of this book are significantly due to the in-depth feedback and commentary of these friends. I will always be grateful.

Then there's staying alive. Here I am due to Dr. Dennis Pessis discovering my cancer and Dr. Tim Kuzel keeping me going. My life has been tenderly and joyfully enriched by my wellness group at Gilda's Club in Chicago, and our fearless leader, Janet Aminoff. For the many friends and family whose prayers and fond wishes grace my life daily, thank you from my heart.

I want to extend my gratitude to John Bennett, acquisition editor at Brill Sense for his faith in this book and his calm guidance in its construction, to Mary Leonard for copyediting it with a light touch, and to Paula Mikrut for my rescue—her management of the layout and proofreading of the final manuscript in the last two weeks before it was due.

To be at peace while writing is an immeasurable bounty. For this serenity, I honor the love of my family, Margery, Matthew and Dan.

About the Author

Raymond Wlodkowski began his work in education as an elementary school teacher in the Detroit Public Schools. For the last forty years he has taught at universities throughout the United States and Canada with professorships at the University of Wisconsin-Milwaukee, Antioch University-Seattle, Regis University-Denver, and Edgewood College in Madison. He is the founding Executive Director of the Council for Accelerated Programs (CAP) and the former Director of the Center for the Study of Accelerated Learning at Regis University. He is a psychologist whose work encompasses adult motivation and learning, cultural diversity, and professional development. Dr. Wlodkowski lives in Chicago and conducts seminars for colleges and organizations throughout the world.

Recent books for which Dr. Wlodkowski shares authorship are *Enhancing Adult Motivation to Learn*, in its fourth edition and twice the recipient of the Phillip E. Frandson Award for Literature (1986 and 2009), *Diversity & Motivation*, winner of the 2010 Cyril O. Houle Award for Outstanding Literature in Adult Education, and *Teaching Intensive and Accelerated Courses*. His books have been translated into Spanish, Japanese, and Chinese. Dr. Wlodkowski has been the recipient of awards for teaching excellence at two universities and has also received the award for outstanding research from the Adult Higher Education Alliance. In October of 2012, he was inducted into the International Adult and Continuing Education Hall of Fame. He has worked extensively in video production, authoring six professional development programs including *Motivation to Learn*, winner of the Clarion Award from the Association of Women in Education for the best training and development program in 1991. His Ph.D. is in educational psychology from Wayne State University in Detroit.

Introduction

When I was 31, I asked myself a question, as much from doubt as from certainty: What if I took the ideas of the scholars I so admired as a psychologist and led an intrinsically motivated life? Now, from the vantage point of today, though I could not have been more serious then, it seems naïve of me to have determined this path with such commitment at a relatively young age. I still hear the echoes of the answers I gave myself, "Don't just teach it. Don't just practice it. Live it."

I don't think I ever told anyone that was my intention. For the person I was then, that declaration would have been too religious, too doctrinaire and too ideological. Yet I wanted something I could believe in, seriously study, and know so deeply that its nuances would continue to awaken me to its limitations as well as its advantages as a belief system for guiding my life. I would not use faith as an excuse to mask its weaknesses and inconsistencies. I thought I could be reasonable and justifiably scientific about understanding intrinsic motivation, advocating for it as a theory for learning, and, within my own life, following it as my true north to give energy and purpose to how I lived.

Every course I ever taught, every workshop I ever led, every speech I ever gave, I designed and delivered as close to an intrinsically motivating experience as I could imagine. Both for the participants as well as myself, this work has gone well.

What I see in this memoir, that I only vaguely realized before is that, professionally, intrinsic motivation as a way of being, where the behavior itself is its own reward, became an instinct as sure as sight for me. Because I could follow its principles, I never had a class or course that left me feeling blameful or hopeless. I knew time was on my side. There were questions I could ask to guide me at the next opportunity to teach. How am I showing respect for these students? What could be more relevant for these learners? What's the best and quickest way I can authentically demonstrate they are becoming more competent at something they value?

One of my most challenging groups of learners were teachers themselves. The audience most frequently interested in my work were administrators who thought their teachers "needed" motivation. Although I was clear I didn't give pep talks and I wasn't a motivational speaker, the subject of motivation drew their interest, and often I would present workshops to faculty who were skeptical, in conflict with their administration, and exhausted from the enormous challenges they faced in under-resourced schools and communities. These included programs among the rougher edges of cities including New Orleans, New York, Chicago, Milwaukee, Memphis, Buffalo, and Boston. On more than one occasion, I found out on the day of a planned meeting with teachers that they had called a strike vote the very morning of my arrival.

Nonetheless, I remained enthusiastic. I had a compass. Intrinsic motivation. The first principle was connection. The question: How could these teachers see me as one of them, a brother, not a judge or an outsider? There were many ways: sincerely asking questions about their circumstances, challenges, goals, and immediate hopes as professional educators; relating vignettes about my experiences as a teacher in Detroit; sharing incidents where I had unwittingly lost my temper with students; using visualizations of students who stumped their best intentions; and often just plain sharing our circumstances and why I believed I had something of value to offer. Then the door was open to many possibilities. I learned very quickly that the most important result of the first fifteen minutes with teachers was not that they liked me but that they took me seriously.

But the toughest of the tough were college faculty. My peers. It's like talking with your family when they don't agree with you. They know the questions to ask. They know when you may have faltered. And sometimes, the knives are out. I loved it. Truly. It was as close as I might come to an Olympian event. Often, there were professors present who would know the theories and research better than I did.

On one occasion, at an eastern university, things were not going well. The workshop had been mandated as part of a grant and the faculty clearly did not think they needed the program. I did not know these circumstances before I arrived. After an hour with the faculty, the air in the room felt like it had turned into a dull lead weight around everyone's neck, including mine. I knew the issue was the faculty's hostile attitude and I had to do something immediately or it would fester into indifference—the surest slayer of intrinsic motivation anywhere. So, I told the participants that I could tell the climate among us felt deadening and that I'd like to suggest an activity to offer us a better direction to make the workshop worth our commitment. A few mumbled okay and a few nodded their heads.

I passed out a set of 3x5 cards, one to each participant, with the following directions: "Without signing your name, please write what would have to happen in this workshop so that you would find it worthwhile and more interesting. Then I will collect the cards, shuffle them, and read each one aloud. Afterwards, we'll decide what to do next." I collected the cards and began reading them.

The first card said, "You have to make this workshop more specific to our subject areas." I thought to myself, "That's a reasonable idea." The second card said, "Divide us into small groups and let us redesign this program." I thought, "More difficult, but possible." The next card said, "A public hanging of the dean." I thought, "Oh, wow! What the...?"

But before I could think any further, there was a roar of laughter. I looked up to see the dean was laughing heartily as well. I smiled and suggested we take a break. It was as though we went from darkness to daylight in an instant. Energy lit the room and everyone began talking with each other. After the break, a faculty member suggested that we continue the program as planned. And by acclamation we did, quite successfully.

To this day, I don't know what the dynamics were among that faculty group that led to such an amazing shift in their mood and involvement. Humor? The exaggeration of a dark impulse? Political history? However, I do know the activity was sound because I followed the intrinsic motivation principle that it is the learners' perspective that has to be involved in the solution of any problem that affects them.

Sometimes I think of intrinsic motivation as a magic divining rod. If I trust and practice its principles, it will lead me to the water, the motivation every person has naturally within them as much as the earth has water beneath its ground, sometimes at a distance but always there. For teaching and learning with adults, I can honestly say that after 40 years of practicing and applying its principles, I don't know a better theory.

David Pink took the idea of intrinsic motivation and for most of his book, *Drive: The Surprising Truth about What Motivates Us,* applied it as a theory for innovation in business and corporate environments. I have used intrinsic motivation as a teacher and a learner with the added perspective of transformative learning to guide my life. As a means to make professional choices and to discern what to study next, intrinsic motivation and transformative learning have worked for me. Since graduation from college, the job changes I made were matters of will—from elementary school teacher to psychologist, to professor, to human relations specialist, to therapist, to adult educator, and now memoirist. All were chosen because I knew I could learn in those professions what I needed without having to force myself. The topics and work they offered pulled me along like a rolling marble on a downward slope. I'm 75 and slowing down a bit, but the energy I had for work and study across forty years was electric. Like there was a current out there I just had to plug into for the light.

I wish this way of life for everyone. I don't think being committed to an intrinsically motivated life means enormous success or status but it is fulfilling, interesting, and usually provides an economically decent living.[1] Connected to a value system that supports the notion of justice in pursuit of the common good, it contributes substantially. But untethered to a value system that is oriented toward peace, mercy, and the betterment of the rights of all people, it can be a destructive energy. Fighting, gambling, and narcissism at their core are often intrinsically motivating behaviors. In personal life and family matters, intrinsic motivation needs goals with boundaries and aspirations framed with a higher purpose.

The second part of this book provides an overview of intrinsic motivation and transformation theory with examples from the memoir in Part 1. It offers activities by which the reader or a teacher can facilitate greater awareness of intrinsic motivation and transformative learning in their own lives, promote this understanding among other adults, and use techniques of storytelling, non-fiction, and memoir to increase adult learners' agency to make intrinsically motivated learning and transformation a means to determine their own future.

As I wrote the memoir, looking back from ages 8 to 48, in every chapter I could see how I benefited from a system where my formally uneducated father could find employment with a living wage, benefits, and health care, and I could find a college with affordable tuition and housing at less than a third of my monthly paycheck. I was able to work continuously with contributions to a pension I now collect. Most of all, these economic conditions allowed me to dream and to make choices to fulfill those dreams with learning and work I cherished. I clearly saw how my choices benefited from an economic context supportive of intrinsic motivation and transformative learning.

As we develop, we need to realize and question the worth of our work for what it means for us and our society. I am grateful for where and how intrinsic motivation and transformative learning led me. This memoir is their testament. I have come to believe that if I do work I love, I never really finish. I stop. Usually I find a way to share it. Then I move on to what's next with confidence as well as doubt about what I've done. As I've grown older, I'm more welcoming of this uncertainty because I've learned that's where the challenge and the new learning are. At such moments, I can hear one my favorite quotations ringing true: To love something is to find it inexhaustible.

Learning is hope. Most of history is not so much finding a way out of the dark as much as it is learning a way into the light. The genesis of a cherished interest is usually an engrossing and successful learning experience that lasts over time. For those of us who teach, we are a medium to that possibility, and for those of us who learn, we can claim it as part of our being, a joy whose greatest value is its benevolent sharing.

Prologue

To this day, I'm not sure how I was able to do it. But there I was, standing alongside him. I knew I had about thirty seconds to say something. It didn't have to be profound. Yet I was scared because I knew I would never get this chance again. The light would turn green. The mass of college students leaving their classes would shove us across the street whether we wanted to move or not. Then there would be no chance to talk. A conversation would be impossible among a hundred jostling students intent on reaching their cars and buses as soon as possible.

I could say hello but what would I say after that? Three ancient history courses with this professor and I had never once talked with him in or out of class. The most I could muster was a nod toward him as we passed in the hallway. He would return my acknowledgement with a glance but not a smile. What did he think of me? I wasn't sure he even knew who I was.

He was so different from anyone I had ever encountered. Men in my neighborhood made their living in factories and wore blue work shirts and heavy khaki pants. The local businessmen and shop owners dressed with a shirt and tie but their clothes were simple. He came to every class in a sport coat, a tie, and a shirt with cufflinks. Cufflinks! The only time I ever wore them was when I was in a wedding party and everything I wore was on loan. He said things in class that surprised me, which sometimes I didn't quite understand but that many of the other students found fist-pounding hilarious. One comment he had said that I still thought about was, "Lyndon Johnson shouldn't be in the White House, he should be home in Texas eating an orange." He had a gift. He could make history come alive like scenes from a film. His classes overflowed with students sitting in window wells and quoting him over lunch and in their other classes. After President Kennedy was shot, he talked with us about the assassination of Julius Caesar. He explained how the Romans heard the news, panicked with fear and grief, and formed a vengeful mob causing the assassins to flee rather than bask in their liberation of Rome from a tyrant as powerful as Caesar. Who was Cassius today? Watch for Marc Antony. He will arrive, if not now, soon.

The light was still red. I took a breath, turned toward him and, as calmly as I possibly could, said, "Hello Dr. Hooper."

He turned, gently smiled and said, "Oh, hello Mr. Wlodkowski. Good to see you."

A pivotal moment with words coming from me that I would not have expected, "I'm not sure if you have the time, but would you like to get a cup of coffee? We could talk a bit. There's a lot from our courses I still think about." I had no idea what the last sentence meant but it seemed right and it held his gaze. Then the light changed and we were moving across Woodward Avenue. He looked down as we walked and I'm sure he was judging the wisdom of accepting my invitation. A few steps after we were beyond the intersection with the crowd dispersing he stopped and asked, "Where did you have in mind?"

I had nowhere in mind. But as Dr. Hooper would surely have approved, the gods were with me and when I looked up the street, I saw a local diner I had been to once before. I pointed it out, "Harry's might be a good spot. It's pretty quiet about now and the coffee's not bad."

"Okay, but I only have about a half an hour."

The half an hour turned into two hours. We talked easily, at first about the courses and his grading policy. Although his classes were filled to maximum enrollment, sixty students, he announced on the first day of each course that he gave only three A's. He said, "Excellence by nature and throughout history is sparse. I follow this maxim as well." As a student taking his first course, Hellenistic History, I was intimidated by such a standard. I received a B. By the second course, Roman History, I was challenged by his perspective and received a B+. There was only one course left, an elective, History of Greece. I took it, telling myself I wasn't trying for a better grade, but for the illumination and transformation his courses offered. But when I received an A, I kissed the page it was written on.

Our conversation took unexpected turns, from a discussion of Rome's wasteful, far-flung wars across the European continent to the U. S.'s growing involvement in Viet Nam. When I told him I had received my draft number, he told me he had been in the army.

"I was not a good soldier. I questioned everything, all the time. Can you imagine me marching in step with everyone else?" he laughed. "I'm lucky there's a university. I wouldn't fit in many other places. But I still believe in duty. It's what kept me going."

Then he asked me about myself and my family. I told him about my father, his immigration to the United States and his kidnapping by the Russian army during World War I. When I told him I once asked my father what surprised him most when he first came to this country and he answered, "Eating a banana," we both laughed. After Dr. Hooper asked me to call him Finley, I realized we had crossed another personal terrain, the possibility of friendship.

I found out he was born in Ontario, Canada. A few comments later and we were talking hockey. He was an avid fan of the game. That's when I took another risk, but a far better bet than my first one. My girlfriend's aunt was the ticket manager for the Detroit Red Wings and I knew I could get a couple of first-rate seats for a game. I told him about my good fortune and asked him if he would be my guest. He answered, "Only on one condition, you allow me to take you to dinner before the game."

I accepted, not realizing my entry into a culture of manners and ideas radically different from my own had already begun.

PART 1

Memoir

∵

CHAPTER 1

Real Life Education

Though emotionally significant, compared with my family's risks, the one I took to reach out to Finley was miniscule. My family had a history of taking chances. Much of what I learned about their forays into troublesome circumstances rife with difficult decisions was from the stories they told. As a young boy, I wanted to be with my elders when they gathered, to sit silently and to listen, never drawing attention to myself so they wouldn't notice me in the hope that my invisibility would allow them free rein to tell their tales as vividly and realistically as possible. Between the two of them, my parents had thirteen siblings and most of them had been through both world wars and the Depression. A short, dark-skinned brood, with dense wavy hair and broad necks, heavy hands, and eyes so deeply set the color of their irises evaded detection, they knew desperation. Some had been refugees and many had experienced combat, displacement, and an uncertain future where hunger and joblessness were counted in months and years. In the fall of 1914 at the outset of WWI, the Russian Army advanced into Austria. My father's village was one of many small enclaves in their path. In order to feed itself, the army took all livestock and harvested crops from each village. Nothing edible was left behind. My father reckoned his good fortune because a cow had been hidden in a neighbor's cellar and the potato crop had not been fully harvested. Until the summer of 1915, his family held starvation at bay on a diet of potatoes, milk, and water.

Their stories were not filled with bravado or tales of courage. My relatives understood that prolonged peril brings out the best and the worst in people. It seemed they used what they remembered to remind themselves of those they loved, what they learned, the total unpredictability of life, and to reflect on how much more difficult the world of their past was in comparison to the lives they led now. Their stories offered them psychological relief and buoyed their fortitude. It was as though they needed to remember their past pain in order to continue, to still be able to struggle, sacrifice, and risk.

Although my father had no formal education and could not write, he fluently spoke multiple languages including Polish, German, Romanian, Hungarian, and English. When we would go to Eastern Market in Detroit, an enclave for buying products from local farmers and artisans, most of whom were immigrants from Eastern and Southern Europe, my father could switch languages with ease, speaking in Romanian at an apple stand and buying potatoes from a Hungarian farmer in her language, then turning to bargain in Polish with another farmer for a better price for a quart of raspberries. He appreciated being complimented for his lingual dexterity but when asked how he had learned so many languages, his standard response was to knot his brow, hunch his shoulders, open both hands waist high and say, "I moved a lot."

Among my older relatives, immigration was a common bond. Their grandparents had been part of the Revolutions of 1848, one of the most widespread political upheavals in European history. In addition to France, most of the countries in central and southeastern Europe were involved. Across this region, loose coalitions from the middle-classes joined with peasants to rebel against the nobility and feudal structures that oppressed their lives. Tens of thousands of people died, many fled or were exiled, and food shortages lasted for decades. Over a period of eighty years, my father's family moved from Prussia to Poland to Austria to Romania, back to Austria and then left Europe to land at Nova Scotia, before immigrating to Michigan, and moving from there to Kansas and then back again to Michigan.

Stories about these travels abounded, with every tale affording a lesson for those who listened, like a wagging finger with a stern reminder for the adults and a moral for the young. Most of the stories were straightforward and followed a similar pattern: Here's the risk we took or had to take, here are the shocks and surprises we lived through, and here's what we learned. If there was a dominant theme, the one I grasped was: Things of your own making, bad or good, follow you, much further than you might imagine.

I had my favorites. The first was about my great-grandfather and the fact that Wlodkowski was not our real name. I found this out when I was eight. My father had an instinct for the theatrical. He liked to tell stories and build a scene, creating these small bits of tension in the context of where the tale was told. In this instance, at the end of what seemed to be a normal meal on a weekday night, my father placed his hands flat on our grey Formica table and with a nod to our mother, looked back and forth to my brother and me and said with a deep voice, "Let's go into the living room. There's something important I want to tell you." Although he made it sound as though we were walking into a cathedral, our house was about four hundred square feet and the living room was one step out of the dinette. I looked at my older brother, Richard. His face held no expression. He also had no idea what our father was going to say.

"Sit on the couch."

Since he had already taken the only chair in the room, it was obvious that if we didn't sit there, we would have to sit on the floor. But I didn't think pointing that out to him was a good idea. My father wouldn't hesitate to cuff my brother or me if he thought we were being "smart alecks." He had our attention.

"Wlodkowski is not your real name. If you ever want to change it, that's up to you. It would not offend me and you should know why. Your great-grandfather changed your real name, von Waldendorf to Wlodkowski. Your true name is a titled name. In the 1880s you could sell your title, which he did because he was a gambler and had many debts. To get some money to keep things going, he sold his title and fled to Romania to escape his debtors. He changed his name there to Wlodkowski so they couldn't track him down. I was born in Bukovina, Romania. At that time, it was a region with many small villages. There, we were very poor. Your great-grandfather was not a good provider. When we moved to Austria, to a small village outside of Vienna, things got better. We had a small piece of land. We could grow vegetables and keep a cow. But our family remained frightened about the debtors. There was always this feeling we might be caught and lose everything. When your grandmother and I came to Canada, we didn't give our real name because of this fear. We used Wlodkowski and that's why you still have this name, a name that's really not your own. You're getting older and I think you should know this."

I wasn't surprised by the story. To some extent, I don't think my mind at that young age could grasp the whole of what it meant. Also, my father had never spoken well of his grandfather and now I knew the reason why. What I felt was more like a huge transfusion of new blood, that there was more to me and my family than I knew. Yet, I didn't ask any questions of my father. I went and did my homework, like I did every night.

After I completed my graduate work, I did consider changing my name back to the original. I was a psychologist and many of the finest thinkers in the profession were German or Austrian—Freud, Jung, Fromm, Klein. The name did have a ring of authority to it. Who wrote that article? Dr. Raymond von Waldendorf! Now, who's going to argue with someone whose surname sounds so distinctive that he well might be a duke in addition to a sterling connoisseur of the mind? But Raymond Wlodkowski, that's another story. Most people can't pronounce the name. There isn't a word in the English language that begins with a *wl*. In every college course I took, when they called roll, I knew when they came to my name before they attempted to say it, not by alphabetical order, but by their hesitation—the double blink as they refocused their eyes to make sure they saw the name correctly, the clearing of their throats as they gave themselves an extra couple seconds to figure it out (because phonetically it just doesn't work), and then the garbled pronunciations: wala, wala, wala, koo, koow, ski. Raymond Walawalakoowski? Now, the devil in me took a little pleasure in this moment of professor insecurity but that's a cheap thrill and I quickly came to the rescue, raising my hand and saying, "I think that's me. Pronounce the W as though it were a V, and it's Vlod—rhymes with flood—kowski, Vlodkowski. Much easier to say that way. Thanks." Most faculty appreciated the assistance, but seldom tried to re-pronounce the name and moved quickly to the next student on the roll.

Yet, I never did change my name. My brother did. His name is Richard Walden. I've kidded him and said, "Nice, Richard. You took the Walden and left me the Dorf. I don't think I'm going to play that hand." For me, it's not an issue. With our history and our mother's family being directly descended from Poland, I feel Polish. Wistfully, I love the story and the possibilities, but not enough to have become a von Waldendorf.

Another story, powerful to this day, had to do with my mother. She was overly shy. Outside of our immediate family, she rarely spoke other than polite necessities such as "hello," "please," and "thank you." Modesty in dress and demeanor were paramount for her. Except for arguments with my father, she never raised her voice. If his badgering edged toward her limit, she would silently assemble her purse, put on her coat, and reach for her hat, at which point he would inevitably retreat to a more reasonable mood before she might walk out the door.

My mother constantly worried that the hem of her dress was too high (which it never was). We could not leave our house as a family without her asking about its height at least once. Then before we left, she made certain the curtains were drawn and the blinds were shut. Though we all objected and teased her, she taped paper across the minute window of our front door so "No one could peep inside our home."

She was the favorite of her nine siblings. Their affection for her was constant, the little things: making room for her at a table, patting her hand with a warm smile, making sure she had a drink, offering to help her in the kitchen. They did this for each other as well, but for my mother there was more affection in their manner and more pleasure in the deed. When her family argued, which was fairly often, usually about politics, union matters, or the Church, they would use her to diffuse the intensity of their differences. At the moment they started pointing fingers, slamming their hands on the armrests of chairs, and shouting, more than once I saw an uncle wrap an arm around her shoulders and say, "Let's ask Dottie, she knows best. Tell them I'm right, Dottie." She would smile with a look that said, "Not a word, not from me, you rascal." Since her reaction was expected, the anger would turn to laughter, and the tension would subside. She liked gossip and would listen with interest but not offer an opinion herself, except for a smile, an expression whose subtlety she used to convey emotions that ran from confusion to bliss.

Because my aunts were outgoing and cantankerous, I wondered about my mother's shyness. Of all the stories she told me, the one she told me most often offered the strongest insight about her tendency to be demure. At first, I heard it as a warning and later as a deeper lesson. When she was twelve, as she was running barefoot in a forest near her home in Boswell, a coal town in southwest

Pennsylvania, she stepped on a rusty nail that went through her foot. From this wound, she contracted gangrene. She came very close to losing her foot and the lower part of her left leg. Although she survived the accident, she was ill for nearly a year. Her story was not so much about the accident itself or her shock at seeing the rusty nail rising out of her foot still attached to the board below, but about being bedridden and often alone. A few months before her accident, her father, after years of being a coal miner, had finally saved enough money to open a small general store. Her mother was needed at the store and the only sister available to help at home was Mary. In my mother's devout Catholic family, Mary was special. Her dream was to be a nun. A lot had been prepared for her to enter a convent in September: the donation to the Felician Sisters, the clothing and supplies for her first year as a novitiate, and the revision of labor across the family. My mother's accident occurred in August and Mary could not go. She was needed at home to take care of my mother. My mother's rehabilitation extended from months into a year. Mary never entered the convent. She married my Uncle John, a tool and die maker, settled in Detroit, and had a child.

Although she knew she had told this story to me multiple times, she told it to me about once a year until I left home. I didn't remind her about the repetition. I liked the story and I liked the way my mother told it, without drama or many extra words, or interpretations like the meaning of sacrifice or what could have been. It was pure and real. She might show me her foot and the scar and how it was changing with time but that was it. The telling did something for both of us. I'm not sure what it was for her, except I knew it drew me closer to her, seeing her as a young girl, playful, alive, and then near death, the courses of her life and that of her sister's changed forever.

When she and my Aunt Mary were together, I would watch them especially when they talked about someone's illness or their own, in hopes of catching a reference to their personal history. They didn't bring it up. Partly because I don't think it was customary for them to say much about it to each other, like soldiers who saw battle together during a war. The most painful, the most difficult to understand lies in the past. Talking about it won't change it. But they were there, and I think I saw this memory rise between them in how they looked and touched, and what was in the air as they listened and cared.

As a young boy I realized money and work within my family had never been and probably would never be secure. Their stories across generations and locales spoke of constant risk, more often than not imposed upon them by circumstance, a swirl of fate, force, and family. This awareness did not worry me as much as it made me wonder. What had gotten them through this chaotic maze? Where did they get the tenacious energy to keep trying? Other than to sustain their clan, why did they do what they did? How could I best prepare myself?

What I didn't know was that their history, their stories, and these questions were laying a foundation which would prepare me for a lifetime of study, engaging a mystery where answered questions led to more unanswered questions, and a universe I would be eager to enter—the field of motivation and learning, the means humanity has always garnered to face the challenges of existence and a fulfilling life.

CHAPTER 2

Sister Mary Desiderata

When I trace back my first sensations of being motivated to learn in school: the delight of joy in a classroom, excited with anticipation by the thought of books and lessons, I'm eight years old in the early 50s. My teacher is Sister Mary Desiderata, a beauty in spirit with a young face, vibrant with energy. My heartbeat would quicken when she leaned near me to help me pronounce a word or pointed out a paragraph for me to begin reading. But that wasn't as often as I wished, because there were sixty of us in that room, two to a desk and sharing the same seat. Boys with boys, girls with girls, and most of us craving another moment with Sister D, as some called her, an affectionate irreverence never to be said in her presence.

Mischief with other boys was a constant temptation. There were two boys within arms' reach in front of me, two boys the same distance behind me, and one sitting next to me, his shoulder nearly touching mine. That's six boys within eighteen square feet. The desks were joined and screwed into wooden strips along the floor. I once saw a photo of a school slashed in half by a tornado, with desks like the ones we sat in, swept out, dangling in the air, but still intact. I warmed to that picture because it reminded me that I never feared anything when I was in school, except those who taught us. We didn't do fire drills or sit under our desks to fend off a nuclear attack. That was for the kids in public schools.

We had nuns with swagger. They knew those beads rattled when they quickly came up behind us. It was the prelude to being smacked across the head, jerked by your shirt collar, and whacked with a ruler, or possibly a pointer, if one were within a teacher's grip. "It's for your own good," was their mantra, an incantation endorsed by our parents and made necessary by us, kids in such close proximity that talking, poking, pushing, kidding, joking, making faces, and dropping stuff to start stuff was as natural as blinking and just about as frequent. Getting physical was the way our teachers toned this sort of thing down.

But not in Sister Desiderata's class. She didn't hit anyone, ever. I waited for it to happen, like expecting a trapeze artist to fall. She didn't. She was the only teacher in my first eight years of school who cast aside corporal punishment, or the threat of it, to maintain order. Once, a fight broke out between Billy Trunowski and Richard Urbanek. A real fight, with fists clenched and blows to the head and face. When it started, she was at the blackboard writing. In the third grade, a fight was the worst thing you could do in school. It was rare, and when this fight began, we were too stunned to jeer or shout. Sister D turned around horrified, the whites of her eyes highlighted by the starched ivory linen surrounding her face. We were as shocked as she was. It was silent, except for the sound of the two boys ramming each other with all their might.

Sister D ran toward them, her face as red as a rooster's comb. I focused on her. I had seen many boys fight but never in her presence and I knew instinctually this was a critical moment. It must have been the sound of those beads, because when she was about a foot away, they both stopped fighting; it was as though someone had pressed the pause button. She looked at each of them, one to the other again, and started laughing, a good hard hoot, so much so she slapped her knees. Billy and Richard didn't quite know what to do. Puffing from exhaustion, they wanly smiled and watched her, still waiting for the ax to fall. Then she said, "You look so silly. Sweaty and lost, like two little pigs in a trough. Now, go to the bathroom and clean up. And when you come back, no more monkey business. Got it?" The two boys nodded their heads gratefully because they knew with any other teacher they would have been slammed, their parents called, and suspended from school. Within less than two minutes, that was the end of any turmoil and things were back to normal. I knew what had just happened was remarkable, but to my young mind, I couldn't make any sense of it. I didn't recall this incident again until I was a teacher in an elementary school where I felt desperate to learn how to help students stop fighting.

As a teacher and a young psychologist, I returned to Sister Desiderata's classroom many times because I could remember that motivated learning could be a regular occurrence, an everyday matter of fact for most students, most of the time, most of the year. Based on my own experience, and well before high school, I knew such teaching might be rare, but not magical or beyond understanding.

It's difficult for me to remember Sister D's methods. From this age, I tend to remember incidents and emotions. What I'm positive about more than sixty years later, is how good it felt to learn in her class: the basics—reading, writing, and arithmetic. Her enthusiasm was palpable. Anything we had to learn was an opportunity, presented by her as a gift, and enjoyed by us as treasured knowledge or a coveted skill. She preceded changes in subject matter with awe and anticipation. When it was time for reading, a daily occurrence, she would go to her desk, look behind it where the books were out of our sightline, and begin to riff with comments like, "Ohhhh, there's something special here. Is it a mystery? A book about pets that everyone one of us would love to have? Or maybe it's a tale from long ago with goblins and ogres (her voice rising) vanquished by girls and boys just like you?!" I wasn't quite sure what the word "vanquish" meant but she had my attention and the attention of every boy and girl in our room without ever saying, "Please pay attention."

What I learned from Sister Desiderata was that motivation trumped discipline. You needed far less of the latter, if the former was in play. Her enthusiasm was essential to an atmosphere for breeding motivation. It infused everything with life. Even arithmetic was no exception. Almost every day she introduced this subject with the same question, "Know what time it is?" And like a single organism, we sat up, and choral responded, "It's board work time!" Then Sister would turn to the chalk board, writing a single problem for calculation: 644 divided by 4. When she asked, "Who would like to come up and do this problem?" all sixty of us raised our hands, waving them madly. I'd make deep guttural sounds from the pit of my stomach, shaking my arm like a jackhammer, and standing on one foot to make my hand appear above the rest. But so were all my friends. I'm not called. Yet, I'm still involved because I'm watching Margaret Mihalski, who has been selected, skipping to the chalkboard with a crinoline skirt dancing up and down with her. When she correctly calculated the answer, we were happy because that meant we were on to another round. The party could continue.

But what if Margaret's answer was wrong? That's where Sister Desiderata was masterful. She'd find a way to give Margaret, or any of us, some credit: "You're close. Just one digit off." Or, "Only missed it by a step. Thanks for helping us get on the right track. Now, who would like to help Margaret? She's giving us a chance to learn together." She was never patronizing. It was always, "We're here to learn. We help each other learn. And don't forget, the wrong answer is the right answer to another question."

As a third grader, I didn't know the word enthusiasm. I would have described Sister Desiderata as "peppy." Or, with "a sparkle in her eye" much of the time. Or, "She seems to really like teaching."

What I know now is that teacher enthusiasm is a cornerstone of motivating teaching. In programs I conduct, I often ask teachers to remember a motivating teacher they have had, someone who taught in a way that evoked their deep involvement and value for what they were learning. I ask them to remember what it was like to be in that classroom, course, or seminar; and to remember the feeling they had as they came in and as they left. I ask them to raise their hands if the teacher they remembered was enthusiastic about what she was teaching them. If I were to count all the people who did not raise their hands in the forty years I've done this activity, there would be fewer than fifty individuals. With groups as large as five hundred, it is the norm to have a unanimous show of hands.

For the rest of elementary and high school, I didn't have another teacher who was as consistently enthusiastic as Sister Desiderata was. I had some good teachers, skillful practitioners, but no one matched her eagerness to teach day in and day out. Some teachers had their moments. They would light up with a particular topic, the stories of Edgar Allen Poe, or the lives of American Plains

Indians, or quadratic equations, but far too much of the time it was, "Open your books and begin reading on page 42." That was it and there is no trouble remembering that many of my peers never did begin reading on page 42.

Yet, I knew instinctively a teacher's spirit for teaching mattered. I knew it like a rock is hard and water is wet. I knew it because when it wasn't there at a minimal level, the class was dismal. This awareness was especially so when I was an adolescent searching for some kind of meaning from adults and the way they lived so I could follow their example. I think I felt most vulnerable during my sophomore year of high school. My best friend's mother died from cancer. I came very close, a micrometer away, from losing the sight in my left eye, when a friend threw a crab apple at me and it shattered my glasses, piercing my iris with needle sharp shards. Soon after this accident, my father lost his job of thirty years as a machinist when Packard Motor Car went belly up on Grand Boulevard Avenue in Detroit. For some kids, and for a while I was one of them, school was the healthiest place you could be.

That same year, I was struggling to learn geometry and feeling the steady diminishment of my will and effort. That class was the first one of the day. It often set the tone for the rest of the periods that followed. When the teacher came in with a cart full of plastic circles, squares, and triangles, she looked listless, dispirited, and withdrawn, qualities her teaching often reflected. Bob Buziak, the boy next to me whose career in geometry was headed in the same direction as mine, dryly observed as he nodded toward her, "See what geometry can do to you." That was it! To my fifteen-year old brain, he was right. We could suffer the same fate. Though we both did poorly in geometry, we never felt bad about it. It's unavoidable: teachers are what they teach. Every student knows it.

The word *enthusiasm* originates from the Greek noun *enthousiasmos,* which in turn comes from the Greek verb *enthousiazein*, meaning "to be inspired or possessed by a god." Enthusiastic teachers are people who care about and value their subject matter. They teach it in a manner that expresses those feelings with the intent to encourage similar feelings in the student. Emotion, energy, and expressiveness are outwardly visible in their teaching.

When teachers care about a topic, they will be naturally inclined to be expressive about it. When teachers do not care about a topic, they will find it more difficult to produce feelings and gestures. They might be able to act out such expressions on occasion but to maintain such zeal is laborious. Without a source of inspiration, it's difficult to be inspirational. Encouraging students to value their subject is important as well. Otherwise, teachers could become so involved in their own emotions that they might teach for their own benefit rather than the benefit of their students. Arrogant teachers often display this shortsightedness.

Donald Cruickshank, an educational psychologist, and his colleagues, found that teachers who present materials with appropriate gestures and expressiveness will have students who achieve better on tests than will teachers who do not gesture, and instead read in a monotone, or generally behave in an unenthusiastic manner. Enthusiastic teaching has a powerful influence on student motivation for reasons both psychological and biological.[2]

Teachers at any level are advocates. They plead the cause of their subjects. Some lobby for math, some for writing, and some for science. Whatever the subject, the message is basically the same: "Learn it. It's worth it." Whenever people are urged to believe something, they perform a keen scan of the advocate, asking in effect, "What will my believing in this do for me?" If teachers cannot show by their energy and conviction that their subject has made a positive difference for them, students are forewarned. If they appear bored and listless with what they are asking students to learn, the students' response will be, "If that's what knowing this does for *you*, by all means, keep it away from *me*." That's survival. Bob Buziak was, in this respect, a wise young man. For most us, *how* something is said will take priority over *what* is said.

Teachers are potent models. Numerous studies in psychology and neuroscience have demonstrated that when people focus on other people, they tend to embody their emotions.[3] As a result, the emotions of observers correspond to those of the people they are watching. In one study, as students watched another describe one of the happiest or saddest events in her life, they felt similar feelings. When people feel pain, the same pain-related neurons are activated in observers of those in the painful condition.[4] Human beings are likely to feel the emotions of others because it enhances their communication with them and their survival in a social world.

Students can see that a knowledgeable, caring teacher's enthusiasm about a subject is the natural emotional outcome of justified commitment to sharing such learning. Because of their biology and pragmatism, students are inspired by such teachers, just as I was by Sister Desiderata in the moment, and for many years afterward.

With enthusiastic teaching there's an entire ecosystem at work. With such instruction,[5] there is constant stimulation that invites engagement with exclamations like "Wow!" "Incredible!" and "Who could imagine?" Impassioned teachers mine this gold because students are more likely to pay attention and understand what they say and demonstrate. Fact: greater alertness produces better learning, which makes future stimulation more likely and rewarding. And on it goes. A constant self-perpetuating chain of events is established. It's no wonder I couldn't wait for the next day to learn with Sister Desiderata, a teacher and a year whose influence lasted a lifetime.

CHAPTER 3

Having a Ball

Throughout the rest of elementary and secondary school, I never had another teacher like Sister Desiderata. I was a learner but not an inspired one. I could grind it out, now and then find a book like *Treasure Island* that would captivate me and propel my imagination, but much of the time I learned despite my teachers and not because of them. The only thing to which I brought the full weight of my being with a constant palpable desire was sports. I can feel it now as I have from the time I was six: What's the game? It really doesn't matter. I can learn. Just please, let me play.

All we needed was a ball. The cheapest and most accessible was a tennis ball. Often bald from use and discarded on the playground, we could get one for free. There was only one criteria: Does it bounce? And that could be known in a Detroit second. Oh yeah, it does! Now the possibilities seem just shy of infinite. There's catch, and you don't need a glove. We can use the telephone pole wire for height, the street for width, and the front bumper on Nancy's dad's car as the boundary for distance. Two drops and you're out. Five tosses per player. We got a game to start. After that, there's keep-away. Catch me if you can! Then, before it gets dark there's cement baseball. We can bounce the ball off the concrete steps of my front porch. All ground balls are strikes. Catch it on the fly and it's an out. If you don't catch it, it's a single. But if it makes it on a fly into the street, it's an automatic home run. Let's go. Baseball? Let's save it for tomorrow.

All children have to play and sports is the organized version of fulfilling that human need. Games are universal, shaped by culture or individual invention. When I was about 12, I can remember sitting on my front porch with my friend, Frank Orlando. No ball. It was a hot August day with the Cicadas in full throttle drowning out any other sounds from the city. Muggy? Yes, the kind of humidity that makes any wetness from sweat or dribble stay with you for the rest of the day.

We were cooling off on my front porch shaded by a green striped aluminum awning. Frank was staring ahead, eyes half open, and glazed with a drooping, somnolent face at the edge of sleep. His elbows were propping up his half bent body and his legs were folded at the knees hanging over the edge of the porch. From the side, he looked like a question mark ready to topple over. Yet, he was holding steady for what must have been a half an hour. Other than looking toward Frank, I can't remember much until this happened: I pulled my hand out of my pocket and out came the lining of the pocket with three things—a copper pellet for a BB gun, a gnarled number 2 pencil that should've been in my school bag, and a dust ball. I blew off the fuzz and viewed what remained.

As I studied the objects in my hand, the grey flat cement top of the porch went from background to foreground. I could see the small craters and holes across the top of the porch weatherworn into its surface. Two words were forming in my brain and as they became clearer I jumped to my feet and shouted, "BB Golf!"

Frank jolted up and asked, "What's wrong, man?"

"Nothing," I said. "We can play BB Golf. Watch." At arm's length, I circled a hole in the cement top with my finger and placed the copper pellet about two feet away. With the eraser end of the pencil as a putter, I stroked it toward the hole. It was about an inch short. When I looked up, Frank smiled and said, "Wow. Let's do it."

I ran into the house, got a roll of masking tape, cut off eighteen pieces, numbered them consecutively, and Frank and I designed our first BB golf course on my front porch. We played the rest of the afternoon. It was so much fun, we invited our friends over to join us the next day. As they might say today, BB golf went viral. By the end of the week, we had charted four more BB golf courses across the neighborhood and held our first tournament at twenty-five cents a head. A nickel for the pencil, the bb was free, and the extra twenty cents went into a pot for the winner. Now, this probably isn't the way it went down for Einstein, Edison, or Curie but to this day, if I want to remember inspiration, BB Golf is the memory that emerges first.

Sports are so commonly used as an example for motivation because at its most elemental definition: Being motivated means being willfully directed toward a goal. We use attention, concentration, imagination, passion, and effort to pursue a goal. Most games and sports have a winner and a loser. There is a clear objective to be reached—getting to home, scoring a touchdown, putting the puck in the net—all requiring focus and energy. So sports is an easy and understandable metaphor. So is the military—a mission to be accomplished, a battle to be won, or an enemy to be defeated. Victory.

But if you analyze behavior, even in sports, motivation quickly gets complicated. How much is his or her effort in this game (pick one) influenced by a family member (which one), a coach (past or present), his or her role in the game, the number of spectators present, friends, other players on the team (again, which ones), the importance of the game for a championship, a scholarship, or a record; preparation, self-confidence, and is it a home or an away game? That's at least ten possible influences on a player's motivation and the reader could probably add two or three more. One of Freud's major contributions to understanding motivation was that it was *overdetermined*.[6]

There are many possible factors that influence one's motivation at a given moment. How to determine which and to what degree may still be more mystery than scientific certainty. Trying to understand one's own motivation is like a bird finding a branch to rest upon. There are so many possibilities and the approach one takes is as much contrived by instinct as by chance. For example, I decide to do my homework tonight and skip watching television. Is that decision and behavior caused by the fact that my mother asked whether my homework was done, or because a homework "buddy" texted to remind me to do my homework, or because I want a good grade for the assignment, or because I like my teacher, and maybe the subject too? There is a score of possibilities for why I'm doing my homework and it's possible all of them might have exerted influence on my motivation. My family and the world about me give me a multitude of reasons for why I do anything.

If we take another simple definition of motivation—why people think and behave as they do—we have to include in our understanding of motivation, not only the likely candidates of the social sciences and neuroscience, but physics, literature, history, and cultural and spiritual studies as well. Many philosophers and religious thinkers have a similar understanding of motivation but use metaphysical assumptions such as cosmology or the supernatural to explain its dynamics. "The devil made me do it," may draw a quick smile or a pitiful glance, depending on who's doing the listening.

Like the national economy, human motivation is a topic that we know is important, continuously discuss, and would like to predict. But just as tomorrow's stock market trend seems beyond our influence and understanding, so too do the causes of human behavior evade any simple explanation or prescription. Yet there are laws in economics such as supply and demand that help us to comprehend, plan, prepare, and influence our economy. Motivation has similar principles and sports can give us some valuable initial insights.

Although I didn't reflect much about it, I tried to fit sports into my life wherever and whenever possible throughout elementary school, high school, and college. Even though I wasn't that good at athletics, I pursued them with a ferocious romanticism. I defied the cliché that success breeds success. I was on a never-ending adventure and the appeal of sports nested within my emotions, not on the facts of how I performed.

During the sixth grade, when the weather was fair, we played baseball in a tennis court enclosure during our lunch break. Again, it was simple equipment: a tennis ball that had to be nearly new (Fuzz and wind resistance mattered.) and a bat. There were three tennis courts surrounded by a twelve feet high, cyclone fence. Including the distance between the courts and the asphalt surface surrounding them, the left field line measured 150 feet. During school hours, the nets were kept down until June. Home runs were rare and every boy knew how many he or any other boy had hit. First and second base were the two net-posts of the first court and woe to any fielder who lost track of the other court posts across the forest green surface.

Lunchtime was an hour. There was no cafeteria and the boys in my class hustled to eat their bag lunches so there would be more time to play. Time wise, I had what I believed to be a great misfortune. Because I lived near school, a matter of three blocks, I had to go home for lunch. My parents' logic was that a freshly made sandwich of peanut butter and jelly or lunchmeat, and an apple and a cookie somehow were better for me eaten at home than if those items were sent along with me to school in a paper sack and eaten there. No amount of argument on my part could change their minds. "A meal at home is much better for you than a meal out of a paper bag at school." Their logic followed the rule of a previously unstated logic they had continuously used for years with me and my brother: *Once our mind is made up, nothing reasonable, unless it's clearly for your own good as determined by us, will change it.*

If I told them the reason I wanted to eat at school was so I could play baseball during lunch time, my father's answer would be, "Baseball? What good is baseball going to do for you? Keep you out of the factory? No. Get you a better grade in school? No. Help you with your homework? No. Maybe, get you hurt? Yes. Now, if you want your mother to pack you a lunch so you can go to the library or study more, that's okay. Otherwise, forget about it." Ironclad and done. The only alternative I could think of was to lie to them and I kept that temptation at bay until the pressing needs of adolescence. Neither my mother nor my father had ever played sports. They considered them something just short of foolishness.

Eating lunch at home translated into the following: I had roughly fifteen minutes before they started choosing teams to play. Since we lined up by two's before the bell rang to leave school, I would inch my way forward without making any fuss because if I did, I'd be sent to the back of the line. When my feet stepped out of the school doorway, I ran pell-mell like an escaped animal. Before I reached my house, I stopped, tried to catch my breath, and calmly stepped in because if I didn't compose myself I knew my mother would start her mantra, "What's the big hurry? It's not good to hurry. Your food won't digest if you hurry."

So I ate in a manner that seemed to be normal, taking bites that seemed to be average in size but were a bit bigger and under her radar. Drinking milk in even swallows but making them as large as possible. And, answering all her questions with one or two word answers, or my saver with a smile, "Mom, let's talk about that when I come home from school." It worked! I'd clock out from lunch in about five minutes. Then I ran back to school as though chased by zombies while praying, "Please God, give me a chance to be picked on a team. Please, that's all I ask."

Half the time I wasn't. I'd get there on time but I wasn't a very good baseball player, just shy of low-average. My fielding was poor. Slow grounders, pop-ups, loopy fly balls, I could get. Send a long fly ball toward me with a touch of speed on it, and it would often be over my head before I could judge its trajectory. At such times, I could hear the groans from my teammates.. Batting? With all due self-respect, I swung like a penguin with a stick in its flipper. Now and then, I would hit the ball, mostly grounders, sometimes a line drive, but I was not "relaxed at the plate." No home runs, not ever.

But here's the thing—I loved to play baseball. Getting picked for a team was the first victory. My teammates put me at second base or in right field, the two positions with least chance of having to field a ball because almost everyone was a right handed batter. If a ball were to come toward me, it was often poorly hit. About half the time, I could catch it. Another triumph. Batting: If you're ninth in the batting order, which I was, any hit is both unexpected and lauded. And something I learned early on—if you're playing with friends and you give it your all, they're quite forgiving, at least during tennis court baseball.

Although I didn't learn until much later in graduate school, there were two ideas that made understandable my desire for playing sports as a sustained and cherished motivation. The first was the concept of *intrinsic motivation*. The brain has an inherent propensity for knowing what it wants. We pay attention to what matters to us. Intrinsic motivation occurs when people act for the satisfaction inherent in the behavior itself. Learning for the sake of learning. Performing for the feeling of performing. The exhilaration of running as fast as you can, leaping, and catching a ball.

Comprehending the phenomenon of intrinsic motivation allows us to appreciate reading a novel for the interest it generates, solving a problem for the joy of encountering the inherent puzzle itself,[7] and conducting an experiment for how it engages our curiosity. Learning, playing, and performing have the potential of being intrinsically motivating experiences. *When people see that what they are learning makes sense and is important according to their own perspectives, their motivation emerges as a physical energy and an emotional state to support learning.*[8] What is culturally relevant to people evokes their intrinsic motivation. They want to be effective at what they value.

Human beings are part of the natural world. Our evolution is directly tied to our capability to be curious and to physically move. Play involves both of these critical capacities and organized sports are a cultural outgrowth of them.

For my generation, listening to a baseball game on the radio was as common as watching a football game on television is today. We played baseball in our local parks in every kind of league imaginable. It was a cultural icon, valued and esteemed. Other than the flights of the astronauts, it was the only media experience offered throughout our entire school. Listening to the World Series was an annual event that the nuns who were our teachers heartily endorsed and enjoyed as much as we did.

However, due to war and economic depression, my father and mother had little opportunity to play sports. Their interest in sports was culturally limited by virtue of their age and gender, respectively. "Making ends meet," and taking care of their children and family were their utmost priorities. In their eyes, they could never afford to let up. I understood this cultural norm as sacred for them. It was a dominant value shared by most of my relatives and the majority of our neighbors. They knew athletic games held importance for other people. But in their lives, feeling any deeper aspects of intrinsic motivation associated with sports such as flow, never had a chance to emerge.

Flow is the second motivational idea for which sports affords a clear and immediately comprehensible platform of examples and insights. I don't want to glorify sports. Today, the most heralded professional forms: football, basketball, baseball, and soccer have become global billion dollar industries with questionable practices and excesses, frequently accepted by the public with vapid scrutiny and a fervor approaching the Roman circus. There are only ten states in which the highest paid public employee is not a football or basketball coach. I understand why and I uncomfortably admit my seduction by the allurement of sports in the face of my own moral code. For decades, after perusing the front page of the daily paper, I have read the sports page before any other section of the paper. Watching the "scores" on ESPN is my last conscious act before I retire in the evening. My exuberance in finding the Superbowl televised at a pub in Sydney, Australia approached what I might imagine I'd feel while viewing a miracle. As participant rather than fan, anyone who's ever sincerely played a sport for the season of its existence, has experienced flow. Other than learning, sports are the most culturally sanctioned venue for experiencing this heightened form of intrinsic motivation.

Flow is when work becomes play, an enjoyable absorption of our total being. When I begin to reflect on flow, I like to think of the lyrics penned by Allen Jay Lerner for "I Could Have Danced All Night":

> I could have danced all night
> I could have danced all night
> And still have begged for more

> I could have spread my wings
> And done a thousand things
> I've never done before.

They capture the spirit of the concept of flow, when, "living becomes its own justification,"[9] as Mihalyi Csikszentmihalyi, the originator of this idea, describes it. Moving in sync with teammates, running the floor, dribbling and passing precisely, sinking a lay-up with grace befitting a ballet company, and maintaining that rhythm and total concentration until the only thing that disrupts it is the shrill piercing arrow of the referee's whistle.

We have all had flow experiences outside of an athletic context: the feeling and focus that sometimes emerges during a taut debate, or in a challenging board game such as chess, or more simply, in reading a book that seems as if it were written just for us or in the spontaneous exhilaration that accompanies a long, deep conversation with an old friend. In any of these endeavors, hours may have slipped by and we have barely noticed.

Whenever we do something in which we can feel vital, creative, and capable, we have the possibility of feeling flow. In such activities, we feel totally absorbed, with no time to worry about what might happen next and with a sense that we are fully participating with all the skills necessary at the moment. There is often a loss of self-awareness that sometimes results in a feeling of transcendence or a merging with the activity and the environment. Later in life, I played racquetball once a week with the same partner, David Oliensis. We were so closely matched that after ten years, possibly five wins separated us. During some of those games, I felt like I became the ball. It was an extension of my arm and racquet and I moved with it at will. I played very well at such moments. "Being in the zone," is a common expression that players of any sport often use to describe this feeling and exercise of exceptional performance.

Athletes, writers, dancers, therapists, surgeons, pilots, and teachers report feelings of flow during engrossing tasks in their repertoire of activities. In fact, when interviewed, they say that flow experiences are among the major reasons why they enjoy and continue to do the work they do. Students can have flow experiences as well. If we think of our best courses and finest instructors, we often can remember being captivated by the learning events we shared with them—challenging and creative activities in which we participated at a level where a new depth and extension of our capabilities emerged. I remember the first time I read, Poe's *Cask of Amontillado*, the trickery and horror of burying someone alive, Fortunato's pitiful plea when he realizes his fate, "For the love of God, Montresor!" still echoes in my mind. The irony of Fortunato's name and his desperate death was a lesson I never forgot.

HAVING A BALL

In tenth grade biology, with Sister Mary Assumpta, not one of my favorite teachers, I had moments of flow misbehaving. I contributed to our mutual hostility by participating in an unkindness for which I now have fleeting regret. Our class was ringed with small stuffed animals placed in delicate balance atop bookshelves: pheasants, rabbits, squirrels, owls, possums, and others sorts of small creatures common to the Midwest. We sat in two's at large wooden desks separated in the middle by a small cabinet, sink, and a curved single chrome faucet. Since the room had wooden floors and the desks had covered fronts that came up to our stomachs, we learned it was possible to move your legs quickly up and down without ever conveying you were making this motion. If enough students participated in this subterfuge, approximately ten, you could shake the classroom enough to cause the stuffed animals to move and tremble. To an observer, all seemed still while the animals spastically shook above us. We chose our moments: her declarations of unexpected tests, too much homework, or criticism of a student would often be followed by "The Dance of the Stuffed Animals." At such times, she became a bit unhinged. Her dark deep set, Eastern European eyes glaring at us as she snorted from a large nose splashed across her contorted face; her head tossing from side to side while she surveyed the room, the black veil of her habit erratically weaving like the tailfin of a spooked fish. When she ran up the aisles to see who was moving their legs, we stopped, and no one dared smile, a response sure to release her wrath. But as soon as she turned and moved toward the front of the class, we started again. When it came to elite trickery, Poe inspired us. Yet, all Sister Assumpta had to do to stop us, was to laugh with us. She never did. Her need to control overran her sense of humor. Our shenanigans in biology illustrate that what some people see as misbehavior may be to others, especially the participants, a form of creative action that evokes feelings of flow. In my opinion, it's one of the reasons rebellious behavior often thrives among adolescents and adults.

I was also able in Sister Assumpta's class to legitimately experience flow while involved in more conventional learning. In biology, we each received a glass jar filled with the animals to dissect over the semester: worms, fish, frogs, and starfish. The worms, fish, and frogs did not interest me. As a boy in the Midwest, I had played and fished with them for years. But the starfish was a different species from the ocean. It was exotic. I had only seen starfish in children's books, often drawn in bright shades of red, blue, and orange. The one I dissected was a gray-rose purple and not as spongy as I expected it to be. I was fascinated by it, examining its tiny tube feet and imagining the coral reef and colorful fish in its habitat. The worksheets and dissection guide helped me to understand the ways in which it did resemble a fish. I followed their directions like a lost hiker with a topographical map. When I completed the dissection,

I knew how starfish could trap small fish and had the organs to digest clams. Class was over before I knew it or wanted it to be. Had I had a better relationship with Sister Assumpta, I would have stayed afterwards to ask questions about predators and how starfish protect themselves.

Because flow can be found across cultures,[10] it may be a sense that humans have developed in order to recognize patterns of action that are worth preserving, a meme to guide our aspirations. Whether we are enthralled by weaving a ball forward through opponents on a soccer field, awed by a chemical reaction we've initiated in a school experiment, or exhilarated by the clever manipulations of a rebellious act, our flow experiences have the following three remarkably similar characteristics:

In flow experiences, goals are clear and compatible. That's why games and sports like baseball, tennis, poker, and a myriad of video games induce flow, but so can playing a musical piece or designing computer software. As long as our intentions are clear and our emotions support them, we can concentrate even when the task is difficult. We absorb ourselves in those dreams to which we commit. In such matters, cultural relevance is an inescapable necessity. Personally, I didn't know of anyone within my sphere of experience who was a scientist. I saw biology as a *required* course. My regard for my fascination while dissecting a starfish was more as an anomaly, than as a vivid possibility for vocational pursuit. Without a better relationship with my teacher, Sister Assumpta, the feeling I had that day in Biology 101 ended when I left the room for another class. Fini.

In flow experiences, feedback is immediate, continuous, and relevant as the activity unfolds. We are clear about how well we are doing when we play games and sports, whether we are advancing or retreating from our goal. In the red zone, third down and six more yards for a touchdown; advance the runner or make the third out; check the king or lose the queen. Writing at its most basic level can be measured by words or pages written, and they do add up! In a good conversation, facial expressions and gestures prompt us and tell us how we're communicating. Every cut I made following the starfish dissection guide concretely revealed organs and an internal system that eventually resembled that of a fish. I was amazed.

In flow experiences, the challenge is in balance with our skills or knowledge but stretches existing capacities. Flow experiences usually occur when our ability to act and the challenge we're facing correspond closely, pulling us further toward greater knowledge or skill. Too big a challenge, one beyond our capability, and we tend to worry, become anxious, or, possibly frightened. "We're in over our head." Conversely, too small a challenge, one below our capability, and we grow bored, restless, or, possibly apathetic. "Please, no busy work." I can remember the starfish was tough to cut, even with my sharp scalpel. It had a tendency to send out flying bits of debris as I made the incisions. I had to concentrate and firmly hold the knife. I was able to, clearly revealing the interior, and experiencing both wonder and new learning.

Flow is why we want great matches in sport or in any field. Where we have confidence, we seek a fine challenge. Beating any team badly becomes as tedious as losing badly becomes humbling. I didn't want to play right field and never get a fly ball. We instinctively want challenges in work and play that require deep involvement and full use of our talents because we know exhilaration lies ahead.

Eventually, I found my niche with the oblong ball. When I asked my father the summer before my freshmen year if I could play football, he answered without hesitation, "No, you'll get hurt." The next summer, I said, "Dad, Frank, Bob, and Mike played (all friends of mine he knew) and didn't get hurt." He answered, "No, you're too small. They're bigger than you." He had me. I was five feet, one inch tall and about a hundred and fifteen pounds. The next summer, preceding my junior year, I asked him again. My friends hadn't been hurt, I had grown to five feet, six inches tall and weighed one hundred and forty pounds. His answer was, "No, you need to keep your job. The money makes a difference." Although frustrated, I couldn't argue with the truth. I was a paperboy and with tips, I made fifteen dollars a week. That paid for everything I needed at school including books, tuition and my clothes. No argument there. I had one more year and one more summer to ask. I got another job working on Saturdays in Walt Haberski's Hardware Store—twenty dollars for one day's work. Luckily, none of my friends that my father knew had been hurt and I was now five feet, nine inches tall and weighed a hundred and sixty pounds. When I asked him, he said, "Okay, but if you become a cripple I won't be able to take care of you. Nothing's worse than being a poor cripple. Those are the people who have to beg."

I played my senior year, never better than second string, but I didn't get hurt and here's where personal culture and flow came together in my football experience.[11] My closest friends were starters. Watching them play in games was a kick, up close from the sidelines and knowing every play called. Also, I got to play a lot—during practice. We scrimmaged three days a week. That's where school and sports differ. I loved playing and I could find my level of challenge with immediate feedback. I was second string but part of a team where practice undoubtedly made a difference with coaches trying to make my skills better because everyone benefited, plus a chance to earn my way to playing on the kick-off team—a few moments of the real thing, mayhem between whistles.

In a classroom: Am I interested in the subject? If I am, is it being taught at my level of capability, or is it beyond or below my capacity to be challenged?

Is there a way to stay engaged and challenged and what is the quality of feedback and how often is it given?[12] What is the goal of the lesson? The subject? How much do I value it and how clear am I about achieving it? Is the course something I finish and move on from, or is it something I cherish and make a part of my life?

Flow is much more possible than many teachers and students realize. One in five people experience flow often, as frequently as several times a day. Generally, it happens when we're with friends or doing favorite activities. In high school, I was a good student but seldom was it flow that forged my learning. It is possible to stay motivated and learn without flow. Yet, who would not choose to make learning a lifelong pursuit of vital engagement rather than the result of a driven dogged ambition? By understanding how to construct engrossing learning experiences for ourselves and our children, we have a means to develop lasting cherished interests that benefit us personally and contribute to our society.[13]

CHAPTER 4

Doing Duty

In high school, I was an above average student. I couldn't afford not to be. My mother expected me to do well but for my father, the expectation was a dictate. Any grade less than an A on my report card had to be explained—in detail. He knew when report cards were distributed and every time I brought one home, I had to sit next to him at the kitchen table as he reviewed it. My father smoked Chesterfields and although his breath was clean, the scent of cigarettes was always present as was the light sweet aroma of machine oil which bathing after work never quite removed. He would not hesitate to place his face an inch from mine and to ask questions that began with "Why?" or "Explain to me…" Only an assessment of all A's drew a compliment.

When speaking to me, under any circumstance, there were no terms of endearment or nicknames. He addressed me by name even when it was obvious that no one else was present. With his heavy Austrian accent, rather than saying Raymond, he pronounced it, Rahmoont. My friends thought this alteration was hilarious. Good naturedly, they often teased me, making requests with an exaggeration of my father's pronunciation, rolling the R and adding emphasis on the T, "Hey RRRRaaaahmoonT! Could you bring me a soda?" But, because no one ever could quite pronounce my name as my father did, I grew to have an affection for his unique rendition of it.

Unless I had received a C, I was fairly calm while my father reviewed the report card with me. These meetings began in high school and had the characteristics of a ritual. The only wild card was my father's temper. It was volcanic and could be released by any behavior he deemed belligerent or disrespectful. At moments like this, my father expected to be taken seriously. Anything less on my part was an invitation to disaster. Once, when my brother and I got into a shouting match over which TV show to watch, my father walked into the room, went to the TV, and kicked in the screen. Boom! Gone. His only comment, "Now watch that." There were enough incidents of this sort throughout the history of our family that taking our father seriously was not hard to do.

He began the report card review that freshman quarter by examining its contents as though they were the prescription for a drug that would make us live forever. His expression was stoic but completely focused on every word and letter on that card. One might think he was committing all of it to memory. Not once did he look up at me. I sat and waited. I was focused as well, knowing the two B's I had earned that card marking would draw his inquiry.

He turned slowly toward me, the only things missing, a black robe and a gavel, "Rahmoont, explain to me why you received a B for Algebra. I thought you were good with numbers."

"I am pretty good. But I'm not real fast with them. Other students are quicker than me. They get the A's."

Now he's leaning in. His expression is genuinely curious. But I know that with him, curiosity might precede accusation. He's holding court and wondering how to help me. "Doesn't doing your homework make you faster? Because it's practice?"

My father had his assumptions about learning. Effort topped the list. "I do my homework, Dad. Look on the card. The teacher says I'm a good student." This was the moment of truth because my father considered teacher comments to be of Biblical significance.

"But look there's another B here. For English?"

Now I know I could be in trouble. Tread lightly. "I know. I was surprised too. I didn't see it coming. It's hard to figure out how she grades. She's kind of boring."

"Boring!? You think boring! Come work with me. You'll get boring, and dirty, and noisy! For the whole week. For the whole month. For the rest of your life!"

Now my eyes are cast down. I'm looking at the table top.

"That's no excuse. What's going on?"

"Probably my writing. Punctuation."

"What's punctuation?"

"Things like where to put periods and commas."

"What? You're not paying attention when you write?"

"No. But I should review the paper before I hand it in to her."

"Just tell me. Can you do better?"

Of course, I said yes. That response ended our encounter. He signed the back of the card and slid it back to me with one word, "Okay." That was it. No hard feelings. We're done until the next report card.

I was relieved because if the situation had amped up anymore, I knew his next move, which would be to pound the table with his fist. Get up. Go into the living room, turn full circle, and come back into the dinette, pound the table once more, and this time shout, "This can't go on anymore!" And then, no one knew what might come next.

I didn't resent my father for the intimidation and guilt I felt at such moments. Partly because his initial anger was predictable. It was after he was angry that we were in a seismic vibration. I had learned what the limits were to provoking him and how to maneuver around them. Partly because there was never a neuron of doubt that he loved me. Partly because when I was a young boy, I felt completely safe in his presence, from the way he would put his arm out to stop me from lurching forward when our car stopped suddenly, to how he would look at me when we were on the streets of the city and say, "Stay near."

Another reason that quelled the potential of antipathy toward my father, I learned later in life when I studied resilient children.[14] Those who live in families where there is violence and parental discord and family fracturing and displacement, and yet, thrive as adults, achieve emotional stability, and find joy and intimacy. One significant characteristic that seems to protect their psychological health is that they tend to appraise the aggression and difficulties enacted by significant others toward them as understandable and not meant to be personally destructive to them.

I knew my father had his demons. To me, he was the face of the paradox: Violent but not mean. I have no examples of him being cruel or vindictive. Controlling, yes. Dictatorial, yes. Prone to rage, unfortunately, yes. My father's greatest stumbling block was how narrow his vision was of what could be a worthwhile life for his family. In this regard, he thought he knew better than any of us, and he was often wrong. That awareness brought me sadness and enormous frustration, but not bitterness. And, he had his ace. My mother loved him. Whether it was the way they danced or hearing the laughter from their bedroom on Sunday mornings, my awareness of the tenderness in their relationship allowed me to reconsider my perspective of my father, to avoid my adolescent, easy dismissal of him as an angry foolish man.

What my parents didn't realize was that the manner with which my father dealt with grades instilled within me the belief that I could do well in school. Getting A's was a duty I could fulfill. They didn't talk to me about being bright or talented or smart. For my father it was, "Do your best and make sure it is your best." High expectancy for learning on the part of teachers and parents is one of the most well researched and most consistent means to enhancing learning.[15] Coupled with an emphasis on effort as a means to improve learning, learners can believe that studying, practicing, and revising matter and are under their control. This combination accentuates the learners' power and responsibility, giving them real hope for future performance in similar tasks.

Stressed as a primary means to learning, effort can have a wonderful effect.[16] Whether it's a comment on a paper or spoken directly to a student, teachers who say, "I like the way you try. Hang in there. I can see your effort is making a real difference in your work," are genuinely encouraging. When effort is more valued than accomplishment and clearly a classroom norm, it means the learners' role is not to perform better than peers, or to avoid looking incompetent, but to strive to learn. In turn, this reduces the pressure of achievement and the fear of failure, letting learners fully embrace learning, which is one of the surest ways to find flow while learning. In the long run, this kind of involvement leads to the highest achievement within an environment of hope and integrity for everyone.

Inadvertently, my father also did something else that was good for me to become a more motivated learner. Although he was stern and could be suffocating, he approached improvement in my learning as a problem to solve. He had never gone to school. Living in a remote Romanian village and being taken at age 11 by the Russian army in 1914 to be one of their messengers until he was wounded by a stray bullet, he didn't know how school worked. His history forced him to rely on me for information and ideas to find my way to a better grade.

He tended not to involve my mother because he believed she was a soft touch when it came to disciplining her children. She was. And, to our later regret, my brother and I sometimes took advantage of her. We were mischievous, constantly roughhousing and pulling pranks on one another, from having fights with butter knives to setting off ladyfinger firecrackers in our basement and hosing each other in the back yard—sometimes all in the same day. When five o'clock approached, the time our father came home from work, we would be on our knees with hands folded begging her not to tell him what we had done because it was sure destiny to a leather strap spanking. She rarely did. So, because my father needed my ideas to be a better learner, I came to see learning as problem solving with me being the sleuth to find a better way.[17] Today, that's called self-regulated learning,[18] an essential characteristic of self-motivated, life-long learners.

Another significant advantage I had in developing motivation to learn was the harmony between what my parents wanted from me as a student and what my teachers expected from me. There was no doubt in my mind that at the top of this hierarchy was obedience to authority. Disobeying, even correcting an elder in my family, was considered worse behavior than doing the same to my parents. It did not happen, nor did I witness any of my cousins transgress this boundary. It wasn't hard to be obedient because my aunts and uncles openly loved us—hugging us, giving us candy, slipping a dime or a quarter into our hands, asking us to dance, and clapping in circles around us when we did. But if they asked us to do something, whether it was to leave the room or help with a chore, we unquestioningly did it. That was the culture, true for everyone, at least in public. The same norms held for school. The teachers were there to help us learn and obeying them was necessary for us to learn. Simple. The problem was that in elementary school, for myself and for many of my peers, with the exception Sister Desiderata's third grade class, the source of our engagement with learning was obedience, not intrinsic motivation. Consequently, for the boys and girls I knew well, we learned but we did not develop a love of learning.

To their credit, most of the nuns were devoted teachers. But their idea of teaching did not include learning for the sake of learning with a sense of vitality and flow as essential. Their mindset was, "Good boys and girls learn and obey their teachers. They do not misbehave or act lazy." To which my parents would have said, "Amen!"

One of my most vivid memories of school is from the second grade when we were using phonics to say new words. Each of us were given a work book page with new words to decipher. After reviewing the words silently on our own, each of us had to go to the teacher, Sister Eucharia, who was, to my eyes, approaching 80, and say the new words, or at least sound them out as best we could. This process meant sitting next to her at her desk and facing the entire class as you ran her vocabulary gauntlet. If you were one hundred percent successful, she stamped your page with the image of a turkey, ninety percent successful, you received a rabbit image, and eighty percent, a blue star. Less than eighty percent, no stamp and you were encouraged to practice more.

While each student was at her desk, the rest of us were told to read silently from a library book that had been distributed to us earlier. But few of us were reading these books. We were watching Sister Eucharia's interaction with the students who preceded us. The range of her emotions ran from elation to disgust. The boy I followed was Richard Okonewiecz. Richard had already achieved some degree of fame in our class because he possessed a perfectly round head. From a frontal view, it looked as though someone had painted his face on a globe and from the rear, as though his neck was blowing a bubble. Richard was also the funniest kid in our class, a role in which he excelled—making faces, doing a Chaplin walk, and rolling marbles to others when Sister Eucharia wasn't looking.

As I watched Richard take his turn, I could see his shoulders slumping as he approached her desk. When he missed the first word, she helped him sound it out. When he missed the second word, she helped him again. When he missed the third word, I saw her sit back, sigh, and whisper something to Richard. He didn't look up. When he missed the fourth word, I could read her lips enough to know she said, "lazy." Richard still didn't look up. Sister Eucharia sent him back to his seat with two words, "Now, go!" When he raised his head and stood up, he was crying. Silently, no wheezing or drama, the tears evident as darkened drops on the maroon top of his Roy Roger's cowboy shirt.

When I took my turn, I said all ten words correctly and received my turkey stamp. I didn't develop a love for reading until college. Until then, there had been too many Sister Eucharias and too many Richards at their mercy. It's easy to blame my teachers for this abscess in my learning history but it was much more due to the culture of my community, my family, and my school. In the

50s, motivation was not a concept used or well understood. Teachers, public or private, didn't have a vocabulary to articulate how to create motivated learning, plan for it, or assess it. The awareness of motivation and research of its role in teaching and learning gathered momentum in the 60s with practical teaching strategies evolving in the 70s.[19]

With forty to sixty students in each class, I had from the first through the eighth grade, it's not hard to imagine why discipline took priority over joy in learning and why the mantle of laziness was a convenient way to use morality to induce student compliance, and to shame us into learning. By keeping the rationale for inadequate learning centered in student flaws, the teacher remained safe and stuck in her ways, the parents had a simple answer congruent with their mores, and the student bore the brunt of responsibility and the need to change.

Today, I would label what happened to Richard a motivational injury. Put simply, people avoid what they're hit with. It's a form of classical conditioning, like being burnt by a hot stove, tripping in the dark, or getting soaked in a thunderstorm. We protect ourselves or stay away from the conditions that brought this pain upon us. Repetition of these conditions cause us to feel fear, dread, anxiety, and discomfort. Richard's experience with Sister Eucharia hurt him emotionally. He wasn't going to forget it because he couldn't forget it. Like being struck by lightning, just the sound of distant thunder can make us uncontrollably tremble. For the future, we protect ourselves by developing a negative attitude toward whatever the subject and its accoutrements were that caused us pain—phonics, fractions, grammar, red pencil marks, revisions, quizzes, tests, exams, GPAs. These eventually evolve into subject areas such as math, science, composition, and possibly school in general. You name it. A person can have a bad attitude toward anything they're repeatedly struck with. A neurobiological understanding is that the person has developed a behavioral inhibition system to avoid such negative places, events, and punishments.

A predisposition to respond negatively to an academic subject is very difficult to change. When students enter a course with a bad attitude, it usually remains a bad attitude or gets worse. Like a phobia, it takes repeated positive proximity to the source of fear to alter it in a more acceptable direction. And, how many subjects or teachers give you that kind of chance? Most of my peers did well in high school but didn't read books, want to write, or think about anything academic outside of school. We did not intend to go to college. Being working class played a role in this situation because we knew so few college graduates and money was scarce for education beyond high school. But what really doused the fire for more learning was the preponderance of courses in which we learned but did not emotionally attach to what we were learning. It was like dancing without music.[20]

I knew how to do school. I could be thoughtful about learning, make sense out of teacher assignments, review for tests, complete homework, and track my performance in academic activities so I would get B's or A's whether or not I found the content interesting or enjoyable. I liked the identity of being a good student, and probably most of all, my parents' approval. I knew what was important in order to get high grades. I had little idea what was worthwhile. This mindset dominated my thinking about school through high school graduation. There were moments of illumination: Sister Avila teaching us how to write personal letters and allowing us to be creative and humorous; Mr. Carson sharing stories about the personal lives of the presidents; designing our own homes in drafting class. However, these interludes of intrinsically motivating learning were too brief to take hold of me or nurture anything that approached a love of learning.

By the ninth grade, I began to internalize a form of motivation that is essential to one's own integrity and self-respect—mental discipline. At the very least it is a means to accomplish personal goals and at the very most it enables us to vitally sustain flow and excel in learning and performance at their highest levels. *Basic mental discipline* is the process of picking a goal and applying steady effort to reach it; as *persistence* mental discipline becomes continuing to stay involved when a solution to a problem is not readily available; and as *gumption* mental discipline is persevering with shrewd common sense. Of the three forms of mental discipline, my favorite is gumption because it requires more creativity and boldness, as the following story about Charles Darwin illustrates:

> When Charles Darwin was a boy, he had a collection of insects in which he took great pride. One day as he was walking in the woods a good distance from home, he saw a large beetle, a specimen missing from his collection, hide under the bark of a tree. Darwin started stripping the bark to get at the creature, and to his delight, he found not one, but three of the large beetles. Since he could not hold more than one in each hand, he popped the third in his mouth and ran all the way home with his catch.

As this story suggests, mental discipline, persistence, and gumption begin to be learned in childhood,[21] often through watching our parents and significant others, as well as through trial and error. In the eighth grade, our teacher Sister Celeste increased the amount of homework we received in order "to prepare us for the deluge we would receive in high school." There were more than a few nights when we had as much as three hours of homework; more reading, writing, and arithmetic. Since on some evenings I couldn't finish it, I started to set my alarm earlier to finish it in the morning before going to school. At first, rising early was difficult. With continued practice, it became easier. By the ninth grade, doing homework in the morning was a dependable alterative to evening homework, and a habit I followed for the rest of my life. I could count on it like a reserve tank of fuel to keep the engine of getting what needed to be done accomplished on time, and in good order.

Often then, and still today, completing useful or cherished work can be a grind. But without mental discipline, how does one sustain intrinsic motivation? Even the most challenging problems about which we care and which fill our lives with creativity require the sweat of plodding through ideas that work and ideas that don't. Who hasn't stayed up most of the night completing an important project or taking care of a sick child? It's how things get done and lucky for those of us who've had people we love and admire show us they've done the same because that's the way most of us begin to learn mental discipline.

I lived at home for twenty-one years. In that entire time, my parents did not take a vacation. Between July and August, when the automobile companies reset their production lines, my father received two weeks paid vacation. He used that time, year after year, to catch up on "work around the house." He painted it one year, painted the garage the next year, painted the interior of the house the year after that. Then he laid a sidewalk, laid a driveway, sodded the front yard, and on and on. He did not do these things happily. Summers are hot in Detroit and all of these tasks cost money. These were also fractious times between my parents because my mother had to help my father and he was a difficult person to work with in the best of times. At night, when he would fall asleep on the couch early from fatigue, she would caution us not to wake him, "Let the bear sleep. We need the rest too."

When I had to rise early to complete my homework, I didn't think of my parents and how hard they worked. Not once. I believed buckling down was in my blood, as much through absorption as through any cognitive process. I didn't see physical labor itself as meritorious. I respected the *will to struggle*, to take on strenuous exertion, because of those who did it and the reality of how difficult it was for them. In my family, the will to toil was a fait accompli. No one escaped it and no one bragged about it. I was grateful that I believed I could persevere with my back or my mind. Mental discipline gave me an asset: the confidence that I could stick with something for the time it took to learn it and get better at it, whatever the subject was. Then, maybe, and here the odds fell sharply, I could enjoy it.

CHAPTER 5

Lucking Out

In my senior year of high school, most of my friends started talking about what they might do after graduation. These were casual conversations. Their matter-of-factness was due to our definitions of future success as well as our limited view of the horizons we might reach. Our rendering of a worthwhile life was not the accumulation of wealth or high status; it was to find dependable, well-paying work, a person to love, and a family to raise. We were Catholic and our character was an essential attribute for any purpose that mattered, and for those who believed, entry into heaven as well. If we had lofty or artistic ambitions, we remained silent about them because of the long odds against ever achieving them and our self-conscious adolescent fear of teasing and mockery.

In 1961, the year I graduated, there were over a hundred Catholic high schools in Detroit. Hardly any had guidance counselors. Our teachers were quick to point out anyone famous who was a Catholic: the Kennedys, Loretta Young, and Dorothy Day. With over 150 million people inhabiting the United States, that was a pretty limited group. I don't remember any nun telling one of us, "You could be a Spencer Tracy." More likely it was, "You know, the way you're acting, you might go to Hell." Above all else, our teachers wanted us to be morally good. They pounded this message like a sledgehammer on a spike. Their advocated vocations included being a priest, a nun, a brother, a missionary, and the willingness to be a martyr. From my vantage point, not much of a fun quintet. Having had the lives of the saints read to me from first grade on, I knew martyrdom and sainthood were a likely combination. By the third grade, after long discussions with my best friend, Tom Wiechy, who had munched his way to the nickname Two-Ton Tommy, I had decided that being a martyr was out of the question. I could not stand to be tortured. I would deny my faith before the first fingernail was pulled. I remember how he stared at me, incredulous at my certainty and cowardice. Then, two weeks later, he closed a car door on his thumb and admitted to me he might do likewise.

Sexism was rampant. Girls were not encouraged to go to college and they were undoubtedly some of our best students. In those times, a good high school education was considered by many to be enough. It would get you into any civil service job, office work, a beginning managerial position, a trade, and keep you out of low-skill factory work. As far as college was concerned, unless you were an outstanding athlete who could be awarded a scholarship, it was seen as desirable but not likely for most of us.

The Catholic college prep schools tended to be the all-white boys' high schools like Catholic Central, De LaSalle, and Austin. They were taught by brothers of various religious orders. Most had two requirements for acceptance: an entrance exam and the capacity of a student's family to pay a high tuition, a provision beyond the means of single paycheck factory workers. I don't think many of us understood the degree to which money and race prevented access to higher education. The entrance exams of these schools had the popular reputation of being "tough to pass." This meritocratic element encouraged the rest of us to think this system of educational distribution was fair and to more readily overlook the potential among us in the co-ed high schools. In this respect, the nuns acted more as midwives than mentors, delivering us at high schools' end like fingerlings—well-equipped in basic academics and of good character—into the sea of opportunity afforded by Detroit, the automobile capital of world.

The only non-religious recruiters we ever saw were in the military. We were visited in my senior year by the Army and the Marines. They came in pairs and were in their late 20s, looking trim, groomed, and sleek in tight-fitting uniforms. Their presentations were high on macho, jokes, and the promise of adventure and benefits: get in the best shape you've ever been in, travel the world, learn a trade, and go to college on the GI Bill after you end your tour of duty. And, if you want to make it a career, after twenty years, you can retire with full benefits. Wow! This was pre-Viet Nam and the pitch they gave sounded a lot better than many of us expected from life after high school. Most of us didn't know what we wanted to do post-graduation beyond finding a job. Among many families, the military was a respectable way for sons to mature, get some experience, practice responsibility, and, in the expression of the day, "Learn to be a man."

With World War II less than two decades in the past, the Korean War less than one, and communism and nuclear war hanging in the air, the 220 U. S. bases across the planet needed personnel. News of the vested interests of the military industrial complex and U. S. imperialism was not being broadcast at my school, St Thomas the Apostle. Our favorite priest, Father Kukler, who taught senior religion, had been a Marine and had the tattoo of a woman's face on his left, well pronounced bicep. When asked who she was, his stock answer was, "Oh, you mean, *Mom*. Nice to have her near." To which we replied, "Yeah, sure," but were impressed nonetheless.

In my neighborhood, about one in four boys joined the service upon high school graduation. I hoped to be one of them. What enticed me was the image and fantasy of being a paratrooper. Seeing them strut the streets of my neighborhood in their powder blue ascots, screaming eagle chevrons, and spit-polished jump boots was an apparition as magnetic for me as Elvis Presley—tough, cool, and sexy. The real plus was that I could actually be a paratrooper.

Larry Zaminski, a boy a few years older than me, who lived across the alley and raised pigeons, became a paratrooper. Before he left for basic training, his face was riddled with acne like potholes on a side street, reflecting a complexion as pale as a duck's egg. He was skinny with wild blond hair and he mumbled. Nice fellow, but not that impressive. When he came back home on leave about a year later, he had "filled out" with a neck as thick as the trunk of a birch tree, no more acne, and a posture so sheer it didn't seem he could bend at the waist. He had a paratrooper buddy with him, Don, with the same build and physical demeanor. They never were out of uniform. When they walked together with such precision and impact, just short of a march-step, it reminded me of how a hurricane looks when depicted from far above, calm in the center with everything else radiating outward—a vortex of cool with Gene Vincent singing "Be Bop Alula" in the background.

They said becoming paratroopers was the baddest thing they had ever done, badder than racing cars at a dragstrip. Basic training was tough but most guys made it. And, when they finished, they went to jump school in Ft. Benning, Georgia. That's where they learned how to parachute and earned their jump boots. "Nothing else like it, looking at the earth below in full gear and jumping out of a plane like it was the top of a flying mountain." They didn't say much more. They were tight-lipped like a couple of Gary Coopers. I wanted to ask a dozen questions: What's it like to hit the ground? How many guys get hurt parachuting? What do you do if your chute doesn't open? Who packs your chute? What's it feel like being in mid-air? But I didn't. I didn't want to sound like some amateur weakling. Yet, I was convinced, if Larry Zaminski could become a paratrooper, so could I.

Early in the summer after I graduated from high school, I went to see an army recruiter. I found out I could take a pre-induction physical before I made any commitments. To avoid the pressure of expectations, I went to have the physical without mentioning it to any of my friends or family. At the end of the examination, I was told that I was eligible for the army but not the paratroopers. My uncorrected distance vision, -500 in the right eye and -525 in the left, was below the standard for that branch of the service.

I didn't take this news too badly. No one had known about this ambition and I had another option, the submarine service. I had a pinball reaction to vocational options after high school. I'd find something. Just keep bouncing around until I do. Some of this attitude was due to naiveté and some to an unremitting confidence in being able to work hard for whatever opportunity emerged.

The Navy recruiter closed out my submarine service option quickly. Once he found out the results of my Army vision test, he told me I would be ineligible for this branch of the Navy as well. Now, I was at a loss for what to do next. My dream of a military enlistment with an adventurous identity had ended. There was no civil service option that appealed to me. I didn't want to look for factory work. As a choice this early in my life, it was too depressing. I also knew it would be a catastrophic wound to my parents' hopes for me. They hadn't told me what to be, but they had told me what not to be. So often repeated by my father that it could have been a mantra, and always with a look that pierced me, "Whatever you do, don't end up in a factory."

What to do? I had a part time summer job that would allow me to stall on any decision until the fall of 1961. I was working landscape maintenance for Greater Detroit Landscaping, essentially pushing a lawn mower from dawn to dusk for $1.10 an hour. I was in great physical shape but the wages were dismal and the foreman's idea of motivating his crew seemed restricted to the word *up* in the only two sentences he ever said to us, "Hurry up." And, "Sweep up."

My brother Richard had joined the Coast Guard and was stationed in New York City. In one of the letters I wrote to him late that summer, I asked what he thought if I were to join the Coast Guard as well. He wrote back with an idea that changed the course of my life, "I'm having a lot of fun in the CG. But I'm not sure I'm learning anything that will make a difference in my future. You did pretty well in school. What about going to college?"

Richard gave me the nudge I needed. Just enough. It's amazing what can be moved with a little help. Like another shoulder leaning into something stuck, his words pushed me from confusion toward a direction that needed a touch more confidence—not through advice but with a suggestion in the form of a question—to lift me to another plane of thought, "Yeah, that makes sense. I might be able to make it in college."

Everything counts. It's just so hard to know when it matters most.

In the early sixties, there were tens of thousands of young people who did what I did next: Without substantial savings, went to their parents and told them they wanted to go to college; requested to live at home paying minimal rent (I didn't have to pay anything as long as I went to school); passed a general entrance exam to enroll as a matriculated student; got a part time/full time job (In the following order, I was a hardware store clerk, bus boy, staging and lighting assistant, and substitute teacher); and paid tuition of roughly $220 for a full semester of credits at a public university or junior college. My alma mater was Wayne State University in the heart of Detroit. Among these characteristics, the one that mattered most was the low cost of tuition. If this were not the case, my desire to go to college would not have been a consideration. Such reasonable tuition was only possible because the state of Michigan provided most of the funding for student tuition. Access to a college education was considered a necessary opportunity to benefit the common good. Thanks to this communal mindset, my generation got a better chance at higher education than has any since.

Personally, I felt lucky. I was going to college at a four year institution. I had not imagined this possibility as a realistic option. Yet, it wasn't simply a matter of chance. I was beginning to live out what Seneca wrote nearly two millennia ago, "Luck is a matter of preparation meeting opportunity."

Going to college was a revelation. I felt like I was being given a high-powered telescope to view the universe for the first time. The scale of difference between Wayne State University and St. Thomas High School was the stuff of science fiction. I had arrived on another planet. St. Thomas had 300 students. Wayne had 26,000. All of our high school was contained on the third floor of a single building. Wayne had a campus measured in square miles. Ninety-five percent of all students at St. Thomas were blue collar, white Polish Catholics. Undergraduates at Wayne represented every race, religion, ethnic group, sexual orientation, and income level to be found in the city of Detroit. But the force that stunned me, slapped me against the back of my seat, mouth agape, were the professors. In the language of the day, "They meant business." Young or old, man or woman, black or white, bow tied or open collared, they took themselves seriously and by demeanor and expectations, indicated that we, the students should do likewise. Many smoked while they taught. Most seemed irreverently quick-witted, making student questions or comments fair game for humorous exploitation—"From the look on your face, that answer sounds like a guess, Mr. Wlodkowski. But it's correct. Better check your back pocket. Might have a silver dollar in there."

Nearly half of the instructors in my freshman year seemed indifferent to student failure, "I grade on a curve. That means some of you will fail or receive poor grades. Take good notes, study for your tests, and keep up with your reading and assignments. If you do, it's far less likely you'll come up with the short end of the stick." I received this declaration like a test dummy: inert, silent, and impotent to defy the impact of their warning. Aware of my good fortune to be at Wayne, I lived in dread of flunking out. Adding to this anxiety was what I believed was a bad omen at my freshmen orientation. The dean gave a speech in which he cautioned us to be diligent learners because of the notoriously high failure rate among first year students. To emphasize his point, he asked us to take a good look at the student in the seat next to us, on the right and then on the left, after which he said, "I'm sad to say one of them will be gone in six months. You won't see that person again." There was no one sitting next to me. I thought I might be gone by default.

Many of the professors seemed like somnolent evangelical preachers, conveying their discipline as if it were the word of God, their ideas unquestioned guides to making the whole world better. Though their expertise seemed astute and certain, I had my doubts, largely because of how dull most of their lectures were. Servants to our note taking and cringing before the almighty grade-giver, I didn't think many of our teachers realized how ineffectual their presentations were. While their ideas could be astounding, their delivery was often mundane. Nevertheless, in a lecture hall filled with nearly 200 students, whether their words were stimulating or stagnant, what most professors saw was the tops of our heads as we labored to record their given knowledge.

Some of the faculty did break up the monotony of their lectures with stunts, a few of which were so famous that students who had taken their courses would return on the particular lecture date to witness their performance again the next semester. In Introduction to Physiology, the following episode had gained such renown. The purpose of this exhibition was to accentuate the difference between the circulatory system and the digestive system. As the class proceeded, a graduate assistant approached the stage with a covered terrarium in which there was a rattlesnake. That in itself was enough to gain my gripped attention. Then, the professor and the grad assistant milked the venom from the rattlesnake's fangs into a glass beaker. Ooohs and aaahs reverberated across our lecture hall in reaction to this sight. Next, the professor drank the venom! At this scene, I was ready to run out of the classroom and into the street shouting with my arms flaying. However, I remained seated to watch if the professor died. He did not. He calmly explained that the digestive system has antibodies and is immune to the rattlesnake's venom. It is our circulatory system that is poisoned by snakebite—a lesson I have never forgotten nor tested.

However, the effect of such a stunt did not carry over to the next day's class. The student next to me smirked, "Wonder what he's going to do today. Have a stroke to demonstrate the effects of blood pressure?" What I began to notice was the better lecturers didn't use stunts; they used interest to sustain stimulation in large classes. They made their topics relevant. Whether the course was in science or liberal arts, the subjects discussed reflected what mattered to us.

Our political science professor knew most of us were familiar with large corporations, the automobile industry, and strikes and other union actions. His selection of legislative bills, Supreme Court decisions, and tax laws reflected those that were connected to our real world: the 1947 Taft-Harley Act, which restricted the power of labor unions and still rankled some of us; the question of whether Joe McCarthy abused the power of the legislative branch of national government was still in the air in 1961. He played recordings of the radio broadcasts of G. Mennen Williams, Walther Reuther, and Father James Coughlin. He took the position that anything worth teaching should make a difference for students or what they value. Our physics professor followed suit with the pertinent question of what were important circles and squares in our own lives before he related them to more abstract concepts and formulas. In order to introduce the human need for compassion, our psychology teacher gave each of us a folded, sealed paper with our name on it as we entered class. After we were seated, she asked us to open it and raise our hand if what was written on it was true. After noting that nearly ninety percent of us had raised our hands, she revealed that she had written the same thing on each slip—"Some people don't realize how sensitive you are." Discussion followed. As I would come to understand later in my own teaching, the closer we bring our topics and skills to the personal lives of our students in the here and now,[22] the more they will be interested and emotionally involved in learning having experienced the essential ingredient of relevance for developing a positive attitude.

However, my attitude toward my courses, though generally good, ran a distant second to my need for survival in college. When I woke up each morning, I felt I should immediately start running. Where or toward what, I wasn't sure. I just knew I should be running. The amount of reading expected was five times greater than in high school. In the introductory courses, there were no make-up tests or opportunities to revise papers. I had little idea how to pace myself. I was a walk-on for football, held two part-time jobs, took a full-time load of classes, commuted by bus to school, and constantly daydreamed of hip ways to talk to the unending phalanxes of attractive women that populated my classes. I seemed stuck on my only conversation starter, "What high school did you go to?" I had no idea what to say next.

But I wasn't the only one floating through this frenzy. The one guy I could talk to, Frank Mackowiak, a buddy from high school, my lunch mate who also went to Wayne, affirmed our mutual distress as he unwrapped the wax paper around two bologna sandwiches, "It's like living in an emergency ward and being on life-support. You could tank out any moment. Miss an assignment, flunk a test, and you're a goner. Like the grim reaper, the Big F is always at your door. The teachers aren't mean but they don't care if you flunk out. It only proves their point. College isn't for everyone."

I agreed, "That might be. I have no idea what kind of grades I'm going to get. I could be one year and out."

"Nah, you belong. Certainly more than the guy in my geography class who said we could solve overpopulation by boarding up the oceans."

Frank and I made it through that first semester. I pulled a 2.86 GPA. Nonetheless, I wasn't certain I should be in college. I had no idea what vocation I should pursue. I was beginning to learn the ropes of being a college student. I was having a more interesting life than I had anticipated. But school still seemed overwhelming and unpredictable. I felt like a pawn in a challenging game that I hadn't figured out. It was moving me; I wasn't moving it. Learning in every course still seemed to be a cliffhanger. The first day and syllabus of every new course remained perplexing. Can I do this? Can I keep up with it? Will I pass? Love of learning was a mystery I had yet to experience or imagine.

CHAPTER 6

Learning to Flow

My sophomore year at Wayne did not begin well. I was getting more minutes playing middle linebacker during practice, but I broke my left fibula early in the fall during a scrimmage. My indelible memory from that season was the first time I came home on crutches. Because of my visit to the emergency room and the necessary x-rays and casting, I was coming home at dinner time. I knew my father would be there. Dinner waited for his arrival. I was more consumed with dread than pain. I had fulfilled his prophecy—"You know, I'll tell you now, you play football, one of these days you're going to break your leg. I can't stop you, but that's what's going to happen." When I came through the door and he saw me, he was sitting at the dinette table. Without saying a word, he stood up, took his chair, raised it above his head, and slammed it into pieces on the kitchen floor. Then, still silent, he went out the front door and did not return until nightfall.

That was it. The worst had passed. I went to my room, undressed, took my pain pills, propped up my leg on a couple of pillows, sighed an interminably long time, cursed my bad luck, called out "Good night," to my mother, and went to sleep. My father did not harass me about my injury. At eighteen, in our home, you were considered an adult. No more handing in report cards, I could smoke, drink, and live according to my own rules as long as I did not act immorally or become financially dependent on my parents. The rules were clear and at eighteen I felt like an adult. Where the rules weren't so clear was in the rest of the world, away from home. But I had bedrock. The basic tenet across my entire family was the same: If you're an adult, you pay your own way. Money, identity and respect were tied together. Unless you were in the military service or married, living with your parents before turning 25 was the norm. The worst fate was to be an unnecessary burden to your family. Losing your job was grim, but not looking for work after losing it was a crisis, intolerable for those I loved most. These rules seemed fair to me. Living paycheck to paycheck, they were born of necessity.

With my cast removed after six weeks, I felt ready to roll. It was too late to resume football practice, so I had more time for work and school. Something I wasn't ready for was being fired from my job as a bus boy. Feeling like an adult is not the same as being an adult. What got me fired makes this obvious. Would you retain a server who ate mashed potatoes with his bare hand as he conveyed them toward the cafeteria in a rolling metal box? It was that glint of butter and paprika at the top that seduced me. With my mouth stuffed so full, I couldn't shut it and creamy pulp dripping from my lips, my supervisor, Mrs. Gillespie, spotted me and fired me on the spot. Still swallowing and gulping for air, I responded with a sound akin to a large splat of mud or worse, landing on the ground. Feeling mortified, I knew I should try for at least one more chance to keep my job. I sucked in the remaining mouthful of mashed potatoes, gave her a submissive look, made sure my voice was below the octave of whining, and said, "I'm sorry. There's no excuse for what I did. It won't happen again." Mrs. Gillespie was a stout woman with greying hair, done up Donna Reed fashion, with cat-eyed black rim glasses. She narrowed her eyes, her face color went from chalk to crimson, and her left arm, finger pointed like a "this way" sign, shot up into a rigid line toward the bus boy locker room. I could take a hint. I was gone and out of the building in less than five minutes.

No job. I had roughly a week to find another one before I felt the loss of money or had to borrow some. I was not going to tell my parents I had been fired. That would've made a crisis into a disaster, mostly for me. If I could find work quickly, I could feint that I had decided to take another job, a common occurrence throughout my family with part-time work. As long as the checks kept coming, not a whole lot of questions were asked.

Ken Dettloff, another regular from our lunch group at Wayne, came to my rescue, "Hey, we could use another person in staging and lighting. Give Frank Smith a call." Frank Smith was the supervisor of set design and construction for Wayne State University TV. Formerly with ABC Television, he was quite amazing. Calm, resourceful, humane, funny, and respectful, he could keep his cool while an earthquake disassembled everything around him. With a slight build hidden by a corduroy sport coat two sizes too big, balding black hair swept straight back, a small mustache, and protruding front teeth, he hired me after a five minute interview, mainly about where I went to high school.

Though his entire crew was made up of hyper college kids who dropped things from desks to spotlights the size of toaster ovens, he never shouted. Everything could be fixed and replaced. "It's human beings that count," and he meant it. Someone once whispered to me that Frank had had a nervous breakdown. If so, I was glad to believe it, reassured to know that a good person could be crushed and come back.

I loved the job. Designing and putting a set together took some creativity. Lighting the "talent" required judgment and finely hewed adjustments. We used a twelve foot high ladder splayed on wheels to spin across the floor and to hang lights from stationary steel rods set two feet apart. Our interview guests ran the range of actors, politicians, sports stars, artists, and musicians who visited Detroit. In the mid-60s that meant anyone from George C. Scott to

George W. Romney and Dizzy Dean to Dizzy Gillespie. Maybe it was because we were young amateurs, and the awe showed up on our faces pretty easily, but these frequently famous people were uniformly nice to us, even Jimmy Hoffa who looked and spoke like a Hollywood thug.

The windfall of this second year was making the adjustment to college learning. I stopped feeling like I had to bolt at the end of every activity. I wasn't tranquil, I just stopped jumping out of my seat and leaning forty-five degrees into my stride. What a relief.

I had learned how to take notes, prepare for tests, economize on studying, judge which ideas seemed worth remembering, tactfully ask questions about things that were important to understand but needed clarification, and most of all, read for pleasure as well as comprehension. I had gotten rid of the quakes, ruminating about all the possible ways I could fail. Part of my relief was due to my own psychological development. I was able to be metacognitive, to think about my own thinking,[23] to realize what I did or did not know well. This capacity allowed me to trust my thoughts about academic work and begin to enjoy it.

It was during this shift toward academic self-confidence that I took my first course with Finley Hooper, History 535—The Hellenistic Period. I had heard about him from eavesdropping on student conversations as a bus boy. I don't think the pattern has changed that much over the centuries—students talk about their teachers, more often about the ones they don't like, but also about the ones they do like. Finley was exceptional because, from my completely unscientific secret listening, his name came up more often than any other highly regarded professor. He was, amazingly enough, a professor of ancient history, a field of study thought to be dead and irrelevant in the 1960s. As students repeated stories he told in his classes, like the great difficulty Nero had murdering his mother, I found myself stalling near their tables to find out how the stories ended or what wisdom might be gleaned from these tales. It was as though I had discovered that Detroit had its own Homer and he resided in Mackenzie Hall at Wayne State University.

For my initial class with Finley, I knew to come early, well before it began because I had heard all seats would be filled. They always were, a prediction that didn't falter for the next three quarters. Many of the students in the class had taken courses with him before. As I talked with the student next to me, Lucas, who was taking his final course with Finley, I asked what grade he had received from him the prior semester.

"I don't know," he replied.

"Didn't he give you a grade?"

"I'm sure he did. I just never open my grades."

He was sincere. I was astonished. "Really? I've never heard of that before."

"I think it is unusual, but I figure if there's a problem, the university will let me know. Until then, I'll assume the best."

"Can't argue with that. What's your major?"

"Astronomy."

"So why are you taking ancient history courses?"

"Dr. Hooper. If he can't figure out the universe, no one can."

I laughed nervously. What I learned in the weeks ahead was that most of the sixty students in the class weren't history majors. They were from every major imaginable including mortuary science. It was like he was on a bucket list for Wayne students—no longer being a virgin, pulling a 4.0 GPA, and taking a course with Finley Hooper. I had to admit I was one of them. I had no idea then that I would take two more of his courses as well.

The atmosphere that day remained for the rest of the quarter: a lively buzz among the students, palpable tension like the mood before a press conference or an important sporting event, Finley entering the room roughly a minute before the bell rang to start class, and a sweep of total silence among us just before he began his lecture.

As I saw him for the first time, he struck me as a small man in his early 50s, a face finely featured and very British in appearance with slightly long, wavy brown hair, a small checkered wool sports coat, a crisp white cuff-linked shirt, silk tie, and polished shoes. More distinguished than handsome, he could have stepped out of a London haberdashery. When he spoke, I was surprised. Although Midwestern in accent, his voice was higher pitched than I imagined it would be. It wasn't sonorous. But he had a confident command of it with the ability to pause and color his sentences with an easy and broad vocabulary, not at all rushed or anxious. He briefly welcomed us and passed out the attendance sheet. Then he looked upward as though bringing a memory into focus, and when he seemed to have it, his eyes swept across the room and he said, "Let's begin with a good, old question: Who has more power, the man who has everything or the man who does not ask for anything?" Lucas flashed me a see-what-I-mean smile and we were flying. Like the first scene in a great film or the first song from a gifted artist, we knew the rest would be magnificent.

Finley did not disappoint. He followed the quote from Diogenes with another, "It is a mark of God to need nothing, and those who are like God to need little." Then he contrasted this Cynic philosophy with the Hellenic ideas of Plato and Aristotle who argued that the application of human reason would make man's life more civilized. Diogenes, disavowing this tradition, taught that civilization was the cause of most of humanity's problems. Finley asked, "Should we today, as the Cynics encouraged the Greeks, 'Look for answers within ourselves, break free from the artificiality of society, and find peace and serenity apart from cities and in the countryside among hushed woods and quiet streams?' Is there wisdom in this idea?"

His question had relevance for our class because it was 1964 and the hippie counterculture was emerging across the United States. We took his query seriously and passionately. In a moment, respectfully but intensely, students began arguing for and against the idea of fleeing civilization and seeking individual self-sufficiency How could that kind of isolated life, however communal, be an act on behalf of universal love or living as a "citizen of the world?" Countered by: How else do you start a new society other than by breaking away from the one to which you belong? Back and forth it went, until Finley, like a jazz pianist moving the music forward after a drum solo, pulled it together with superb timing and a knowledgeable historic insight—"The time of the Cynics' greatest influence was the same time that Alexander, a student of Aristotle, was conquering Persia, when no one could escape Greek overtures to empire. Is this not parallel to the United States militarism today?"—deftly moving our thinking further and deeper.

I was fascinated. The discussions were like solar eruptions, unpredictably shaped and stirring. With their spirited questions and responses, students weren't just listening to themselves talk. They cared about what they said. In those moments, it was as though we were debating the future of our lives and our world. This wasn't a classroom, this was the *polis,* a small community of fellow citizens deliberating and sharing what life means and how it should be lived. When a student would mask a challenge in a question—Why admire the Romans?—Finley would tease it out with a gambit I used later in my own teaching. "Sounds like there's a statement behind that question. What do you think it might be?" Students' answers ranged from, "They were murderous, vindictive conquerors." to "They kept slaves, raised taxes, and decimated native cultures in favor of their own." Whatever the answer, by making a declarative sentence along with and after the question, the student gave the entire class a better sense of what she was thinking and more specifics for a fruitful discussion.

Finley never let any idea or story become final. Among a dynamic citizenry, nothing ever is complete. Answers beget more questions and knowledge seeks more knowledge. He had his beliefs and values but he didn't *know.* One of his gifts as a teacher was to show confidence in his own uncertainty, to be a scholar humbled by what he discovered in his search for enlightenment. No dogma. He continued to explore the realm of ancient history, using its heroes, art, and philosophy to raise questions and answers still worthy of concern for us all.

I felt transported in his courses with the ache of ideas that shook my entire belief system. I'm sure I had heard ideas as profound as those he related before, but not in a secular setting, not from people who were regarded by my religious teachers as pagans or mythic figures. The first thoughts that pierced my defenses were political and moral. Why Viet Nam? Why segregation? Finley didn't use history to explain why things turned out the way they did, he used history to question things as they were. How do distant wars with imperial intent weaken powerful nations as they did Athens and Rome? How does the cultural superiority of "civilized men" breed exclusiveness and chronic class struggles in cities, taking a toll and leading to a populace that is insecure, anxious, and constantly in strife? Where are the signs of these conditions among us today? How do we respond?

When Finley's classes began, I immediately felt absorbed and in flow. Fully present, he took himself seriously. Because of his gifts of rhetoric and scholarship as translated through stories with which we could identify, we took ourselves, as students, seriously as well. Although not stated as such, *the goals were clear*: understand the world more deeply, find your role in it, and influence it. Discussions *provided feedback* with our own self-generated examples and questions.[24] The *challenge* was also apparent. If we understand and value these ideas, how do we fit them into our lives and use them as guides to form a better world? This felt meaning was the significance of each of Finley's courses. Such vital engagement meant making an attempt to realize what our purpose in life might be.[25] If we could grasp it, what did that mean today and for the decades ahead?

After three courses with him, I was being transformed, though not comfortably so. I no longer needed to believe in an anthropomorphic God or accept a Catholic hierarchy to be a moral person. This was not easy for me to accept within myself. Along with my family, most of my social life was with friends who were Catholic. The historic sources for my reasoning about what was good and what was evil were Catholic teachings and I knew I still depended on them. Living at home, I went to mass every Sunday. I didn't think I could just stop. But once I started to trust my own thinking about what was just, I started to trust less what the Church said.

My distrust of priests and their homilies accelerated. They seemed simple, predictable, and controlling. Most of all, they offered a superficial relevance. Be truthful. Be pure. But we're not going to talk about Viet Nam or segregation, especially in the light of the perspectives of Martin Luther King, Jr. or God forbid, Malcolm X. Although my neighborhood was desegregated and a black family lived next door, the church I went to, St. Louis the King, was white, Polish Catholic. There was no public mention of the black community among us, ever.

When I went to hear Malcolm X speak at Wayne, I left his powerful presentation in an auditorium packed with students and faculty feeling scared, confused, shaken, and with little doubt that I was complicit in a racist society. Though he didn't say it, I knew that a core connection to my own prejudice was anchored in my Catholic upbringing, where my character was formed and influenced, where charity was praised for the poor as though they were an abstract, distant, colorless, and impotent entity, deserving of our pity but not our political will.

The place where I found authentic discussion of inequity, race, and war were Finley's classes. The only current reading I found other than books that confronted social and governmental injustice was Wayne's school newspaper, *The South End.* Wayne State University was both my haven and my provocateur for issues that unsettled me. I didn't know it at the time but I was going through *the first three phases of transformation* as described by Jack Mezirow, a leading thinker in adult learning theory.[26]

I was feeling disoriented, my thoughts dissonant with the assumptions I had learned in my family and schools. My church was not the leader in moral thinking. Its priests and bishops were not at the forefront of social change for the betterment of society. They were not addressing urban poverty, racism, gender inequality, or an unjust war shouldered by the poor and black. Instead, they seemed invested in the status quo, ignorant or afraid to speak out. While rattled to the bone, I believed I couldn't talk about these things in my home. My mother trusted the Church. My father didn't trust the Church, but he respected the President and if I challenged him about his loyalty to Lyndon Johnson, he would explode.

As a result of my *self-examination of my beliefs*, I felt vaguely guilty. Did I lack the strength of my convictions? What were those convictions? Maybe I needed more time to know them and test them. Discussions in an ancient history class weren't the same as those with my friends and family. I needed to start to bring these questions up, not in some kind of pompous or know-it-all manner, but as ideas that were on my mind. The first time I did was with Bob Schroeder. He was a football teammate and a friend that I respected. He was generally quiet, thoughtful, and honest about his opinions, a natural leader on our team. We were waiting to register for a class and I told him I had some reservations about the uptick in the U. S.'s involvement in Viet Nam.

"You know Ray, I do too."

"Like what?"

"For one thing, I don't like the draft. For another, I don't think we know the people we're fighting."

"But would you protest it? You know, Martin Luther King has come out against the war. I'm thinking I should be more public about opposing it. Demonstrations are starting and I'm beginning to think I should join them."

"Well Ray, you're further along than I am. I've got to think more about it. See what the government does."

We left it at that. I didn't want to try to convince Bob the war was wrong. But he was the first one in whom I confided my thoughts and he was respectful of them. That brief exchange gave me an incentive *to keep on questioning my assumptions.*[27] I could stay critical. My doubts about my religion had substance. In some ways, I had already begun to leave the Church; I just hadn't told anyone yet. Like a friendship that's fading, my emotional intensity for religious involvement was growing dimmer. I wasn't looking for opportunities to join any church organizations or to volunteer for any of its functions. Going to mass was the last vestige of my connection to the church. As a consequence of the ideas that Finley Hooper and the courses I took with him had generated, my trust in Catholicism had waned.

Without knowing me personally, and before we became friends, he challenged my beliefs, which made me think more deeply, motivating more unsettling reflection about my faith in the church. But it's important to note that "unsettling ideas" are also stimulating ideas. I wasn't anxious or depressed. I was in flow with an eagerness to explore other ways of thinking about what existence meant. With this questioning, I became more open to another font of ideas on the horizon and to which my fidelity had begun to grow:[28] psychology and the belief that science held relevant answers for the life I wanted to live.

CHAPTER 7

Transformative Friendship

It wasn't as though everyone else stepped away. In 1964, I still lived at home, played football at Wayne State University, began a serious relationship, and had close friendships with college friends and schoolmates from way back when. But every year in one's history has something unique about it, and I believe, a chance for making a difference. As my friendship with Finley evolved, I had the focus of a thoughtful person, deeply immersed in another reality, and as other worldly to me as life two thousand years ago would have been.

Emerson's idea of friendship was that a friend could be anyone with whom we could be sincere. I think personal honesty was the first emotional step between us. Before we went to the hockey game, he took me to The Caucus Club, a small gem in the city, with lights that glowed like candles and an intimate, dark rich atmosphere, hinting at any moment Edith Piaf might sing a song or two. At first, I felt self-conscious, concerned about my manners, but Finley made me totally at ease. He read a few items off the menu, asked me if I might be interested in them (Of course, I was. It was the first time I had been to a restaurant of this sort in my entire life), and ordered our drinks. That was one of his gifts—to relieve my discomfort in new situations. I didn't have to monitor myself. I told him I was interested in becoming a teacher. He was delighted. He asked me about what and where I would teach. In his opinion, all worthy leaders were essentially teachers.

"Raymond, it's a great place to begin and a wonderful place to end. And, even if you change your mind, the experience will give you a better direction for what comes next."

"I think so. But I haven't taught yet, not even student teaching. I don't know what teaching feels like—for real. And, I'm not sure of the grade level or students. Teaching in Detroit would be so different from the suburbs."

"You're right. Students do make a difference. Seneca was Nero's tutor and look how he turned out," he smiled.

I nodded.

"But it's also important to remember the good ones. Fronto was the teacher of Marcus Aurelius, one of the best emperors Rome ever had. You can read their letters to each other. They're filled with mutual admiration and telling details about the importance of truthfulness." Finley looked around and beckoned me with his hand to lean in closer toward him, "I'm pretty sure we'll be the only ones in the Caucus Club tonight talking about Marcus Aurelius," he whispered with a laugh.

I laughed as well, a bit louder I'm afraid. Then I felt a rush of warmth because I knew the night was going well and I'd be with Finley again, listening to his stories, having a drink, bemused with ourselves and our world through the prism of a firmament far away in time and place.

The hockey game was memorable, not only because it was our first sport's outing together but because Gordie Howe of the Red Wings scored a hat trick. When the red light went on for the third goal, the crowd rose with a roar like the drunken beast it was. Finley was so taken by Howe's feat that he raised both arms forgetting that his left hand held a beer. The red waxed paper cup flew out with a trail of lager and foam streaming away like the top of a wave in a windy sea. Then it landed face down in his lap with all of its contents across his thighs and shoes. He looked at me while the crowd was still screaming its ovation, a guilty shocked expression that quickly turned into a deep throated hearty laugh ending with, "Having a good time, aren't I? Go, Gordie!!" The game was against the Toronto Maple Leafs. In the years ahead, we would often recall it. Our cue being the spilling of anything on either of us, a more frequent occasion than we might have imagined during that unforgettable evening.

After that night, unless he was travelling, I would see Finley about once a month. Most of our time together was over coffee, a drink, lunch, or dinner. For me, these occasions were precious. I cherished them as I would the most beautiful sights I would ever see, except that each also had wisdom as an inherent bountiful gift bonded to it. Finley was interesting because he was interested in subjects outside of himself. His curiosity about ancient and modern times was infused with unique knowledge. I sat with a man who had been inside pyramids, read Latin and Classical Greek, knew curators of museums across the world, spent summers in Athens, Rome, and Cairo, and wrote books reviewed by the New York Times. And, the beauty of it all was that Finley was being Finley. He did not try to impress. He listened to me as much as I listened to him. He genuinely believed that anyone concerned about present problems would profit from learning how the ancient peoples went about solving theirs—with the added advantage of knowing how it all turned out.

When I told him about my father's temper, how he would rage, how I feared him, and hesitated in his presence, wary that I might offend him with my behavior or my words, Finley's eyes left my gaze for a long while. When he looked at me again, his eyes were glistening and tearful, "You know, Raymond, a father among the Romans had the power of life and death over his children, even when they were adults. From what you've told me, your father's life was extremely harsh, that he was beaten by his own father. Although he may despise himself for his fury, it may not be an instinct he can control. I know this: you love your father and he loves you. Here, the psychologists are probably wiser.

As Freud said, 'It is not our dislike of our enemies that harms us, it is our hate for those we love that destroys us.' I don't think there's an easy way out. I'm sorry."

Though I came to love Finley, I never wanted to be him. That kind of identification would have seemed like a transgression, a violation of our trust. Becoming him would be a kind of idolatry that would destroy our friendship. We both liked our differences. I could kid him when he criticized Lyndon Johnson as a bit of a hick or pronounced the end of Latin as the official language of the Roman Catholic Church as a travesty. "Come on, Finley, you've been in those tombs too long. I think cobwebs in your brain might be the real thing."

He'd laugh and say, "I think that calls for another drink. Never found a spider in a bottle of Scotch yet." He enjoyed irreverence and that's one of the things I had to offer. What I admired about him and *did want* was the way he thought. He wasn't knee-jerk about almost anything. He had a reservoir of knowledge that seemed endless and charged with originality. He could always go into it and draw something that made what we were talking about more complex, but saner. When I told him that if I were to be drafted, I might opt to be a conscientious objector, he asked, "Is this your best conception of what is right?"[29]

I answered, "I'm not sure, but I don't believe in the war or killing."

Finley responded, "Socrates would say, 'Be master of your own destiny, your own happiness. It's not what other men can take from you. It's the power you have over yourself that gives you freedom from others' power.' What happens when you think of it that way?"

"Going to Canada and escaping the draft comes to mind. Still not sure though."

"Well at least that's another option that keeps you in control, more so than being in the Army. There may be other options worth thinking about."

Having immediate certainty about hard choices was not as attractive to me as it once was. Being Finley's friend continued my transformation because he offered *exploration of alternatives for new roles and actions* by what he said and did. He helped me to enjoy thinking.[30] It was contagious. Like most transformations, it carried over to other important aspects of my life. Rather than taking a course and being controlled by the syllabus, I saw that I had much more control over the course and syllabus by how I thought about it. Motivation is about more energy for a given purpose but transformation is about changing a mindset. Now, I looked upon my own ideas and beliefs as guides for what courses should offer me. From this perspective, I derived more energy for learning, and consequently, greater motivation.

This personal transformation affected my psychology courses. Introduction to Child Study was essentially memorization of definitions like development, maturation, and sets of age related behaviors, but I concentrated on defense mechanisms, memorizing all of them, because they helped to explain not only other people's motives, but my own as well. I came to understand human beings can *rationalize* anything and often do, from greed to genocide. So, when was I rationalizing? Was my difficulty with authority a projection growing out of my troubles with my father? More important, realizing the pervasiveness of defense mechanisms cautioned my own self-righteousness, fired by my youth, idealism, and incalculable ignorance. Yet, I felt charmed because I could reach back into Greek history and see how Sophistry was a precursor of psychology with its emphasis on the individual, and the notion that there was no way for a single person to know the absolute truth for everyone. What that awareness left me with was that knowledge was both reassuring and unnerving, freeing and restrictive, and the words of Finley about the Sophists ringing in my ears, "You know Raymond, you can be educated enough to be dangerous, but not intelligent enough to see beyond self-interest." Conceptually, I didn't know then what intrinsic motivation was, but I was feeling it when I walked into a classroom to learn, especially about what mattered to me.

Transformation doesn't take place in a vacuum. According to the phases cited by Jack Mezirow, one transformative experience can connect to the next one, building a succession of integrated ideas that become *provisional for trying new roles* and *building confidence for new relationships.*[31] Though I had not yet come to know him personally, once I had taken two of Finley's courses, I realized I had to leave home for a period of time, to live on my own with my own thoughts as my guide, beyond the influence of my parents and old friends. Otherwise, the centripetal force of their expectations would draw me in so firmly I might never act on what I imagined I might become. Like hordes of young adults before me, I wasn't ready to surrender quite yet. In May of 1964, before my senior year, I knew I had to leave Detroit.

Where? I didn't know. I knew where I couldn't go—another Midwest City or Great Lakes countryside—too familiar, too close. And, I knew wherever I went I had to be able to earn some money. Otherwise, I'd be depleting my savings and putting my college education in jeopardy. Wayne State University had a counseling office with large binders filled with summer jobs. In less than two hours I found my destination: Rocky Mountain National Park. I could work at the Estes Park Lodge which included complete room and board and twelve dollars a day for expenses.

As soon as the spring quarter was finished, I was on my way. I still relish that feeling of adventure, not knowing anything but the sight of a few photographs in a crumpled brochure with a vista of the lodge and enormous mountains behind it. I took $36, half of the train fare I needed to get back, because I knew myself well enough to know if I actually had enough money to buy a return ticket, I would be tempted to do just that when things got tough.

They did. Ed, the man at the lodge who was in charge of temporary help, a euphemism in the brochure for what he referred to as "mostly dumb-ass college kids," greeted me with, "Could you pronounce your last name for me? That's the weirdest name I've ever seen." After I did, he said, "Pick yourself a cabin out back. There's two left. You'll have to share it with the next guy we hire. You start work in the laundry room at 6:00am tomorrow. Don't be late or else you'll lose a day's pay."

I nodded my head and moved quickly through the doorway of his office, glancing back one more time. He was placing his feet up on his desk, his square head, brush-cut grey hair, and rimless glasses in perfect tune with a white shirt, cheap thin black tie, and a plastic pocket protector overwhelmed with pens and pencils. I thought, *Okay, the boss isn't too friendly. I've had that experience before. But I get a cabin. Wow! And all to myself, at least for now.* When I went behind the lodge, I saw the cabin was a small wooden shed, 8 x 10', on stilts, along the side of a mountain. If I ran good and hard and threw a cross body block on it, I think I could've knocked it over. The steps up to the door were nearly break-thru thin. When I stepped inside, the entire floor seemed to move. It wasn't a weakness in the floor, it was a scurrying army of insects, most of which were larger than any I had ever seen in Detroit. At that moment I felt my stomach clutch and I remembered what my brother had told me when he first went into his boot camp barracks, "I thought I knew what to expect. I saw the rows of thin steel bunk beds, and then I looked at the end of the room and there were five toilets with no doors facing me. I could feel a giant cork wedging into my butt. I didn't crap for five days."

I had to step back out. I looked at the lodge and tried to keep breathing. At 7,000' elevation, I felt faint and it was legit. I stepped back in and the floor moved again. This time, I heard it, like a piece of sand paper being rubbed on a cardboard floor. I looked up because I was scared to look down. I saw a single light bulb on a wire dangling above me, with three holes in the roof, about the size of college textbooks. Then I saw the bunk beds with rolled mattresses on top of them. I pulled at the string around the first mattress. It popped like a spring loaded jack-in-the-box. When the mattress unfurled another swarm of insects darted in every direction, some flying into my face. Again, I stepped out of the door. I told myself to stay calm.

It took me about twenty minutes to resume normal breathing. Then I got angry and shouted, "Dammit! No!" I went down to the kitchen, introduced myself, and told the head cook about my cabin. He nodded knowingly, told me where the frozen turkeys were stored, and suggested I use the plastic bags they were wrapped in for the holes in the roof. Then he told me where a ladder was and wished me luck.

It took me until nightfall to shape up the cabin, but I couldn't get over the bugs and I had the shakes. When I went to sleep, I swaddled myself like a baby with only my face showing, which I buried into my pillow. I knew I was desperately homesick because I had no appetite and the sight of food roiled my stomach. The laundry room was my salvation. A friendly woman named Beth, tall, fit, and with a single length of braided grey hair reaching down her back to her hips ran it. Our only rule was, "Work hard and leave early." Most days we were done by noon. The seismic shift came on the third day, when Larry was assigned to my cabin. He was a twenty-six year old, rail thin, bearded vagabond from Scotland, wearing a winter cap with the flaps over his ears. He looked like he stepped out of a Lil Abner Cartoon. Larry walked through the door, looked around, and said, "Ah, the palace. How refreshing!" That broke the spell. I started laughing and could feel the wisps of home sickness dissolving around me.

It took about a week before my appetite returned and I could appreciate the mountain paradise that surrounded me. With little money, I spent most of my free time hiking. My travels in the park were a feast of firsts: the first time I saw a black bear in the wild; the first time I saw trout jumping in a mountain stream, the first time I saw endless groves of aspen, their leaves flashing green and silver; the first time I rode full gallop through a mountain meadow; and the first time I reached the top of Long's Peak and saw the boundless spillway of snowclad crests reaching out into the infinite distance. At that moment, I knew why the gods made Mount Olympus their home.

Although I danced in the Estes Park bars, and my Detroit moves were fairly well received, there was no summer romance. I had graduated to another variation of small talk, "Where are you from?" which was usually followed by a state being named. Then, with confidence, "What city?" Cited easily. Then, with continuing confidence, "What's your name?" Given easily. More confidence, "I like that. It seems to fit you." Followed by her smile. Then I was lost, with the conversation dribbling away.

I left the Estes Park Lodge before August began. I had saved another $36 for the $72 train ticket back to Detroit. I needed a more sizeable salary to build some reserves for the fall quarter. There were still about five weeks before football practice began and I knew I could earn a heftier paycheck doing landscaping.

I didn't tell anyone I was returning. This was one of my only chances to truly surprise my family and friends. I got back to our house in the late afternoon on a Friday. I knew it was likely that my mother would be out shopping. I called first to make sure she wasn't there. After I let myself in, I took a seat in the living room and read. When she came through the doorway and saw me sitting there, she didn't say a word. She quickly crossed the room as I rose to greet her. She rested her cheek against my chest and held me. It's an image I hold dear to this day. When my father came home from work, I made sure I was sitting at the dinette table. He came through the side door, put his lunch pail down, and saw me. He stood there for a moment surveying me. No smile. He was making sure I was physically okay: no marks, no casts, no crutches. Then he came up the small stairway toward me. I didn't rise to greet him, but I did look up with a smile. He put his arm around my shoulder, pulled me in toward him. His words not quite a whisper, but deep from within, "Glad you're back. Safe and sound." Then he looked at my mother and I knew they were happy. Feeling the same, I was thankful for it.

I had lived on my own, and I knew I could do so again. I had made some friends with people unlike myself, nothing deep and lasting, but with more time, I felt that would have happened. I knew I wanted to travel and I could be at ease away from home. I think Colorado prepared me for reaching out to Finley. It may have been what spurred me to talk to him at that corner stop light and to ask him to have coffee. But of this, I'm more certain: one transformation sets the foundation for a deeper similar transformation. After my trip to Estes Park, I *wanted to travel.* As my friendship with Finley grew, I knew I *would* travel. I also knew I would leave Detroit. That was something I didn't anticipate before we became friends. Because of our sincere rapport, I was *building competence for new roles and relationships.* I had been deemed significant by a man I deeply admired. His esteem for me helped me to look further *to reintegrate my life with a new perspective a*bout with whom I might be intimate and where I might live.[32]

In my senior year, when my relationship with Finley was deepening, I knew teaching offered the surest route to a vocation with which I could identify. I liked kids. I got along with them easily whether they were my cousins or my neighbors. However, what really attracted me to teaching was that I now knew I loved learning.[33] How better to nurture this feeling than to be a teacher. Just one more step. To teach. Then I would know for sure.

CHAPTER 8

Teacher Newbie

In terms of hard evidence, other than being a good student and sociable, I had little reason to believe I could be an excellent teacher. I wasn't particularly patient. No one had ever said to me, "Raymond, you'll be a great teacher someday." When I asked myself what had I ever taught someone? The list was sparse. In high school, I had helped a few of my friends with their math homework but that was the norm for those of us who had actually done our homework. Nothing special there. My biggest success, still in high school, was coaching my friend, Frank Orlando, for his fifteen minute speech when he ran for class treasurer, "Tell three jokes, one in the beginning, one in the middle, and one at the end, and promise you'll listen to students and keep the money safe." His jokes were good. He won.

Another possible clue to my potential as a teacher was winning three trips to cities outside of Michigan for selling Detroit Times newspaper subscriptions to strangers. The contests lasted six weeks. Although it wasn't competitive, a carrier had to sell at least 35 subscriptions. Sales for each carrier were posted on the paper station wall. The "station master" (This term was the first example I thought of when I learned the definition of a euphemism) was usually a guy around thirty, who was paid to hang around with adolescent boys while they folded papers and to take them canvassing to sell subscriptions. I peddled papers for five years and I never met another paperboy who considered this occupation as a future career choice.

The entire city of Detroit was eligible for canvassing. Working in pairs, one boy on one side of the street, the other on the other side of the street, we went house to house to sell. This arrangement was also our safety system. If one of the pair saw the other was in trouble, he was to knock on a door for help. We knew this precaution was bogus because fights and muggings usually lasted less than a minute. Harm doesn't waste time. When we told the station master that we could be dead by the time someone came to the door, much less helped out, he said, "If you don't trust the system, carry a knife." None of us did. Living in Detroit, we knew that having a weapon only increased the odds for personal immolation.

They never took us to a middle-income or higher-income neighborhood. It was always a lower-income neighborhood. I knew why the first time I canvassed and the neighborhood changed as its fringe edged into a middle class community. People there didn't hesitate to tell me to get off their porch or slam a door in my face, especially other adolescents. Worst of all was the look I got.

I called it the scum-of-the-earth stare. This treatment wasn't from most of the people but it happened often enough that I knew I wouldn't canvass such an area again.

In the lower-income neighborhoods, most people who answered the door gave me a chance to speak. A few would interrupt and say, "No thank you," but most listened until I was done making my introduction. However, there were other dangers: gangs or just a tough kid who didn't like your look, and blue-collar burglar alarms—vicious dogs. On more than one occasion, a dog penetrated the screen of a bolted door to bite me. For all predators, I had learned the same routine: not to run, try not to show fear, keep my posture, and move quietly away. I was bitten twice but I was never beaten up.

The main thing I learned from this experience was some degree of compassion, an essential ingredient for any excellent teacher. Disrespect and making someone feel less-than was an invitation to their dislike and anger, possibly violence. Feeling dismissed was painful. I knew this awareness had registered within me because at my own home we often had people who came to our door selling everything from candy bars to car insurance as well as people who didn't have a home and were hoping for some food or funding. When my father answered the door, I would not describe him as nice, but he was respectful, listening and answering with a grim, "No thank you." Or, "Sorry, not today." After I had been canvassing, hearing him and watching the person at our door walk away left me with a feeling near loneliness. I knew the caller's life could not be at its best. These visceral memories served me well when I began student teaching. Not learning something, especially when one honestly tries, may have something to do with life circumstances far beyond individual intellect.

Looking back, it's difficult to know if I chose elementary teaching because I was confident or insecure. I remember saying to friends, "You know, kids who are 9 or 10 are just about perfect. Still innocent, but aware, thoughtful, and able to have a really good conversation with you. Being with them is fun." This was true, but I also knew that at twenty, I was capable of being threatened by adolescents. Sullen, strong, and macho, there were plenty of young guys around Detroit to give me more than a second thought. I had my last fist fight at 19, and I had enough of a temper to know I wasn't predictable when confronted by someone in a physical way. I worried that the discipline needed to teach in high school might be beyond what I could handle calmly and firmly.

Getting to know Finley and my ambition to be a teacher had made me realize that fighting and hostile reactions like shouting had to be a part of the past. Although Finley saw unnecessary violence as something tragically foolish, an urge to be avoided, he could be overly anxious about his physical well-being. Once, I saw him react to a paper cut in a way that I found hard to believe.

The cut was deep enough to bleed, but it took him a good quarter hour to stop talking about it. My reaction would have been to hope no one noticed that I winced, and to put my hand in a pocket until the blood coagulated. When I finally raised my eyebrows, smiled, and gently asked him, "Want some cheese to go with that whine?" he was startled. He gave me a who-do-you-think-you're-talking-to look, then smiled, shook his head, and chuckled to himself.

I knew that one of the reasons Finley liked me was my comfort in situations he considered rowdy. Once, at a Detroit Tigers baseball game, while we were sitting in the bleachers, a fight broke out about ten seats away from us. It was more pushing and shoving than anything else. When the police quickly approached the two combatants, they stopped. The police hauled them off by their shirt collars to the applause of a good many fans. Finley watched with fascination. I was less sanguine and said with an air of bored disgust, "Too much to drink."

Finley responded in a respectful tone, "You know, Raymond, you'll never be a fop."

I could feel it was a compliment. I faked a knowing nod and responded with a stoic, "Thank you." Later I looked up the word to know how I had been praised. Nonetheless, Finley's regard for my ease in less predictable urban settings did not diminish my apprehension that outside of his company, I could still be too easily provoked: an insult, someone putting a hand on me, or raising their voice ignited a similar reaction from me.

However, when children were aggressive, I had enough sense to react with humor and acceptance,[34] deflecting or distracting their anger. If not, my presence or an admonishment usually would suffice. This self-awareness and the fact that at 20, I looked about 16—a certainty due to the children who mistook me for that age or younger—led me to request a fourth or fifth grade as my initial student teaching experience.

When I walked into Mrs. Musgrove's fifth grade class at State Fair Elementary School, I knew I had made the right choice. The children were beaming. They looked at me like I was a professional athlete. Introducing myself and telling them that I was from Detroit too, about four miles away, only seemed to make things better. When someone genuinely likes you, wants to do their best for you, is eager to learn with you, then as a teacher, you cannot do enough for them. There is such a thing as a mutual admiration society and we had it going from moment one in that class.

Mrs. Musgrove made this happen. She looked patrician: tall, mid-fifties, hair nearly white pulled back into a tight bun, always in a tasteful dress, and as she said to me on our second day, "I'm a lady from Tennessee. These are good kids and we're going to have a good time teaching them." She spoke the truth.

She had primed the children for my arrival. In 1965, male elementary school teachers were rare. Though there was no evidence that we were better teachers than women, a general idea in education at the time was that it was good to have men teaching young children because of they offered a healthy male image, especially for children from single parent families. There was no evidence for this claim. I benefited from this bias and I think Mrs. Musgrove was proud to have me as her student teacher.

The down side to this situation was that my skill to discipline children didn't get tested or challenged because Mrs. Musgrove was a teacher who had that classroom humming before I got there. During the second week, when I began teaching partial lessons on my own, a boy became sarcastic with me. Mrs. Musgrove, who was watching from a seat in the back of the classroom, rose quickly but walked slowly to the side of the room. Like a tennis exchange in a rally at Wimbledon, all heads turned in her direction. She said nothing but she gave the boy who taunted me a withering look for a full few seconds. The boy looked away, hunched his shoulders, and slid down in his desk. I found myself scared as well. I thought, "Henry Kissinger could learn a thing or two from Mrs. Musgrove."

At the end of the day, when I spoke to her about the incident, she responded, "You have a few tools when it comes to disciplining children. Used wisely and in variety, you can apply them effectively. One is to remain silent and look firmly at a child. Most know when they're misbehaving and don't need much more than this kind of reminder. You can also use a reprimand, tell them what they've done wrong, and ask them to stop. But sometimes you have to issue a warning and its consequence. That should be a means of last resort because the next time they misbehave you'll have to follow through on the warning."

I asked, "What warning do you prefer to use?"

She looked at me seriously, "I warn them that I'll call their parents, and I do. I don't like doing it because for most of the boys that means a spanking or the belt. This is a working class neighborhood and corporal punishment is widely used. But when you like children and they know you like them, and you're fair—that's why the classroom rules are posted on the front board—they will accept these consequences. Be consistent. And no grudges," her eyes widened. "When it's done, it's done. I welcome the child back and we move on."

After that meeting, I watched Mrs. Musgrove more closely. I saw that she followed the ideas she shared with me like they were a binding code. The children knew what to expect and she did not deviate. I had little need to use many discipline techniques while I student taught with her, the furthest I went up her hierarchy of classroom management was to a warning, and that was only once.

I learned a lot about teaching as well. Mrs. Musgrove was extremely well organized. Her lesson plans were detailed and thorough. She did transitions (assembling materials, getting ready for recess or lunch, dismissing the class, and so forth) beautifully. Her homework assignments were clear and reasonable, as was her grading system. I could see why she was considered an excellent teacher. I appreciated her approach to teaching and I realized I was personally quite different: more physical with the children, roughhousing or picking them up to reach something above their height; kidding them, playing games with them, running on the playground with them, and more openly enthusiastic about our lessons. I had not forgotten Sister Desiderata.

Mrs. Musgrove and I were a good match. We liked each other. In the back of my mind, I wanted to ask her to go out for a drink, but I couldn't imagine how to say it. She drank tea and that stopped me cold. My mother drank tea and I couldn't imagine asking her out for a drink either. When I finished my student teaching at State Fair Elementary, Mrs. Musgrove and the children gave me a lovely party. A few of the children who played instruments (accordion, clarinet, violin), played songs for us. There were home-made pastries and punch. They asked me to give a speech. Beyond thanking them, I remember telling them three things I had learned with them, "All children are beautiful. All children can learn. And, all children like to fool around," which drew a laugh. Each child had made a card for me with a personal note. The class gift to me was a small trophy on which was engraved, "To the best teacher in the world." Until I lost it in a move to Seattle, I kept it in a drawer in my office as a talisman against despair.

I had one more student teaching assignment before I graduated. I wanted a contrast from Detroit. I asked for a fifth grade class in Bloomfield Hills, a wealthy suburb north of the city. Other than driving around it a few times to view its mansions and manicured landscapes, I had no knowledge of this city. With a teaching shortage in the area, I knew I would have some choices about where I could work after graduation. I wanted to stretch those possibilities and I was curious about how schools in wealthy communities worked. I also knew I had a bit of a chip on my shoulder—blue collar boy among the rich. How would that feel? Could I cut it? Would I be dismissed or relegated to a lower status because of my background? Being Finley's friend had given me more confidence among people different from myself. However, Finley appreciated my rough edges. Partly due to youth, partly due to naiveté, I told myself the only way I might ever find answers to these questions was to be a student teacher in an affluent milieu.

Charmed. Guilty. Expectant.[35] Those were the feelings I had at the end of my first day with Mrs. Alice Gocella, my supervising teacher, at Pine Lake Elementary. Fifth graders seemed to beam everywhere when presented with the rare male species of a student teacher. Mrs. Gocella had friends who taught her to say my name before I arrived. Not only did she know how, but so did all the children, who greeted with me the only chorale pronouncement of my name that I had ever heard. I blushed and before I could recover, the principal walked into the room to greet me, addressing me as Mr. Wlodkowski, of course, with proper Polish pronunciation. Within ten minutes, I could feel pressure mounting to meet *their* expectations. Again, I was wrong. The principal took over the class and Mrs. Gocella and I went to his office to "have a chat and coffee." Before I had completely seated myself, she asked me to call her Alice and if I would be comfortable being addressed as Raymond, or if I preferred Ray. Then she told me there were no expectations from me during my first week other than to report to school on time, jot down questions as I observed her, get to know the students in a manner that was comfortable, and to meet with her at the end of each day regarding my questions, observations, and suggestions. She said, "I'm here to learn from you as well. Please enjoy the children and learn about our school. The rest will work out fine."

There were no rules posted on the chalk board. The modus operandi was polite consideration. When someone misbehaved: took a book from someone without asking, made fun of another student, pushed another student away, copied during a test, or shouted, Mrs. Gocella called their attention to their behavior by way of its effect on the student possibly harmed, or the negative effect on the student misbehaving. She explained these things to them as though they were adults and always in a voice that was more therapeutic than accusatory. "When you take Alice's book away from her without asking, it interrupts her learning. What can she do?" Or, "Treating Sean so roughly and throwing his pencil on the floor threatens him. Please return his pencil and I think you know enough to apologize." For most of the children, her suggestions worked very well. She would give those who were more resistant a time out which meant sitting alone in the back of the classroom to reflect on why their behavior was wrong. Then, after about twenty minutes, she would counsel them in the hallway. It was a very effective method. The classroom had an air of civility that was impressive. Politeness and consideration were highly valued and practiced throughout the entire school.

Mrs. Gocella's approach to teaching was more flexible and unstructured than Mrs. Musgrove's methods. There was more group work, more independent work, more projects, and rather than sitting in rows, children sat in quartets, their desks symmetrically arranged in neat squares. The class was noisier and seemingly a bit chaotic but learning was going on and the children were more in charge of their own learning. I liked it. I could see I had much more to learn about being a teacher. Finley's words echoed, "Knowledge begets more knowledge."

I guessed Mrs. Gocella was in her late thirties. She was fit, with short brown hair, large lively eyes, and a gentle voice. She was more physical with the children than Mrs. Musgrove but no less affectionate. As a teacher, she was more experimental. If she used a system, she would never call it that. In her view, it was a philosophy of teaching. Children are natural learners; teachers are there to create situations so children can learn at their best and become self-directed learners throughout their lives.

In terms of physical fitness, energy level, mischievousness, and wonder for learning, the children were not noticeably different from Mrs. Musgrove's class. Their clothes were more expensive, their manners were more conventionally apparent, and they were more ethnically homogeneous. Most seemed to be at least third generation descendants of families from Western Europe. There were no African Americans or children of recent immigrants. Another difference between the two groups that was apparent was the amount of travel that Mrs. Gocella's students had done. Many had been to Europe. When I talked about Colorado, more than half the class had already been there. That difference indicated many other economic differences beyond spoken awareness: leisure time, mobility, and the means to afford extended vacations. Teaching them was a pleasure of its own kind, but not discernably more or less than teaching the children in Mrs. Musgrove's class.

Mrs. Gocella's commitment to relevant and self-directed learning would include me as well. At the end of the first week, she asked which two subjects I might prefer to begin teaching the following week. I chose social studies and reading. Then she asked me if I had any suggestions or personal ambitions for my student teaching experience with her. I didn't know how she would word it but I knew this request was coming because she so often asked the children which topics most interested them and how to fit these into their regular lessons and projects.

I had given this expected opportunity some thought. A guest lecture by Fritz Redl that I had attended at Wayne State University had inspired me.[36] Dr. Redl was a pioneering behavioral scientist and therapist who had co-authored *Mental Hygiene in Teaching*, the first theory-based set of guidelines based on group dynamics to help teachers understand and deal with student misbehavior. An immigrant from Austria, with an accent as thick as my father's, but with the demeanor of a jolly grandfather, he made the point that student misbehavior in most instances is only group behavior. If teachers treated it as such, rather than as a discipline problem, pain on everyone's part could often be avoided. "Most fights in elementary school start like spontaneous combustion. Somebody steps on someone's toe, somebody accidentally knocks a book out of someone's hand, or someone takes teasing beyond its humor point, and a fight starts. It isn't that the children don't like each other or are holding a grudge. Like a small fire, it can be dowsed out quickly. Nobody needs to go to the principal's office." I thought of Sister Desiderata and how she handled the fight between Billy Trunowski and Richard Urbanek. Dr. Redl made sense. By virtue of her own experience, Mrs. Gocella was practicing some of his ideas for talking with children to establish classroom norms. His lecture ended with a question that kept me thinking, "What would change if we thought of discipline as character development?"

When Mrs. Gocella asked me that Friday afternoon for suggestions, I answered, "What if I started a character development project with the students?"[37]

Her smile was immediate, "Great idea! Please do. How can I help?"

The next week, we held a class meeting to discuss the children's perspectives on the idea of character. We asked them who they thought had character and why. Popular choices were family members and friends. Their why's were often heartfelt, "My mother helps people who need it. But she doesn't wait for them to ask and she doesn't expect anything in return. And, she doesn't tell anyone she's doing it. I only know because I see her. She takes meals to people and drives them places like hospitals and drug stores. Once she *made us* take in a family when their home burned down."

We talked about how we might build character in our own class. Less complaining, stop blaming, and offering help without being asked, were some of their suggestions. The children's ideas weren't too dramatic but they seemed sincere. They wanted to interview their parents and do reports. They wanted to make posters. I suggested a social studies project on ancient peoples and their ideas of character. For a culminating event, we invited a couple of the neighboring classes and the principal to hear our reports and view the posters. I think the children were proud of their accomplishments, and better yet, it seemed they were kinder and more thoughtful with each other. They had gained the insight that what develops character isn't studying it, it's practicing it.

When my student teaching assignment was completed after three months, sadness was my strongest emotion. I felt grateful and competent and better prepared for teaching. I had developed skills and techniques to create learning environments where students were more included in mapping their own learning and able to be self-directed. I had a firm grip on the importance of relevance as a constant in learning. I knew I had a lot more to learn about children's group behavior and the downside of too much emphasis on discipline. However, on the last day, I could feel my gratitude for the ease of all

I had learned and experienced. Mrs. Gocella had become a true colleague, a partner in teaching who was a mentor without the need for hierarchy. I would miss her.

As a result of both student teaching experiences, I knew nine and ten year-olds were an excellent age group for me. I enjoyed them and how they learned. I was often in flow while teaching them.[38] There was a thrill to seeing someone and, in certain instances, entire groups *learning*: going from multiplication, to division, to decimals, to fractions, or from writing sentences, to paragraphs, to stories. Simply knowing someone had learned to ask better questions was striking. It was like watching one of those rapid photo montages of flowers and trees growing, seemingly in minutes. I believed learning more about teaching could sustain me as a person who wanted an interesting life.

I had yet to teach on my own. I hadn't been challenged in more formidable misbehavior situations like fighting and gang behavior. I had to develop my own materials and lesson plans. I saw how much commitment goes into creating a vital learning atmosphere physically and emotionally. I had no doubt that learning was hard work; it required effort, repetition, practice, and mental and physical exertion.

At the end of the term, the Bloomfield Hills School System offered me a position as a fifth grade teacher. I was exceptionally happy about their tender. It affirmed my capability. Yet, with what I hope was a gracious response, I did not accept it. I wanted to teach in Detroit. Being native to the city, idealistic and aware of the need for change, feeling myself as a part of the Cultural Revolution of the mid-sixties, it had to be my choice. I didn't need to soul search. As a student teacher, I had passed through two realms of educational experience. I believed, as the recruiter said, "Detroit is where the action is."

CHAPTER 9

Teaching Troubles

Six months later, as I approached Winterhalter Elementary School, I wanted to see it as my new professional home, a school not without challenges, but one where I could anchor myself, learn the nuances of becoming a fine, fifth grade teacher, and make a difference in the lives of my students. I was filled with feelings of possibility: fresh approaches to teaching where children talked about their learning preferences, worked in cooperative groups, wanted to come to school, left at the end of the day eager to return the next morning, and learned in ways that made them love learning and develop the will to make it a lifelong pursuit inside and outside of the classroom. "Schools without Walls" was a sweeping educational gale crossing the Atlantic and into the United States from Great Britain: large educational spaces that expanded educational potential rather than constricting it in tedious box-like rooms. Maybe not immediately, but somewhere down the road, I might try something that innovative as well.

As I drove up to the school, I was impressed by the building and the neighborhood. Located on the near west side of Detroit, it was in an older area of the city with many large brick and Tudor homes built, as the school was, during the second and third decades of the twentieth century. It was largely a black community with many of the houses being homes to multiple families. There was some poverty but also a spectrum of income levels broad enough to provide comfortable shelter for Mary Wilson of the Supremes and several professional athletes who played for the Detroit Lions and the Detroit Tigers.

The school building was two stories high and took up most of the square block. Its centrally located, large wooden double doors, framed in thick grey columns embedded in maroon bricks, had a tongue of concrete steps descending into a broad sidewalk, giving the school a traditional medieval look. I appreciated the fullness of the shrubbery and the manicured lawn that surrounded the front facing windows and walls. It was a well-kept school, a good sign.

The interior of the building was dark, a common trait among older schools. The lighting was from the original installation, hanging ivory orange globes in the shape of large cooking kettles formed a single line down the middle of the hall, casting light below but not much further. Things seemed quiet. Classes were in session.

Before I began teaching the next morning, I had an appointment with Mr. Levitsky, the principal. He greeted me warily, like Humphry Bogart taking his measure of Peter Lorre in the Maltese Falcon. I knew his reputation. He was considered one of the better high school basketball referees in the Detroit area. Still refereeing games, he was widely respected as a no-nonsense kind of guy. Coaches did not challenge him because he was not shy about calling technical fouls and because most of the time he was right in how he managed the game. High school basketball in Detroit drew thousands of fans. He had a backbone. Balding and fit, with grey close-cropped hair, he dressed well, preferring grey suits and red ties, looking more like a corporate executive than an educator.

"Before we go to meet your students, I want to let you know about a few things. We're glad to have you. We need you here. There hasn't been a regular teacher in your room since September. This is December. That's a long time, far too long. So, you may have a bit of a rough start. You'll probably have to be firmer than you expected to be. We have good morale among our staff and people pitch in. Don't be shy about asking for help. If you need me, let me know. But I don't want the principal's office to be a dumping ground."

Mr. Levitsky made no request to review my lesson plans and only smiled once during his orientation. I found out later he had an excellent sense of humor. He was quick-witted and liked to kid around, especially about clothes and how we looked—"Hey, Mr. Butler's got a new pair of shoes. Though, I don't think he broke the bank." I think he wanted to forewarn me and make sure I wasn't cavalier about my responsibilities. I found out later from the other teachers that his meetings with everyone tended to be brief. As one said later, "He's no schmoozer."

Seeing my class for the first time left me wondering. As we approached the classroom, I could see through the window in the door, the substitute teacher, a woman in her forties with shoulder length grey hair in a black, loose fitting dress with an angry expression on her face, moving quickly toward the back of the room as a boy ran away from her. The class was watching them, laughing or smiling with apparent anticipation of a scene of amusing chaos, like seeing The Three Stooges running to shut off a spraying fire hydrant. Their sound was not kind, a mix of jeering and merriment. When Mr. Levitsky swiftly knocked and opened the door, some of the children gasped. The boy quickly walked to his desk and sat down. The teacher, looking mortified, didn't say a word. Mr. Levitsky looked over the room and in a quiet voice said, "That's better."

He introduced me to the class and told them I would be their new teacher. I would be there on a regular basis. No more substitutes. The children, most of whom were black, looked at me. About half the class smiled, but most of the rest had an expression that my experience in the city would lead me to describe as "sizing someone up." Being a male teacher didn't seem to make much of a difference to the students. I wasn't surprised because they had had substitutes for such an extended time, many of whom were male. It was one of the best paying part-time jobs in Detroit. All you needed was sixty college credits to be eligible. These were nine and ten year olds—concrete thinkers. From their experience, there was little reason to expect me to stick around. Glancing at Mr. Levitsky, I kept my comments calm and brief. I told them I was looking forward to being their teacher. I'd see them all tomorrow morning. As we left and I said goodbye to the substitute teacher, she responded, "Good luck," with a smile more sardonic than sincere.

I told Bob Schroeder about my experience at Winterhalter. He had started his first year of teaching as well. He said, "Sounds like it could be difficult, but I think you said you wanted a challenge. Looks like you've got one."

"You're right. Yet I wish I knew a bit better what to expect. Then I'd have a more strategic plan. Like in football, when one play doesn't work, you can go to another."

"You mean a playbook?"

"Yeah."

"Not in teaching. I don't think it would work. Too quick a game and no time for a huddle."

"Hey, I'd settle for a compass."

He laughed, "Keep that funny bone. Sounds like you're going to need it."

When it came to adversity, most of my younger friends were pretty stoic and tough minded. They relied on instinct rather than theory or psychological methods. There's no doubt they wanted me to do well as a teacher. They'd certainly listen to me and offer encouragement, but not much in the way of specifics. To some extent, this was because they were not experienced teachers themselves. For the first time, I realized this was work I was going to do alone.

∴

The next morning, as I drove to Winterhalter, my mind was throbbing with self-talk: *You didn't expect this to be easy. It won't be. It will probably take at least a month to have a classroom climate with trust and discipline. Be patient. Let the children get to know you and you get to know them. It's like Purgatory. Things will get better. Keep your sense of humor. It's your saving grace. Teach like your family and friends are watching you at every moment. That will keep your temper down and in touch with your better instincts. You're there to help children learn. You're prepared.* I was so psyched, I had one of those experiences where I only realized I had stopped driving when I shut off the ignition and saw the cyclone fence at the edge of my front bumper in the school parking lot. I had driven the entire way without any memory of doing so.

The best thing about the first morning was that I started to see the children as individuals. I had 34 students, a fourth/fifth grade split with no student younger than 9 or older than 11. After I had told my name again to the children and had reviewed it phonetically, a girl whose name was Tanya, wearing a rose-colored dress with her hair in pink-bowed braids, raised her hand, "Sorry, I'm still having trouble with your name. Could we just call you Mr. W?"

I liked it. I said, "Sure Tanya. That's fine." Some of the other children nodded their heads approvingly. A boy named Willie, the only boy dressed in a white shirt and tie, who looked like he stepped out of a Sunday magazine ad, chirped in, "That's cool." I thought we were off to a good beginning.

When we began our first lesson, things started to crumble pretty quickly. In order to form reading groups, I had to hear each child read. Although I had given seat work for the rest of the children to do as I listened to each one read, only a few were on task. The rest were talking, joking, or starting to push each other, or take each other's materials without permission. I could feel things starting to disintegrate. I issued a firm reprimand that quieted the room for about ten minutes. The next one worked for about eight minutes. Two more reprimands later, their effect was lasting less than five minutes. Then, I saw a boy, Tyrell, punch another boy, Joseph, hard in the arm. Joseph had tears in his eyes. Disintegration again, a bit nearer this time. No more reprimands.

I asked Tyrell to come out into the hall with me. With my back to the door, I asked, "What happened?"

"Joseph, called me a name."

"What name?"

"You're not going to like it."

"That's okay. Just tell me."

Tyrell looked down at the hallway floor and whispered something I couldn't hear.

"Tyrell, I can't hear you. Please."

"My momma says I should never say words like this."

I put my hands gently on his shoulders and began, "Tyrell..."

Raising his voice and jerking his shoulders away, he hissed, "Don't touch me!"

I heard rumbling noises and laughter coming from behind the door. When I looked in, I saw about three students out of their seats and Willie was dancing in one of the window wells. Students were starting to clap and join him dancing next to their seats. I quickly moved back into the room and told Tyrell to take his seat. By the time I shifted my gaze, Willie was back in his seat with his hands clasped on his desk. I took a breath and told the children we were moving on to another lesson. For the rest of the day, we did lessons involving the entire class. Some I made up on the spot. I refrained from any one-on-one discipline techniques. I chose to ignore any behavior that wasn't outright disruptive. I also had the children whom I couldn't afford to ignore move their seats next to me while I continued to teach. There were four students in a semicircle within arm's reach by the end of the day.

After the children were dismissed, I sat at my desk exhausted. I declared a moral victory: I had not sent a single child to the principal's office. But what was I going to do tomorrow? There was another teacher across the hall, Mr. Clifford, who taught sixth grade. I went to his room. His door was open. A tall man, about 50, lean and goateed, with round glasses and a modest Afro, he smiled and motioned me to come in. We shook hands. I introduced myself and leaned against the wall a few feet from his desk.

"How was it?" he asked pleasantly.

"Oh, I got through the day, but it wasn't easy." Then I briefly told him what happened and asked if he had any suggestions.

"You need Hector," he raised his hand and pointed his thumb toward the chalkboard.

I saw a wooden paddle, the kind used for beach tennis. It had holes a bit smaller than dimes symmetrically drilled in a square of four rows across it. Emblazoned in red paint along its diagonal was the name, Hector. For a second, my mind flashed on Hector, the Trojan hero, killed in mortal combat by Achilles in the *Iliad*. The paddle was hanging on a string in plain sight.

Mr. Clifford continued, "The students need to know there's a limit. It's only your first day, but not having a regular teacher for so long, they don't know what the limits are. They're going to test you until they find out. Hector tells my students there's a limit."

I looked at him and grimaced, "That thing looks pretty painful."

"It is, but I don't use it often. Mostly just in the beginning of the semester. After that, I just have to point to it and things usually settle down quickly. I don't strike anyone more than three times, always on the bottom, and in front of the other students. With the holes, I don't need to hardly swing. It's more ritual than anything else."

Feeling humbled but not convinced, I averted his gaze and said, "Thanks, Mr. Clifford. I appreciate the time. I'll think about it. Good to know you're across the hall."

He looked at me and said with warmth in his voice, "Yeah, give it some thought. That's a good idea. Many of the teachers, men and women, use a paddle in this school. The students know it. They appreciate having boundaries. I think that's the important thing. Boundaries."

That night, I thought long and hard about what Mr. Clifford had said. I wasn't going to use a paddle but he was right about the boundaries. I needed to have them. They had to be clear and the children had to know I would follow through with them. I reviewed my notes from Dr. Redl's lecture. He had used the metaphor of a bank account when working with children with whom teachers have a new relationship: "They don't know you. You have little emotional trust deposited in their account. Unlike their parents, who've taken care of them when they've been ill or played with them for the joy of being with them, new teachers, substitute teachers are essentially strangers. So, when a parent disciplines a child, even harshly, the parent has a lot in that emotional bank account and can draw quite a bit out of it with large sums of trust still remaining. But as new teachers and substitutes, you have little to none in that account, and children will likely be more obstinate and less forgiving. They're just being children. Remember that."

The next morning, I woke up and thought, "Thank goodness there's another day." I was eager to meet with my students. When they were all in class, I reviewed with them three rules I had posted on the board. I said the rules were there so we could learn better together. (1) *No talking out loud without first raising your hand and receiving permission.* It's okay to talk in a quiet voice or a whisper. (2) *No leaving your seat without permission.* It's how trouble starts. (3) *If you misbehave, you'll receive a warning and your name will be placed on the board with a checkmark. If you misbehave again on the same day, and receive a second checkmark, your parents will be called at the end of the day.* Everyone starts every day with a clean slate.

The third rule had made an impact on the children. They asked many questions. Some with hostility or disbelief:

"What if no one answers the phone?"

"Then I'll send a note home to make an appointment."

"What if we don't have a phone?"

"Then I'll have to come to your home in person."

"You wouldn't do that."

"Yes. I would. We have to have an atmosphere that helps all of us to learn and we can't let a few people stop us from learning."

"My momma's going to believe me. Not you!"

"I hope we don't have to find that out."

Our discussion of the new rules did not leave me with a good feeling. Too much of our exchange was testy and we didn't end it with a sense of mutual acceptance. I felt more like a new warden who had laid down another set of prison regulations. I accepted their resistance as part of the process, again recalling Redl's comments, "It's not just children. When anyone receives a rule that confines their behavior, don't expect them to cheer or thank you. That's not human nature."

I also had three more announcements that I hoped would draw the children closer to me and I to them. The first was that I was starting a "craft club." Twice a week we would meet after school for an hour to build models, make drawings, and work on anything we wanted to create as a project. I would supply the initial materials and models. At the end of the day, eight children had signed up to be part of the craft club, six boys and two girls.

The second announcement was that every day for twenty minutes I would read to the children from a book of their choice. By majority vote, their first selection was *Charlotte's Web*. Most students were openly enthusiastic about this announcement. The last announcement was that if we could go three days straight without any names posted, we would have a class party. I wouldn't call their reaction to this idea scorn, but it was close to it. Like a gift promised but never attainable, some of the children were openly doubtful with their remarks, "Not going to happen!" "That's a party we'll never see." With this last announcement, I immediately felt regretful but tried not to show it. I clapped my hands and vacantly cheered, "We can do it."

For two weeks, the warning rule seemed to be working. During that time, on any given day, there were as many as nine names on the board and as few as three. The class was more orderly, but to me it felt like an active volcano in a brief state of dormancy. The lava was still red, hot, and simmering. I felt continuously tense. On several occasions, I pretended not to see a child, whose name was already on the board, knock over someone's book or pull someone's hair. I didn't want to call their parents. I wanted us to create a new mood in our class, where disruption became undesirable because learning felt better.

However, I knew I was failing at this goal. I was too often creating lesson plans meant to keep the class engaged but of little learning value. I would have them role play or act out concepts from social studies like the solar system with one child being the sun and the other children the planets revolving around her. Then, they could draw what they saw as observers and felt as actors. But I didn't do what was necessary for them to learn the planets' names, sizes, and features because it took more practice, repetition, and effort. I was afraid of the ensuing turmoil that might develop and shied away from that part of the lesson.

In the third week, Tanya, after receiving her first warning for kicking another girl, ran back at her and put gum in her hair. I said, "Sorry, Tanya, that's two. I'll have to call your home today." She scowled at me, returned to her seat, and, although remaining sullen for the rest of the afternoon, did not cause any further problems. At dismissal, when she was leaving, she stopped at my desk and said, "I was good until the bell. Please don't call."

I did. Her mother answered the phone. She was cool toward me but she was interested in what had happened. When I explained to her the rules I had been using, she seemed to understand. She thanked me and told me, "Tanya will not be a problem again." The next day as Tanya passed my desk, looking straight ahead, she whispered, "I hate you." I ignored it. Yet, I felt stung. Before January was done, I had to make about five more calls. A similar pattern ensued. The child would return to class, less likely to act out, but deeply resentful toward me.

In February, I became more certain of the reason for their dislike. Jaylen, a muscular boy with a close cropped haircut and a dominant physical presence, started two fights in one day, the second right in front of me, punching his fist into the spine of another boy who didn't move when he told him, "Get out of my way!" I called his home after school but there was no answer. After our class craft session, which was going well (We had added a once-a-month Saturday session and now had eleven members.), I went to Jaylen's house. It was a modest brick bungalow. His father answered the door. A stocky man in a white round-collared t-shirt with grey work pants, he invited me into his home. When I told him what had happened, he didn't question me. He called out for Jaylen to come into the living room. When Jaylen saw me, I could see the fear in his eyes. Then his father grabbed him like a coat off a hanger, wrapped him in a headlock with his left arm, bent him over, whipped off his belt with his right hand, and strapped him on the spot. Hard. When he released Jaylen, the boy ran sobbing to another room. Then the father thanked me for coming, and told me to let him know if there were any further problems with Jaylen.

I drove home feeling guilty and ashamed. I told myself that what Jaylen's father did was probably what my own father would have done, had a teacher ever come to our door with a similar complaint. That realization only made me feel worse. No less than the executioner who carried out the punishment, I was the judge who gave the sentence. I was not becoming the teacher I thought I was going to be. I told no one about what had happened with Jaylen, using stoicism to batten down my vulnerability.

After this incident, the children whose parents I had called seemed to form a clique. Other than frequent dirty looks and an ongoing sullenness, they didn't openly misbehave. What they did do was to make fun of me. They mimicked me. When I turned around to write on the board, they imitated my motions from their seats. When they went to sharpen a pencil, they frowned at each other like I frowned at them when they misbehaved, eyes squinting with a deep furrowed brow, and pursed lips. When they said, "Excuse me," or "Thank you," to each other, they exaggerated the words in their version of my voice. The rest of the children thought their impersonations were hilarious. They guffawed and chuckled. I smiled, but it was a phony, thin smirk. The serious tone in my voice that followed my wan recognition told everyone these children had affected me, hurt me, which only further reinforced their mockery. There were so many better ways I could have handled the situation. I had lost my sense of humor. I remembered Sister Assumpta and felt a chill run through my body. I had become only a part of the human being I once was.

To an outside observer, in three months our class had made progress. We were more orderly. Children were more on task with their lessons. I had not sent anyone to the principal's office. Both announced and unannounced, Mr. Levitsky had come to our class to observe me teaching. In his presence, the children were responsive during our lessons, appearing to be interested and behaving well. The craft club was a success. The children who attended it were the quieter and less outgoing students. I appreciated my time with them. The daily reading also went well. There were tears across our entire class at the passing of the spider, Charlotte. That may have been our most intimate and trusting moment together.

Here's what I thought that no observer or my closest friends knew about the class. Being orderly does not reveal the tension or threat that maintains that order. I believed we were a hair trigger away from disaster. I never left the class unattended. Too dangerous. I kept the lid on at all times. I didn't dare release my grip. Unless there was havoc before he arrived, just Mr. Levitsky's presence would keep the children well-behaved. Being on task is not the same as learning, nor is it being interested in the lesson. There has to be substance, study, and assessment. All three of which I did not think we were doing well. I was feeding the children an educational version of junk food: high on taste, low on nutrition. My lesson plans looked great. Staying up to 10:00pm every night to design them made them so. But I thought they were camouflage, concealing the holes in my teaching of which I was well aware. I had trapped myself. Looking apparently so good to others, I had an image to maintain. I was too ashamed to admit to anyone my misgivings and to ask for help. This included my closest friends. I thought they would've understood, and yet I wouldn't allow myself to tell them. I had wanted this challenge. I couldn't risk looking so incapable and impotent in their eyes.

In March, we received a new student. With a light coffee brown complexion and crystalline blue eyes, Pauline was striking. Slightly taller than the other girls and broad shouldered, she was well-coordinated and immediately made friends with her jump roping skills. It took me about a week to be more certain, but there were some things that were unusual about her. She would sit perfectly still for as long as twenty minutes, her eyes seemingly vacant, like she was daydreaming, but it was more trance-like than being lost in one's imagination. At times, she would whisper and then raise her voice in the same sentence.

Without request or provocation, she made animal sounds: dogs barking, cats meowing, cows mooing, and so forth. If children bothered her, she would snarl or growl at them. She could be frightening. I noticed the children, including the more aggressive, beginning to avoid her.

Although I realized I was young and inexperienced, I could not remember encountering another child like Pauline. I knew I needed to talk to her parents. Her mother, Mrs. Daniel, met with me the same day I called. A friend had brought her. Mrs. Daniel was blind. A woman in a grey business suit, she appeared to be in her early 30s, with Pauline's same complexion and shape of shoulders. I told her there was no serious misbehavior. However, since Pauline was new to our class and what I had seen had struck me as so different from the rest of the children, I wanted to avoid making any mistakes of judgment. I felt I needed to be better informed. Mrs. Daniel indicated she was a single mother, new to the area, and that she shared my concern. She came to the point quickly, "I think Pauline may be a troubled child."

"Why do you say that?"

"She's very difficult to discipline. She has moods. She gets very angry over small things like a spot on her dress, or going to bed, or being asked to help with the dishes. She hides from me in the house for no good reason. And sometimes it takes me hours to find her. She writes with crayon on the walls. She runs out of the house and doesn't answer me or come back when I call her. At times, I think she's uncontrollable."

My heart went out to Mrs. Daniel. I had no experience with what she was describing and I could only imagine how painful and distressing such a situation might be. Even though it was K-8 and over 800 students, our school had no counselor. Mrs. Daniel approved my idea to involve a school psychologist from central office. The next day, I spoke to him and found out that Pauline would have to be tested before any suggestions could be made about teaching or communicating with her differently from the rest of the students. With his current schedule, there would be no opportunity to test her for three weeks.

When I talked the matter over with Mr. Levitsky, he gave me the tired look of a man who had heard my story once too often. "That's a shame. It happens all the time. Our psychological services are understaffed. Testing and diagnosis are backed up. Frankly, I'm surprised to hear it's only three weeks. Sometimes, it's well over a month."

"What do I do in the meantime?"

"Well, here's how it works. If she's a danger to the other children, herself, or you, we can place her in the care of her mother. Right now, other than some strange behavior, there's not enough to send her home. And, there are no infractions to suspend her. Keep a paper trail. Evidence of threat is what matters. Don't hesitate to talk with me."

What bothered me the most about Pauline was that she was so unpredictable, with a physical strength well beyond the other students. I didn't want to overreact and I couldn't say anything to the children. My mouth became dry from thinking about her. A week later, I felt more in control. Pauline continued to act strangely but nothing beyond "her normal" until the following incident.

I had given the class an innocuous request, asking them to open their geography books to a particular page. That's when Pauline came out of her seat. She was in a pink fluffy dress with her hair in two looped strands with matching light blue bows. Her thin lips opened into a snarl. She dropped to the floor and into a four-point stance with her knees and hands for support. Then she started to bark low and gruff sounds like those of a large dog. She wagged her head, bared her teeth, and with a stuttering motion came at the other children who were in their desks, nipping at their legs, not quite biting them but ferocious nonetheless.

A small girl, Carla, in a blue jean jump suit with her hair in two long braids with satin red ribbons, about three seats ahead of where Pauline had stopped and was emitting a low long growl, jumped to the top of her desk, stood straight up and shouted, "Do something Mr. W! I don't want her to bite me! Please!!"

Most of the other children in the class began standing in their seats, trying to get a look at Pauline who was still on the floor, barking again and shaking her head. Some of them started shouting, "She's crazy! She's crazy!" Others were making a sound I had heard before when fights started on the playground, a shrieking with a whistling that was contagious and grew louder and louder in milliseconds with more children joining in. Oooooooooooooooooweeee! Ooo ooooooooooooooooooooooooweeeeeeeeeeeeeeeee!!

I could hear a boy, I didn't know who, yell, "Stop her, Mr. W.! You got to stop her!!" Like a dog rising on its haunches, Pauline started barking louder. I had no idea what to do. I didn't know what to say and I didn't want to start shouting. I was frozen, standing in shock. My mind racing across the question, "What should I do?" The only answers coming up were those that said what I shouldn't do—Don't touch her! Don't lose control! Don't leave the classroom! Don't call the principal!

The class had catapulted into bedlam. Everyone was up on their feet. Most seemed to be shouting. I had lost the ability to decipher what they were screaming, but I could see that some children had now jumped up into the window wells and were standing in them, watching Pauline who was trotting on all fours toward the front of the class, barking and growling as she went. I ran to the front of the class, dropped on all fours in front of Pauline, and looked her in the eyes as I might a dog, using the same fierce expression I had learned as a paperboy when I wanted any animal to think twice before approaching me ready to bite. Putting my face inches away from hers and locking my eyes on hers, repressing my voice to a menacing whisper that I'm sure sounded like an animal, I said, "Stop it, Pauline. Now, I mean it. You just stop it!"

She halted. I could tell she was afraid. Then I moved quickly, taking her wrist and holding it tightly in my hand, like a padlock on an eye-bolt. I stood straight up, lifting her off the ground with me. I pulled her behind my back to her seat. As I went I could hear her cry, "You're hurting me, Mr. W.!" I didn't look back. I knew I was going to put her in that seat no matter what happened. That's when I heard the other children, "Watch it Mr. W. You're gonna hurt her." I realized at this moment, I wasn't *with* them, I was apart from them. They had morphed into my enemy. I needed to calm down and I didn't know how.

I told everyone to put their heads on their desks and to take a five-minute break. No one objected, including Pauline. Trembling, I sat down behind my desk, using my elbows to prop up my clasped hands, I rested my chin on them until my breathing returned to normal. Leaving the classroom door open, I briskly walked across the hall and asked Mr. Clifford to watch my class. Without any questions, he came over immediately. I took Pauline to the Mr. Levitsky's office. When I told him what happened, he nodded his head, called her mother, and suspended her. The next week, when she came back, she seemed happy to return. While her behavior still seemed erratic, there were no more incidents.

At about the same time of Pauline's return, I began to have trouble sleeping, accompanied by severe headaches and night sweats. I had mononucleosis. For most of April, I stayed home and did nothing but rest. I watched the most guilt-free television I ever have in my entire life. Later, my study of psychosomatic illnesses would confirm what I knew then: my mind would never have allowed me to leave Winterhalter, so my body took me out of there.

The break gave me enough distance to gain another perspective.[39] It was a heavenly negation: I didn't have to be a perfect teacher. I didn't even have to come close to perfection. Accepting this realization emotionally, and letting it sink in released me from feeling demoralized. I read *Mental Hygiene in Teaching*. It made so much sense, I couldn't understand why every new teacher wasn't given a copy of it. Searching through its writing, I found a wisdom I could now be open to, *"In short, love and affection, as well as the granting of gratifying life-situations, cannot be made the bargaining tools of educational or even therapeutic motivation, but must be kept ... as minimal parts of the youngsters' diet, irrespective of the problems of deservedness."*[40]

I saw how contagion, the shrill yelling and excitement of the children's reaction to one of their peers acting out, was not a personal venting against me, but a matter of group dynamics. Absorbing this understanding released my feelings of guilt. After three weeks, I was amazed by an awareness I did not suspect would emerge. I wanted to get back to my class. I was able to work with the substitute teacher who replaced me, designing lesson plans together, but as time continued, the urge to return was undeniable.

When I walked through the classroom door with Mr. Levitsky at my side, the children cheered and clapped. Tanya ran up and gave me a hug around the waist. Later, I would reflect, "Contagion works for good and bad. Remember that."

Mr. Levitsky surprised me as well, saying to the children, "Maybe you would like to say something to your teacher or ask a question." They asked me a lot of questions about mononucleosis and my recovery. At that time, mono was less understood and some of the children mistakenly thought I was near dying. I said that was not at all the case, but that I did have an enlarged spleen and if anyone had hit me hard in the chest, it might have burst. I ended my explanation with a smile, "But since my family has stop beating me, I'm okay."

The children laughed. Mr. Levitsky gave me a look that said, "You're at the edge here. Don't go over it." After Mr. Levitsky left, I think the children and I knew without saying that there was a new mood in the room. We were like a family that's had troubles, but emerged from a crisis with an appreciation of how precious it is to be whole again, unharmed, and with another chance to live together. I had brought a copy of Jules Verne's *Twenty Thousand Leagues under the Sea* with me. We put our books aside and glided into this fantastic story for our first half hour together.

Our last six weeks of the semester were exceptional. It was as though a veil of patience had descended upon all of us. There was less pushing and shoving and more tolerance for frustration. I kept the three rules, but I sanctioned them differently. I became far looser in their application, less like a meticulous accountant and more like a joking, benevolent uncle. If I witnessed someone hit another child, I'd be more likely to say, "Saw that Jaylen. You trying to put me in the sick bed again. I can see by the way you hit Derek, you might want to put him in there too. Now, come on up here and sit next to me for a while." No mean look. No frowning. No name on the board. In my first week back, with some luck, a better climate, and a less stringent application of the rules, we achieved our first three consecutive days without any names posted. We had a party the next day. It was a hit. For the first time ever, I danced with the children.

Pauline was still with us. The results of the testing were inconclusive. It was the psychologist's opinion that because the family had moved several times and because her mother was blind and often isolated in their house, there was substantial instability in the home. Pauline's behavior might be more a reflection of this fragmentation than any deep-seated emotional problem. Putting her in a classroom for the "socially maladjusted," made up mostly of older boys, this late in the school year, would not do her any good, and might be harmful.

Though I understood and agreed with the psychologist's rationale, Pauline was still an enormous challenge. I moved her desk next to mine. Although I wasn't as anxious about her as before, I kept a psychological tether to her, never letting her out of my sight, and quickly buffering her from any altercations with the other children. She had stopped snarling and barking. Yet, every day I remained vigilant in her presence until she left the building.

Two weeks before school ended, we went on our one and only field trip. This was a big deal. Each class received only one. The city was at our disposal: parks, museums, professional ball games, automotive technical centers, and the River Rouge Ford plant to see a car made from scratch. The school system rented a bus for the class trip. We had a month to plan for it. I was proud of the children because through consensus, not majority vote, they had decided to go to the Detroit Zoo. The trip became a galvanizing event for us. From studying the animals to selecting treats for the trip to meeting with the parents who would chaperone us, we had an opportunity to learn about each other as more complete human beings and to see ourselves in each other's world.

∴

Now and then, to improve my mood, I play a mind game: ten best moments in teaching. Always on the list, and often the first one I go to, is sitting on the bus with the Winterhalter children on our way to the zoo. They are all in their seats. They are all snapping their fingers. They are all singing Hank Ballard and the Midnighters' "Finger Poppin' Time."

Hey now, hey now, hey now, hey now
It's finger pop poppin' time
Finger poppin', poppin' time
I feel so good and that's a real good sign

The children and the parents are smiling, swaying to the rhythm of the music. So is the bus driver. So am I.

I didn't return to Winterhalter in the fall. I knew I had much more to learn about teaching. Another transformation was in the making. There was little doubt in my mind that I was far too dependent on discipline with little knowledge of a much greater force for learning—motivation. Reading *Mental Hygiene in Teaching* had convinced me to take another path. It seemed to me that more illumination and guidance were to be found in the behavioral sciences. I would become a psychologist.

CHAPTER 10

There Are Ways

The shallowness of my knowledge of psychology became apparent when, barely a year into graduate school at Wayne State University, I volunteered to take a Rorschach test in front of my peers. Our professor, Dr. Juanita Collier, a tall, impeccably dressed clinical psychologist in horn-rimmed glasses, introduced the exercise, indicating it would not be too revealing, only a few inkblots would be used, and any probing of the volunteer would be safely done by her. In a course on projective testing, the demonstration would give our seminar a relevant introduction to the rapidly evolving field of personality assessment.

I thought it was a great idea. All of us seemed interested. But no one volunteered. After Dr. Collier asked a second time, a tense silence filled the room; it was obvious no one was willing. I had one of those, "Oh, what the heck," moments and raised my hand, more to put an end to the tension than for any other reason. Other than its use of ink blots, I knew very little about the Rorschach. I didn't know it was standardized largely on the basis of responses from people with mental health problems and tended to reveal unconscious conflicts. Since the class's apprehensiveness hadn't abated as I sauntered to the front of the room, I thought, "My classmates know more about this test than I do."

As I looked at the card in front of me, I gave myself an immediate internal directive, "Don't say anything sexual." Then I responded, "I think it's two angels fighting. There's a child in the middle that each angel wants for itself. The child is trying to get away."

Although no one moved, it felt like the entire class had leaned in toward me. Dr. Collier showed me the next card. The palms of my hands were wet with sweat. I cancelled my first thought as too strange ("Two monks playing pattycake.") and searched my mind for a quick reasonable response.

"Mr. Wlodkowski?"

"Well, it looks to me like two elephants with their trunks touching. There's cotton candy floating above each of their heads because they're having the same dream."

I was trying to keep my responses safe. I hadn't had that much attention from the students in any psychology course I took prior to that moment. I think Dr. Collier realized my hesitancy. After one more card, she concluded my participation, asking the rest of the seminar members what some of their responses to the same cards might have been. This diffused the group's attention toward me. I was relieved. During the break, a student asked me if I knew what the Rorschach test usually revealed. When I admitted my ignorance, he remarked, "It's easy to reveal personal problems taking a Rorschach. Unless you wanted to publicly expose one of your own personality disorders, I think you just dodged a bullet."

I had enrolled as a Master's student specializing in school psychology with slightly better than an inkling of what was involved. Wanting to learn more about motivation distracted me from realizing how little I knew about psychology. I had barely an idea of what encompassed a psychologist's repertoire. In terms of what a psychologist did, my awareness was just above the threshold of the stereotype of a bearded man sitting with a notebook, listening to a patient lying on a couch talk about her dreams. What brought me above this meager level of insight was my contact with a school psychologist as a teacher. I was certain I wanted to work with students in a school environment. Schools were the best place for me to learn about motivation: how it could infuse teaching and learning, and how it might replace unnecessary, destructive disciplinary interventions. When I stepped into the behavioral science landscape, I was like an explorer with a compass but no map. I knew the general direction I wanted to go, but had scarce idea of the terrain I had to travel.

In 1966, in my neighborhood, the only thing weirder than having to see a psychologist was to be one. In the same year, Thomas Eagleton was receiving psychiatric treatment for clinical depression at the Mayo Clinic, an admission that in 1972 would remove him as a vice-presidential nominee from the Democratic ticket and label George McGovern as crazy for backing him "a thousand percent." Peter Sellers' portrayal of a dippy psychoanalyst in *What's New, Pussycat,* a popular film at the time, only fueled the flames of popular misgivings about psychologists and psychiatrists. The other stereotype—a white coated, maze-crazed, rat-running scientist—did little more to enhance the profession's image.

When I told my parents I was going to become a psychologist, they didn't object because, in their eyes, more education was good education. Finley's reaction was serious but supportive. "You know Raymond, the Greek tragedies are filled with despair, lost causes, and hopeless odds. They didn't believe in a heaven to end their lives with a reward. Fulfillment of life was in the living of it. They would have had plenty of use for a few skilled psychologists. I think you'll be good. Your first instinct is usually to try to understand. I think that's fundamental to this work." Then, with a smile, "Should be interesting. More for us to talk about."

In a paradoxical way, not knowing that much about psychology made every course more relevant because I knew I had so much to learn to increase my knowledge of the discipline as well as to converse with my peers, many of whom were psychology majors as undergraduates. I realized knowing something well is what allows spontaneity and improvisation,[41] the core requirements for nuance, humor, and useable knowledge in any field. I couldn't afford to only *finish* my courses, I had to learn from all of them.

In the school psychology program, many of the courses were in psychological testing and clinical measurement. I found myself attracted and repelled by these tests. I was fascinated by what they could assess: intelligence, emotional stability, achievement levels in numerous subjects, unconscious desires, vocational potential, and mental health. I was wary of the sorting function of the tests: who should be classified as mentally retarded or emotionally disturbed, common clinical classifications in the mid-60s. The Wayne State University School Psychology Program did an excellent job of making sure we were competent in administering these tests. Generally, we had to memorize the directions for giving each test, be observed by an experienced clinician through a two-way mirror while giving the test, file reports that were assessed by experienced clinicians for accuracy and comprehension, and practice, practice, and practice in order to make our testing as fluid as possible.

I enjoyed having this testing expertise. I knew something few other people my age knew. How beneficial was this knowledge? was a question to which I remained open. Beyond using testing results to designate students for placement in special programs, how could the results of these tests help learners solve problems, build new skills, make friends, or decide something of real value to them? Most important, how could my knowledge as a school psychologist help teachers to help students learn?

Many individual intelligence tests have a Lego quality to them. For measures like the Stanford-Binet Intelligence Scales and the Wechsler Intelligence Scale for Children, there are materials to assemble and manipulate. Giving these tests can actually be fun for both the psychologist and the student. For me, the Cracker Jack surprise in learning how to competently use these measures was practicing them with my family and friends.

When I asked Finley and my parents to "let me practice with you," they turned me down cold. Feigning outrage, Finley said, "You've got to be kidding! Not in a million years. You could raise Julius Caesar from the dead and I wouldn't take your test. Don't you realize I earned a doctorate so I wouldn't have to take any more tests?"

Without any histrionics, my mother said, "No." She looked to the side for a brief moment and then again said, "No." That was good enough for me.

My father thought I was joking when I asked him. He said, "Really?"

I said, "Really. It will be the best intelligence test you've ever taken."

He said, "It will be the only intelligence test I've ever taken. No, better yet, it will be an intelligence test I've never taken."

I laughed and said, "Come on, Dad. We'll have fun. I need to practice. Don't you want to know how smart you are?"

He looked at me more seriously, "Sorry. I know you need to practice. But not with me. That's what you have friends for."

Fortunately, my friends were more open to helping out. They were good-natured about it, took the process seriously, and with each of them I had conversations we had never had before. We discussed a topic seldom revealed: our own self-images of how intelligent we might be. We knew I was only practicing and my skills were not refined. However, how intelligent we think we are has an effect ranging from whom we marry to what we choose as a vocation. The impression from these talks that stayed with me was how influential our families are upon our self-regard for our own intellect.[42] If there is such a thing as a curse, it would be to make one's child believe he is stupid.

∴

The more courses I took, the more I knew I wanted to be either an educational psychologist or a clinical psychologist. As the former, I could focus on learning, motivation, and transforming schools. As the latter, I could focus on helping families through therapy, another powerful process for change. I was becoming more familiar with the field of psychology. I was also being influenced by the great tumult in education and society at the time. Jonathan Kozol had written *Death at an Early Age:* [43] *The Destruction of the Hearts and Minds of Negro Children in the Boston Public Schools.* His experiences in Boston in his first year of teaching had, in some ways, mirrored my own in Detroit. On July 23, 1967, when police raided an African-American, after-hours unlicensed bar, Detroit exploded with racial violence, looting, and chaos, leaving at least 43 dead and 1,189 injured, with more than 2,000 buildings destroyed. By far, most of the destruction and killing occurred in black communities.

Yet, even in the largely white neighborhood in which I lived in Detroit, I could hear the whiz of stray bullets flying by. I slept for four nights on the living room floor of my second story flat until the city settled down and the gunfire ceased. With the 82nd and 101st Airborne Divisions sent into the city by President Johnson to quell the disruption and stationed at the Detroit Fair Grounds, I continuously heard the trembling whir of their helicopters as they moved equipment and kept surveillance on the city. I didn't feel fear as much as a sense of awe at how unreal life had become.

Anyone breathing and living in Detroit knew there was discrimination in policing, housing, and employment. For blacks, the poorer quality of public education was undeniable. Michigan law stipulated class size could not exceed thirty-five, but in inner-city schools, I had seen up to forty students where I substitute taught. Blacks had a profoundly legitimate question, "Why are things so much better where I'm not?" When I returned to Wayne State University that July, there was still an armed machine gun nest guarding the Woodward/Grand Boulevard corridor, where the university edged against the General Motors and Fisher buildings. As a psychologist, I didn't think I was going to end racism. I had difficulty openly talking about race with my white friends in ways that were authentic and constructive.

After five days, when the killing and upheaval in the city ebbed, I knew Detroit had received a death blow. Without my asking or bringing up the topic, whites everywhere were talking about leaving the city. "Let the f_ _ _ _ _ s who burned it, have it," was a common refrain. Though sad, Finley saw Detroit's demise as destined, "The white middle class will leave. They won't stay to watch things get worse. There are over twenty factories in the suburbs to work in, and plenty of land for housing. Then, what can a city do without a middle-class? It's the backbone of every civilization."

It wasn't an exaggeration to say that white residents were frantic to leave Detroit. In the last half of 1967, 67,000 people left the city; 80,000 left in 1968, followed by 46,000 in 1969. With them went jobs, city income from corporate, property, and sales taxes, retail dollars, mortgages, city investment, and tourism. This exodus was a far greater devastation for Detroit than the toll of the fires and destruction of the summer riot. Hopelessness. Everywhere.

During the city's upheaval, Wayne State University closed. After five days, it reopened and I was able to return to my office, a room designated for research and teaching assistants in the College of Education. My office mate, Mary Rogers, was at her desk. Mary was one of the few black students in our program. She was in her forties, wore her hair short, favored tailored linen suits, and, as she said, "I don't suffer fools gladly." We were in the early stages of getting to know each other. When I entered the room, I think she realized the difficulty both of us might have trying to say something earnest about what had happened in the city. With a staunch expression, Mary raised her hand, palm up and shook her head, "Let's talk about it later. For now, let's work." I nodded and turned to my books.

Mary had a smoldering wit. She could readily caricature the odd habits of some of our professors. One, in particular, was known for wearing wrinkled shirts and khakis, with white tennis shoes. We were sitting next to each other the day we first saw him. Mary remarked, "That man looks like a hankie with a human head that's just been taken out of my dryer. No black man who's a professor would ever dress like that. Shame ... it's a shame. And, you know it, he's gonna grade us."

Mary and I got along. Our relationship was friendly contentious. She repeatedly told me I was naïve and I repeatedly told her I was an idealist. "Too young to give up quite yet."

"Yes, but you also *might* be a bit ugly. Though, in your case, you'll probably look better with age."

Mary and I eventually did talk about the riots. Mostly, I listened. It took away the burden of having to talk about something I didn't know much about. Mary had lived in the South. She was a reading supervisor with considerable experience in the Detroit Public Schools. She had an intimate friend, Mac, one the McFall Brothers, who were preeminent funeral directors for the black community in Detroit. They were responsible for collecting the bodies of those murdered during the riot. Because of her close relationship to Mac, she knew much more than what the media revealed about how horrendous this strife had been for black families. There was cold-blooded killing with people being shot in the back and by snipers. Of the reported 43 people who died, 33 were black. She was dismayed. Her experience gave credence to how difficult the city's recovery would be.

I still grieve Detroit. I believe it makes an enormous difference in a community to hold steady when things seem to be getting worse because, if one doesn't, they will certainly deteriorate further, quite possibly beyond imagination. There is value in keeping a situation from deteriorating even when improvement seems far off. Someone has to shovel against the tide until the dike gets built. From my perspective, nowhere is this truer than in public schools. Those who work to give us honest hope are precious and should be treated as such.

∴

I knew I had to learn more about my own limitations and prejudice. The best way that personal change could come was through experience. At a professional level, I thought psychology held possibility. I believed psychology was alive with new ideas: T-group theory, re-education, inter-group processes, and motivation theory, ideas by which change benefiting all people seemed possible. And, at heart, although I thought I was politically informed, Mary was right: I was ignorant and extremely naïve.

In fall of 1967, I applied to four doctoral programs: The University of Chicago, Columbia University, The University of Illinois, and Wayne State University. The University of Chicago was my first choice. My favorite aunt, my mother's sister, Ann, lived in Hyde Park, figuratively a stone's throw from U. of C. I had spent vacations with her, loved the vibrancy and excitement of Chicago, and knew the university was home to the Sonia Shankman Orthogenic School. This residential school was world famous for its innovative treatment of children and adolescents with profound emotional issues. Its director was Bruno Bettelheim,[44] by 1967 a legendary figure in psychology, who had written *Love Is Not Enough: The Treatment of Emotionally Disturbed Children*. He had also led the development of milieu therapy, in which children had a structured, caring environment that enabled strong attachment with adults.

I believed I had a good chance to be admitted to the program. Dr. Collier wrote a strong letter of recommendation for me. She was a graduate of U. of C's clinical psychology program and knew Dr. Bettelheim. Finley also wrote an excellent letter on my behalf. I had made the first two cuts and I was in the final field of candidates for admittance. When the letter came, I considered it to be the most important mail I had ever received. The message was unmistakably clear and brief: "Dear Mr. Wlodkowski, You have not been selected. Students of greater merit have been chosen."[45] The directness of the writing reduced my pain: like immediately being cauterized after receiving a bullet wound. How could I argue with something so blunt? I saved the note. I did not want to forget how different my life might have been had I been accepted, living the next three years in Chicago and being part of a prestigious doctoral program with a world renowned faculty. I wanted to always know how close I had come. That awareness would motivate me the next time, and I believed there would be a next time.

Columbia University had either not received or misplaced my application. I found this out in early 1968 when the protests and occupied buildings on its campus were gaining national attention. That left Wayne State University and the University of Illinois. I was accepted by the University of Illinois with a caveat: I would have to enroll in 1969 because their cadre of doctoral students was filled for 1968. Wayne accepted me with no restrictions. I was grateful and extremely pleased. I immediately enrolled.

What Wayne's College of Education had that would last me a lifetime was an educational/clinical psychology doctoral program with a committed urban orientation. I had the opportunity to study in small, conversational seminars with Fritz Redl, Jack Kounin, and William Wattenberg, each of whom had a profound influence on my understanding of motivation. What these men helped me to know was the importance of a person's momentary situation in understanding his or her behavior, rather than relying entirely on knowledge of that person's past. Their theoretical stance contradicted the popular notion that an individual's behavior was a product of the person's nature (inborn tendencies) and nurture (how experiences in life shape individuals). There were other powerful forces at work such as group dynamics influencing a person's behavior. Understanding those dynamics could give the teacher or parent a means *in the moment* to alter that individual's behavior.

Unforgettably, I learned this maxim on the first evening of my first seminar with Professor Kounin.[46] There were about ten students in the class. The course was held in a basement room in Old Main, a building dating back to the late 19th century. It was a dark and musty setting with exposed water pipes, clinking sounds, and dismal overhead lighting. Dr. Kounin, a man in his late fifties, his voice distinctly hoarse and deliberate, was wearing a large checked sport coat and tie. I was sitting in the first row to the right of the class in the seat closest to the doorway. As he introduced himself, he caught my attention for two reasons. The first was he referred to himself as "the second doctoral student of Kurt Lewin." Kurt Lewin was considered by scholars to be the founder of social psychology. Dr. Kounin made this statement with a kind of reverence I found appealing. The second reason he caught my attention was because he seemed distracted by something in the back of the room. As I glanced at the last row of seats, there was a student reading a fully opened newspaper. Dr. Kounin, noticeably irritated, said, "This is a doctoral seminar. You don't read a newspaper while the professor is teaching. Leave the room."

The student quickly folded the paper and said, "I'm sorry Dr. Kounin."

Dr. Kounin, his eyes fixed on the student sternly, said, "Leave. Now."

The student apologized more profusely, "I'm sorry, it won't happen again. May I stay?"

Dr. Kounin, with his voice rising, said, "I mean it. Leave this room!"

The student rose from his seat, pleading, "Please, I made a mistake. I'm sorry."

Dr. Kounin did not respond. He looked at the student and then at the doorway. The message was clear. He was not changing his mind.

I could hardly watch the student leave. It felt like the floor had sunk two feet. There was total silence in the room. Except for Dr. Kounin, everyone was looking at their shoes. Then he said, as though nothing had happened, "Please copy these notes from the board."

I copied his notes as though they contained the secret to the meaning of life. I didn't skip a letter or a punctuation mark. I think I could say the same for my classmates. Then I spotted the student returning. He was walking briskly toward the doorway. I thought, *Maybe he's flipped and he's coming back to punch out Dr. Kounin. This is Detroit. Things like this happen.* When he walked through the doorway, I was hunched in my seat, ready to tackle him. When Dr. Kounin saw him, he smiled and offered to shake his hand. The student had been a plant. With him, Dr. Kounin had just demonstrated the *ripple effect* (an expression, he and his colleagues added to the English lexicon): how a teacher's method of handling the misbehavior of one student influences the *other* students who are an audience to the event. It is a lesson I have never forgotten. When witnessed, how we treat others affects the entire community.

As the seminar continued, I learned that Dr. Kounin had identified a host of techniques that effective teachers used to manage a classroom rather than resorting to punitive discipline.

Positive alerting cues such as:
- Creating suspense before calling on a student to respond—pausing, looking around the room, and introducing the question with, "I wonder who might know the answer to this puzzling dilemma ..."
- Asking for a show of hands in response to a question before selecting a respondent.
- Alerting students that they may be asked to explain or give an example for another student's response during a discussion.

Overlapping: Attending to two classroom issues simultaneously such as listening to a student read while helping another to find her place in the book being read. Today, that's called multitasking.

Variety in learning activities: Varying the content as well as the style of learning such as moving from math work to social studies but also from individual work to small group work.

Fritz Redl also had a number of interventions that were not punitive and applicable in the moment such as *emotional first aid* which may involve helping students to manage their emotions,[47] e. g. "I realize you didn't get a chance to participate during the discussion and you're feeling frustrated now that the bell has rung and we're moving on to another class. I'll keep that in mind so you have a better opportunity tomorrow."

What I saw through my eyes as a teacher was that these professors had ideas that kept children learning by sustaining their interest in tasks and preventing distractions from undermining their attention or focus on learning. From my perspective, some of these "management techniques" were also motivational strategies,[48] deliberate actions teachers could take to enhance student motivation to learn: to maintain the energy to initiate, continue, and complete learning.

The wonderful benefit was I could test these ideas in the classroom as a Detroit Public School substitute teacher, my part-time occupation while in graduate school. They worked! I found out that without any remarks to "Settle down," I could gain the rapt attention of inner city high school students when I said, "I'd like to tell you my name. (Pause) My hunch is you've never seen a name like mine before. (Pause) It's a difficult name to pronounce. Sometimes, even for me. (Smile, Pause) Please watch as I write it on the board." By creating this kind of suspense, a positive group alerting cue, I would gain enough attention to also set a few rules with the students.

There were two more benefits. The first was the pure pleasure of being intrinsically motivated to study motivation. Some of these methods didn't work or didn't work all of the time. I could always ask why. I could reflect and experiment with another approach the next time I substitute taught. This self-questioning led to the second life-long benefit. *I learned to think motivationally.* What kept students involved, interested, persevering, or excited to learn was *what teachers did,* even if it was as simple as handing them a book they thought the student might enjoy reading. Through such judicial musing, I had edged myself, my insecurity, my ignorance, and my hope to another way of looking at learning, classrooms, and schools.

There was no doubt that the personal characteristics of students made a difference in how they behaved. But those characteristics interacted with the students' social situation. As teachers, there was little that we could do to influence those personal characteristics. There was no time and we didn't have the skills to do therapy in the classroom. But we could influence the social situation. I was learning there was much more we could do than I ever thought was possible.

∴

I think most students who enter a doctoral program and complete it are transformed by it. That's usually one of the goals of the program: to immerse a student so deeply in ways of thinking according to the discipline in which a person is specializing that its language, literature, values, perspectives, and ideas become second nature to the doctoral candidate. I wanted this kind of professional absorption and I believed the deeper my knowledge of motivation, the more likely I would be to discover a contribution to the field. What I liked about many of my professors was they didn't quote research, at least not very often. What they could do that I wanted to do was to be conversational *with* theory, to see things and make sense of them through the prism of a body of knowledge.

Jack Kounin was a master of this approach,[49] using a set of ideas to understand effective teaching with language that was simple and direct. He would use the analogy of travelling in a car. "Your destination won't be reached if you can't get the car started and keep it moving. Your educational objective won't be achieved if you can't get children involved in learning or keep them from disturbing others." He used videotapes of classroom teaching, analyzing how group management techniques used by a teacher maintained higher involvement and lessened misbehavior whether or not the teacher seemed to be patient or enjoy children. He had an entire language of concepts such as "desists," "slowdowns," "flip-flops," "jerkiness," and so on to make these analyses. He had essentially reframed teacher and student behavior to make better sense of what happens in a classroom. I wasn't sure how I was going to do it, but I wanted to use a motivational lens to see teaching more insightfully. To accomplish this goal, I believed I needed to understand human motivation to learn as deeply as I could. In this way, my transformation and changed world view was self-generated. I wanted to change my way of thinking about teaching and learning.

My ambitions were also fueled by the era in which I lived. Thinkers, books, and ideas abounded with the notion that the world could be changed and education as it stood was a Neanderthal structure in desperate need of reformation and reinvention. Doctoral students from my program were going to Mexico to study with Ivan Illich whose book *Deschooling Society* would,[50] in 1971, describe how to de-institutionalize education. *Teaching as a Subversive Activity* was in galley proofs in 1968. Campuses across the country were vibrating with debates about cultural and political revolution. There seemed to be a grand momentum moving forward like a shattering sound morphing society into another shape. When Timothy Leary spoke at our campus, his opening band was Jefferson Airplane and his opening line was, "Are you turned on?" Students roared their approval. We listened carefully to his admonitions to come to Chicago, only 220 miles down the road, to radicalize the 1968 Democratic Convention. Radios were playing and students were singing Graham Nash's anthem, "Chicago."

> Though your brother's bound and gagged
> And they've chained him to a chair
> Won't you please come to Chicago
> Just to sing?
>
> In a land that's known as freedom
> How can such a thing be fair?
> Won't you please come to Chicago
> For the help that we can bring?
>
> We can change the world
> Rearrange the world
> It's dying to get better

I wasn't radicalized or even a radical thinker at the time. I was, however, profoundly affected. I believed that a change was occurring in the world. There was a ferment going on. Something had to shake loose. I wasn't sure what that was going to be. From the music, art, politics, and norms of the day, conventional society's grip on the way things were seemed to be unravelling. "Revolution" was a buzz word being touted throughout the media. Cultural Revolution. Sexual Revolution. Political Revolution. Educational Revolution. The change wasn't just a matter of marching in the streets.[51] It was everywhere: Like going to my friend Catherine's home for dinner and asking her, "While you're up, could you get me a glass of water?"

Her reply, "What's the matter?" Is your ass nailed to the seat? Get it yourself, big boy." No one blinked.

Now, psychology was getting hip. One of the most common questions among students on campus was, "What are you studying?"

"Psychology."

"That's cool."

This was a response I hadn't often heard before, but I was frequently hearing it in 1969. I didn't argue with the apparent compliment but I didn't buy it all the way. Too easy. Detroit, Summer, 1967 was vivid in its aftershocks and my professors looked and sounded much as they did before. They had important knowledge to share. Being cool was irrelevant to them. I saw their implacability as a strength. I did believe psychology was relevant to the times, an avenue for innovative thinking and new ideas. I was impassioned by its potential. With my doctoral research ahead of me, I had a chance to discover knowledge that could make a genuine contribution to my field of study. I needed to pick a topic for my dissertation. I was excited by the opportunity, a real chance to learn something so deeply that I would be one of the few people in the world to know it with such thorough comprehension. In addition, this study would set the course for my future.

In 1968, Robert Rosenthal and Lenore Jacobson wrote a book, *Pygmalion in the Classroom,* which, like the times it was written in, offered a view that the world might be changed with a different mindset.[52] Based on their study of a California elementary school, they found that when teachers were told that some of their students could be expected to be "spurters" due to their performance on an IQ test, those students would perform better over the school year in comparison to their classmates. But the spurters were a randomly selected group who *did not perform better than their classmates* on the IQ test. However, the spurters' names were made known to the teachers. At the end of the school year, all students were again tested with the same IQ test used at the beginning of the study. First and Second Graders showed statistically significant differences in gains favoring the experimental group of "spurters." This led to the conclusion that teacher expectations, particularly for the youngest children, can influence student achievement.

Many educators, reformers, and public officials generalized from this study that "the obvious had been made obvious." Teachers treat children differently based on their expectations of them. From this generalization, accusatory suppositions flooded the popular media: Teachers with negative expectancies toward their students are responsible for their poor learning. Teachers should not examine a student's records ahead of time as this may cause them to make a negative expectancy of the student. And possibly the most radical and popular, IQ tests should be abolished because they create negative teacher expectations. Over the years, these bromides have not dissolved. In 2004, President George W. Bush made headlines when he referred to "the soft bigotry of low expectations" as one of the challenges faced by low income and minority students.

But back in 1969, I, and more than a few others, didn't think teacher expectations were so simple in their effect to cast such an easy diatribe, like a flashy lure in a still pond. When I brought up the idea of teacher expectations as a dissertation topic to Dr. Kounin, he had a strong reaction, "Yeah, teachers have to do something to make an expectation stick with a child. I don't think they get their expectations across to students with magic or mental telepathy. Or the evil eye," he laughed. "They might say something differently. Whatever they do, it probably has an effect based on what students expect of themselves. I think it's worth a look." Predictably, his words made a difference. His assurance and value for my research proposal, strong characteristics of a positive expectancy, left me highly motivated.

Within a year, I had completed the study.[53] Simply stated, my findings were: For working class fifth grade boys whose teacher displays a positive expectancy for them on a simple math task like solving calculation problems, this positive expectancy can significantly raise their performance. For the same group of boys, performing a complex math task like solving word problems, there was no positive teacher expectancy effect. The characteristics of a task—simple/complex, long/short, familiar/unfamiliar, math/social studies—can influence an expectation's impact.

What I personally learned from doing this research was that I should be thoughtful about what I said when I gave assignments and tests. However, there was a small group of students who improved their performance when they were given negative expectations. They seemed to be the "I'll show you!" learners and exhibited defiance as motivation to achieve. I started to imagine how carefully expressed goals and contracts between teachers and students need to be in order to help them learn.[54] The personality of the students could make a difference as well. Most of all, I was still fascinated about learning about motivation. I had found a universe to explore for the rest of my professional life.

CHAPTER 11

Entering a Life of Study

A blind future may be one of youth's best friends. That seemed to be the case as I prepared to leave for the University of Wisconsin-Milwaukee (UWM) as a new Assistant Professor of Educational Psychology. I had been hired by Dr. Robert Ingle who was a graduate of the Ed. Psych program at Wayne State University. I had one other serious offer from Miami University of Ohio where I interviewed prior to UWM. The campus at Miami was stellar, with ivy covered Tudor buildings and a large mall precisely dotted with venerable oaks and maples. When I looked across its vista, I half-expected Sean Connery to walk out at any moment smoking a pipe. The faculty was cordial. The program was solid but there were two things that deterred me. The first was location. Miami U. was in Oxford. The largest city near it was Cincinnati, over 40 miles away and more than an hour's drive on a single lane road. The second was the answer to my question, "What do you do for fun on Saturday night?" A young professor without a trace of sarcasm said, "A lot of us go bowling." At that moment UWM looked much better.

I had been to UWM once before my interview when Wayne's football team played UWM. The city impressed me because of its unexpected beauty. Milwaukee sits on the southwestern shore of Lake Michigan and has beaches and parks that run along its entire length from downtown to its northern suburbs. Seeing surfers along the city's shoreline was a stunning surprise. The university is located near Lake Park, a thickly forested greenway, designed by Frederick Olmsted.

However, I thought I might not get the position because of a faux pas I committed after dinner with the Ingles during the weekend I visited. We were in the elevator going down to the parking lot and I noticed that Mrs. Ingle had a small piece of lettuce and a radish slice in her hair. I have no idea how they got there, but when I said, "Mrs. Ingle you've got the beginnings of a great salad going on in your hair," she smiled, but Dr. Ingle didn't. Though I worked with him for seventeen years, neither of us ever brought up that moment again.

Like so many people in their late 20s with little money to spare, it was my friends, Frank and Ken, and my brother, Richard, who helped me to move to Milwaukee. We were an inexperienced but enthusiastic crew. All we needed were strong backs and a U-Haul truck. The first pick-up was an upright piano from another house. Heavy—yes. Could we handle it? Of course. It wasn't easy, but we had it on the truck without any mishaps.

Now, to pick up the rest of the furniture at my flat. We decided Ken would stay inside the truck with the piano as we drove there. Rambling down 8 Mile Road, I think it was my brother who first asked, "Do you hear screaming?"

Frank and I listened carefully. I said, "No. Maybe it's the tires on the pavement. We're going pretty fast."

My brother responded, "Wait. Listen. If it's not's screaming, it's someone shouting."

Frank said, "Let's roll up the windows. There's too much noise from the highway to tell where the sound might be coming from."

As soon as we did, we knew it was Ken from the interior of the truck. We couldn't make out what he was shouting, but there was no doubt he was alarmed. As we pulled off the road and stopped, his cries became louder and more frantic. When we rolled up the back cover of the truck we saw the piano on a diagonal in the center and Ken pinned against the side wall of the interior. None of us had thought to tie the piano down.

We tied up the piano. Other than heavy rainfall, the rest of the move went smoothly. After we had unloaded the furniture in Milwaukee, we went out for pizza and a few beers. By that time, we were laughing about our collective dumbness. We knew "Ken playing dodge-m with the piano" was already becoming a good story for looking back on some of our Milwaukee misadventures.

∵

Living 350 miles from Detroit was not too difficult. It was close enough to be able to return for holidays and to have friends visit. Beginning life as a young university teacher was exciting. Randall Jarrell said that the only thing better than being a college professor was inherited wealth. He was on the mark. To be paid to study, advise students, conduct research, teach three courses a semester, and write felt incredible.

I could be the best possible teacher I could be. Part of that realization was practical. Where else but in the College of Education should excellent teachers thrive? We taught teachers how to teach. We were activists for what we professed we loved to do: be inspiring exemplars for one of the most important professions in the world. It was 1970. Wayne had left me with a legacy to make a difference. I had seen faculty there who did. Who could say without irony, "This is important work. We learn from doing it well. It might not turn out how we planned, but if we stick with it, chances are we won't be ashamed when we die."

Though it didn't come without arrogance, I had the faith. I wanted to find the best teachers in the college and get to know them. A name that kept coming up from both students and faculty was Norm Bernier. He was a philosophy of education professor considered brazen and outrageous, a master of the Socratic method of teaching, using a respectful argumentative dialogue with students to draw out their ideas and assumptions. Students in the classes I taught frequently talked about provocative incidents in his classes. He openly dealt with issues of race and gender. He would say, "You know, I don't like to admit it, but when I see a black man and a white woman walking down the street holding hands, I feel uncomfortable. What do you think of that?" Then a student would respond, often initially timidly, either supporting his discomfort or critical of it. In either case, he would then ask the student, "Why do you say that?" After that student's response, he would ask the rest of the class their opinions, probing deeper and deeper into their given assumptions with questions, gentle yet laser sharp, like small sting rays. Students often would leave his classes upset. However, there was no disputing the fact that his classes made them think deeply. His reputation was that over the course of a semester, he changed minds and won many of his students over to a liberal philosophical perspective. Changing education meant fundamentally changing how racism and sexism played out in United States schools. I was intrigued with what I heard about his teaching and admired his willingness to risk, to put himself on the line to teach well. He co-taught an advanced graduate course on racism and education with a black graduate student, a woman widely known as an activist and militant. Some of the professors were critical of him, framing his teaching as egotistical and flamboyant. Nonetheless, he was the only professor out of more than two thousand faculty who had ever won the university award for teaching excellence twice. I knew I wanted to meet him.

I had been at UWM for two months and I hadn't yet encountered him. We had a large faculty in education, more than 90 professors scattered throughout three buildings. In my ninth week, students from my course gave me a good reason to visit his office. While I was offering my considered opinion on the topic of stages of psychological development and learning, a student, Jason, without raising his hand, spoke out. "Dr. Wlodkowski, this is complicated stuff. Even if I learn it, I doubt if I'll ever use it as a teacher."

I found myself stammering as I attempted to respond. But before I could say more than, "Ah, um ...," Jason interrupted me again.

"You know, Dr. Bernier said in class yesterday that educational psychology is a useless subject."

"Really? What rationale did he give for that opinion?" I asked.

"He said, 'Teachers never refer to Ed Psych as a resource. It doesn't even deal with discipline problems. And, although Ed Psych provides a definition for learning, few teachers ever remember it and most never use it.'"

"That's quite an indictment. Did he say anything else?"

"Yeah, when students are asked in surveys which course is the least helpful to their profession, Ed Psych ranks number one. The only subject that ever beats it is Statistics."

"So how do you feel about our course?"

Jason hesitated ... "The jury's still out."

"Now, that's a diplomatic response, Jason. I think I'll have a talk with Dr. Bernier."

I relished the opportunity my students had given me to meet Bernier. Even if in name only, as a colleague, I felt he shouldn't make disparaging remarks about another department in the same college in which his own department was housed. When confronted, in addition to his presumed feelings of guilt, I would have the element of surprise because I intended to visit him that same day and I doubted he knew who I was. This was gamesmanship. As a cocky young professor, I was having fun. I had one more card to play: my opening gambit.

What I noticed about professors, all the way back to undergraduate school, was that most of the men, although sometimes politically, intellectually, and emotionally courageous, were not physically very brave. Take them out of the classroom, put them in the street, and they tended to avoid physical confrontation. In parking lots, or driving, or outside of bars, more than once I saw academics shy away from the more volatile construction and factory workers. They knew these weren't students worried about their grades. I thought the same observation would hold for him.

He was one of those professors who kept daily office hours and whose door was always open. He wore glasses, was slim with short straight brown hair, exposing an early bald spot at the crown of his head. He favored crew neck sweaters and khakis. Raised in a French-Canadian neighborhood in Boston, he spoke with a strong Northeastern accent.

When I walked quickly into his office, I stood straight up at the edge of his desk, not quite over him but definitely into his "space." It surprised him. As he began to stand up, I motioned for him to sit down. He did. He looked a little discombobulated. With an expression mirroring my father's, when he would say to me as a boy, "Now, don't touch that again," I said, "My name is Raymond Wlodkowski. My students tell me you've been slandering Educational Psychology. I'm an educational psychologist and I'm here to get physical with you about that insult." Then I looked him in the eye for about two seconds before I slightly smiled. As I did, he began to look amused.

"Now who are you?" he asked still grinning.

I motioned to check if it was okay to sit down.

"Sure. You've got my attention."

Then I leaned toward him to shake hands. As we did, he asked with an edge of perplexity, "Were you trying to scare me?"

"Absolutely. As a representative of a worthy profession, educational psychologists might be questionable, but we're not wimps."

He laughed. He seemed intent on figuring me out, "Have we met before?"

"No. This is the first time."

He looked at me affably, "Well, you're leaving an impression."

I nodded. I knew I was making a friend. We decided to meet later that evening for a drink. It turned into dinner and about four hours later we were still talking. Norm didn't worry about being agreeable. He also didn't worry if his questions were too direct: "Why do you think that way? What have you read that makes you so sure? What have you done to see if your ideas work?" Although he left the impression he was the better thinker, he didn't insinuate he was the better person. For him, life was about learning. He believed that a deep dialogue with a trusted person could change either mind. Conversation with him was like a chess game—fastest mind in the west—let's see who wins.

At the end of dinner, I asked him, "What do you think you'll learn from me?"

"I'm not sure. But we're off to a good start."

After that evening, we met every week for dinner and drinks. Within a month, we trusted each other enough to diminish our verbal jousting and begin more intimate conversations where who knew more counted less and less. One of the beautiful things about this early time as a professor was how effortless it was to enter into friendships. How those intense, unpredictable beginnings offered so much to learn because of how exhilarating it felt when deepening trust enhanced our vulnerability, questioning things to their core because neither person feared knowing less.

⁘

One of the most important things I learned from Norm was that if I wanted to be a critical thinker, I had to take seriously other perspectives and bodies of knowledge. He thought everything was open for debate. He was a dialectical thinker. He believed ideas competed with each other. Each viewpoint had to provide reasonable support, counter objections, and include evidence from other disciplines. If biology said men were physically stronger than women, what did psychology say? What do you mean by stronger? How does having a baby reflect physical strength? Does longevity indicate strength? How does culture influence how physical strength is perceived and how it is nurtured? What about other cultures? Although he didn't always live up to his own ideal, he espoused being fair-minded while arguing: One had to concede points that did not stand up to critique and integrate strong points from other views. His ultimate question was: What does any idea mean for human rights? Minorities suffered at the hands of majorities everywhere. Only those at the very top and those at the very bottom knew what was really going on. A philosopher led people away from pap.

For Norm, one of the biggest hoodwinks going on in education was operant conditioning. "Raymond, don't deny it. It's educational psychology that's pushing for rewards and punishments to control kids in schools. The Nazis would have loved B. F. Skinner."[55]

"Hey, psychology is a giant field, not like philosophy that's shrinking by the minute. There are plenty of psychologists that oppose operant conditioning. Carl Rogers, Kurt Lewin, and Anna Freud to name a few."

"But who are the teachers following with their gold stars, threatening grades, and free pizzas for reading books?"

"Skinner. That may be true, but I don't hear any teachers quoting Plato or Kant to oppose those methods."

Norm thought for a moment, "Maybe we're not doing our job. You don't find operant conditioning in any of the upper income school systems. They wouldn't touch that stuff for their children. It's for the other kids, whom eventually they want their kids to control."

"I wouldn't argue with that, but you have to have an alternative to replace something as convincing as a rewards and punishments mentality. We have to look at motivation as ideas that work in the classroom; ideas teachers can use so that, in their minds, student learning pre-empts their need to control students."

Norm affected me deeply, not only by his thinking, but by his warmth and generosity. If you were his friend, anything he had was yours: books, food, car, apartment. He didn't keep tabs on who paid for what or when. He was the only person I ever knew who would not repair furniture or interior decorations that were damaged during a joyful event, like a party or celebration. His home had more than a few stains, nicks, and dented lamp shades. He said, "Each of those comes from a memory I never want to forget."

While both men heavily relied on philosophy to guide their thinking, Finley's fealty was more to values such as honesty, duty, responsibility. That's how he took the measure of a person. He believed great leaders nurtured and defended universal values: Pericles and democracy, Jefferson and freedom, Martin Luther King and equality. Norm was invested in philosophy as an agent for change: How Socratic thinking or John Dewey's pragmatism might be used to challenge the status quo. Listening carefully to him and strenuously arguing with him led me to transform the way I taught. Without directly trying, he helped me to take seriously fiduciary responsibility: the idea that there is a public trust in professional education, that what we do in college classrooms should significantly affect the way future teachers teach.

As a college teacher, I moved from lecturing to doing, from learning about ideas to experiencing them. I asked myself how I could make psychology come alive in the classroom. How could I make a psychological idea or concept become an experience or a practice or a strategy? My internal guide for teaching was, "If we don't do it in here, we won't do it out there." Essentially, I turned my course into a workshop. I initiated small collaborative groups so every student could get a chance to role play or problem solve based on realistic challenges in schools such as discipline problems, boredom, and resistant students. We rehearsed communication techniques like paraphrasing and making assertive statements. We analyzed and acted out scenarios such as conflict with an angry parent or conferences with students to solve homework problems. If a student saw something troubling in a school or remembered something that caused frustration for a teacher, we enacted it on the spot. I kept Sister Desiderata's memory handy for these moments:

"Okay, Sarah, what did the (high school) student say that stopped the teacher in his tracks? If you can remember, say it to me, just like the student said it to the teacher."

Sarah raised her voice, "I'm not good at anything and my teachers don't like me!"

I responded calmly, "I don't think that's true. Maybe you're good at making your teachers dislike you."

"What!?"

"In fact, you might be very good at making your teachers dislike you."

"You're putting me on."

"No. Let me ask you, 'What do you think you do that makes teachers dislike you?' And, please answer honestly."

Sarah hesitated and then she said, "I come late to class. Teachers don't like that."

"Anything else?"

"I don't bring my homework."

"Is it possible there might be one more?"

"Sometimes, I slam my book on my desk when I get frustrated."

I smiled, "Sounds like you're pretty good at making some teachers dislike you." Then I asked the class to analyze what happened between me and Sarah and how they might understand and use what I did in their own classrooms. They refused. They wanted first to brainstorm ways they made their teachers in the past dislike them before doing any analysis. I wrote their examples on the board as they called them out. There were easily over fifty items ranging from smacking gum to pretending not to hear a teacher when she spoke to them. After about two years, I had developed my introductory Ed. Psych. course into a relevant set of psychologically sound teaching methods that my students found useful.[56]

⁂

In 1971, not long after I moved to Milwaukee, my father died. I was teaching an afternoon class when I found out. A graduate student came to our classroom and told me the dean wanted to see me immediately. I knew it wasn't going to be good news.

My father died of a stroke in a small plastics factory where he held a part time job as a sweeper. My first reactions were a calm resignation and concern for my mother. I wasn't surprised. My father's personality was a breeding ground for hypertension, an ailment he had most of his life after middle-age. I was able to drive back to Detroit the same evening of the day I found out. I felt grateful for having him for so long in my life. The quiet trip along I-94 in the late night gave me time to reflect, the darkness a still canopy to hold my thoughts. Most were appreciations. My father was physical in his love, easily putting his hand on my shoulder with affection, wrestling with my brother and me when we were boys, and quick to hug us as adults. A presence for the rest of my life, whose faith in the redemptive hope of education never wandered, never detoured, and seeped into my soul.

The last time I saw him was when we drove off on our move to Milwaukee. We had said our good-byes in my parent's home but he wanted to accompany us to the cab of the truck. It wasn't tearful. Spirits were high. I had a good job. He knew that. It made our departure necessary and he celebrated my good fortune. He was in his light blue work shirt. His thinning grey hair swept back, he was smiling carefully because of bridgework yet to come. He leaned in the front window, a light scent of Ivory soap drifting off his arms. It was the last time I felt his touch. His hand pressed gently on my wrist. "Be safe."

CHAPTER 12

Human Relations

In 1975, my mother's life changed dramatically. Her sister Ann came to live with her. If the texture of my father's temperament was sandpaper, Aunt Ann's was silk. In her 20s she had modeled in Detroit, appearing in full page automobile ads in Collier's and The Saturday Evening Post. She was what was known in those days as a "looker." I was not surprised when, in her 60s, she drew wolf whistles walking along Woodward Avenue. She wasn't brassy. Her clothes were tasteful and sedately colorful, what one would expect of someone with her background in fashion. I never saw her in a house dress. She favored low heels, light make up, and chic hats. Her hair was a deep honey blond and she had a posture Jackie Kennedy would have envied. I may have been in love with her, at least until I was 16.

She and my Uncle Pete led the high life in Chicago. He was an industrial sales representative and she was a buyer for Carson, Pirie, Scott and Company. They traveled, went to professional sporting events, ate out on a regular basis, and were the best dancers in my family. On their fireplace mantle was a photo of my aunt, holding a drink, surrounded by the offensive line of the Chicago Bears. When I asked my Uncle Pete where the photo was taken, he just laughed and said, "You know, I can't even remember. We were having so much fun."

My Aunt Ann taught me how to Charleston and play poker. She called a three a "trey" and, when we were boys, she never visited us without taking my brother and me out for hot fudge sundaes at a Sanders Confectionary. When we visited her as adults, immediately after giving us a kiss and a hug, she would take a step back and ask, "Want a drinkie?" Sure.

It was obvious Aunt Ann and my mother were quite dissimilar—different temperaments, different lifestyles, and different personal histories. Yet they were at ease with one another. There was a mutual kindness and respect. Uncle Pete had died of throat cancer. My Aunt Ann had no pension and only slight savings. My mother welcomed her into her home. She opened up my mother's life to a broader world. They vacationed together in Chicago and California, played cards and games, and visited friends and relatives.

In order to be more mobile, Aunt Ann decided to learn to drive in her late 60s. She had my father's car, a 1949 Chrysler in 1975, and she decided to put it to good use. Although she was able to get a license, driving did not go well for her. The last straw was when she went to take the car out of the backyard garage, put it in reverse, and forgot to open the garage door. No one was injured and, fortunately, little damage was done, but that accident put an end to her ambitions for a more freewheeling life.

Among all the people in my life, Aunt Ann had the strongest influence on motivating me to leave Detroit, to live in another city away from friends and family. Out of eleven siblings, she was the only sister who left. She *modeled* a successful and interesting life in a world class city with which I could identify as a young adult.

Modeling works on both a conscious and unconscious level. Whenever we see people who are similar to ourselves successfully performing a challenging task, whether it's designing computer software, rock climbing, or conducting an orchestra, we can believe in the possibility that we could perform such a task ourselves. If we can connect with those people in ways which afford us an understanding of how these models accomplished such goals, our chances for similar success become greater. And, if we can be mentored by them, then odds in our favor increase again. We can practice their skills and receive feedback directly from them.

As a young child, seeing Aunt Ann at least once a year, visiting her in Chicago, walking the streets of that city with her, and, perhaps, most of all, just plain liking each other in a joyful and tender way, made her life appeal to me. The wondrous thing about all of this was I wasn't aware of it until I was much older, in my 40s. Before this time, I never thought that Aunt Ann's presence in my life motivated me to move away. It happened unconsciously. That's why it's so difficult to know what one's influence on a younger person is when you're an adult. It's an unseen harvest neither person may ever realize, though today we better understand the impact of mentoring and modeling.[57] There's plenty of research by eminent scholars like Albert Bandura that demonstrates how we derive information from competent models to alter our sense of personal effectiveness.[58] In regard to my professional aspirations, the person who most fulfilled this role was Finley. He did so without ever mentioning the word mentor. He simply wanted to be helpful where he could.

⁙

I thrived at UWM. Along with Norm, I had exceptional friends and colleagues: Dick Larson, Alex Molnar, and Dick Wisniewski. We had read Paulo Freire's *Pedagogy of the Oppressed* and had begun to use his ideas as stepping stones to foster school change,[59] primarily in our courses. We agreed with Freire's premise that schools were inherently political in nature, where political views were constantly modeled and acted upon: teacher-student relationships (authoritarian or democratic), the readings offered to students (how liberal or conservative, how roles of women and men were depicted, and the sustainment or interruption of racial stereotypes), and course content (a shared decision or solely the teacher's), what's discussed and what's glided over. As Martin Luther King,[60] Jr. wrote in his *Letter from Birmingham Jail,* "Injustice anywhere is a threat to justice everywhere." In our minds, this was as true for pedagogical practices as it was for employment practices.

I adopted a teaching philosophy that my courses should offer students the opportunity for critical inquiry that addressed their real-world issues in an action-oriented manner. The first course in which I attempted this orientation was in my graduate adolescent psychology course. Rather than coming in with a pre-written, completed syllabus, I left ten weeks of topics open. The subjects for each of these weeks were created by the students on the first night of class. Using small collaborative groups, I asked them to respond to this question: What's a problem you are facing with an adolescent that you think the behavioral sciences could help you to understand and, possibly, resolve? Within forty-five minutes, usually fifteen or more problems emerged. A sampling:

− I think my son is addicted to marijuana.
− A close relative who's twelve years old claims she is a lesbian.
− There's a teenage gang terrorizing my school.
− I've got a daughter who's gotten so sullen, I don't even recognize her.
− Most kids I work with don't seem motivated to learn in school.

The class and I used these problems to form cooperative research groups.[61] Each group created a presentation and a paper for the course, discussing the possible causes of their selected problem and personally useful, promising ways that might resolve the problem. They also had to address how issues of income, race, gender, and conventional biases, values, and media might contribute to sustaining the problem. Serving as a guide and co-learner to each of these groups provided me with wonderful learning opportunities: visiting schools, first-hand contact with local and state politicians, access to juvenile detention facilities, and deliberations with counseling centers and health providers. I was learning how the city of Milwaukee worked for kids.

I continued to study motivation to learn. It was my abiding interest. Anything I could get my hands on about motivation, I read. I was like one of those small terriers who knows his master has a treat for him and perks up his ears at the sound of its impending arrival, usually the word, "Wanna ..." as in "Wanna biscuit?" For me the word was "motivation." All things related to it mattered to me. I once said to my students, "This class is only three hours in your week, but for me, it's everything. It never ends. And, gladly so." A few looked up with expressions of what might best be called mixed admiration; most did not pay that much attention; and a few shook their heads with mild pity. Afterwards,

I thought it might be wise to keep my more exuberant feelings about motivation to myself. Nonetheless, if I were asked a question about motivation, I could feel the hairs on my neck rise and I would remind myself to contain my response in the direction of brevity.

Partly due to my enthusiasm about motivation, partly due to my experience with kids, and partly due to being in the community, I began to receive requests from schools to speak on the topic. Another reason, I believe from the responses I received to my work, was that it was useful to teachers and parents. What seemed to be most interesting to them were motivational strategies: deliberate actions they could take to encourage motivation to learn among their students and children.

Any strategy I shared had to be supported by my own experience. For example, I understood that relevance—when something personally matters— evoked personal interest and motivation. That being so, I knew I was more likely to read and study about prostate cancer than cancer in general because a number of my close relatives had suffered from prostate cancer. This particular form of cancer was far more relevant to me than cancer as a general topic. For this reason, I used relevant problems as a motivational strategy throughout my workshops to generate participant interest as well as a strategy to be enlisted by these teachers and parents with their own students and children.

Relevant problems evoked passion in people because they sincerely needed to solve them. I would ask participants to offer an example of a problem that's on their mind and that they'd like to solve. People spontaneously spoke. "I can't even get my son to open a book!" One could feel the energy surge through the audience. Finally, the motivational strategies I espoused had to be supported by theory and research. I wasn't going to advocate a strategy that hadn't been rigorously considered, examined, and found to make a significant difference in increasing motivation or learning.

This work allowed me to develop a catalogue of solid, useful motivational strategies. I believed I was beginning to have something worth sharing on a broader scale. I started to envision writing a book. But a powerful thing happened to interrupt this goal: school desegregation.

My friends, Dick, Alex, and I were doing snappy workshops at the invitation of schools with topics like affective education, school leadership for change, and motivation to learn. However, with rare exceptions, most schools didn't change. We affirmed and expanded what some teachers were already doing. We had a few testimonials that teachers had changed their teaching practices: "After your workshop, I transformed my entire curriculum!" But most teachers seemed to enjoy us as a kind of educational vaudeville featuring classroom skits and plenty of humor. Beyond stimulating guilt and displaying a kind of with-it-ness as hip urban educators, we didn't have many levers to push. Other than consulting with a small number of innovative school administrators, we weren't conducting sustained, programmatic professional learning. We knew desegregation was a serious attempt to change urban schools. Along with the threat of mandatory busing, it was coming to Milwaukee under federal court order.

The unanimous Supreme Court Brown vs. Board of Education ruling on May 17, 1954, was the landmark opinion that separate public schools for black and white students were unconstitutional, a decision that would drive school desegregation efforts around the country. My teaching experiences in Detroit and Milwaukee allowed me to see that schools that were almost exclusively attended by low-income black students were inferior to schools largely made up of white working class or white middle class students. Locked into zones gerrymandered by politicians, segregated housing practices, and high unemployment rates, these schools were older and more poorly maintained, had more substitute teachers and inexperienced teaching staffs, and all too often, administrators and teachers who openly stated low learning expectations for their students. The attitude was: What do you expect from us? Many of these families don't care about learning and some don't even care about their kids. They have too many problems to even get to learning. Don't blame us.

When I began teaching, the correlation between poverty and low achievement was a well-documented fact.[62] There was no doubt in my mind that as a racial group in the Midwest, white citizens were not going to voluntarily change inequitable schooling in urban areas. Many would prefer to leave, seeing their exodus as essentially common sense to avoid less effective schools and to acquire adequate financial compensation for their homes before their value plummeted because of realtor-driven blockbusting and "white flight." Their migration from Milwaukee to the suburbs had already begun. The city's black population increased 18 percent between 1970 and 1975, while its white population decreased 11 percent. This rate of decrease for those five years was three times the rate for the entire decade of the 60s.[63]

In 1975, during the first year of court-ordered desegregation, whites rioted in the streets and schools of Boston. Molotov cocktails flew through bus windows and hundreds of students rampaged in South Boston High School. When the police were called to prevent residents and students from blocking the buses transporting black students, the white mob turned on them. For months, white residents openly attacked and beat black students. Some black youths countered by throwing stones and beating white students. Neither black nor white leaders could calm the violence. To be the wrong race in the wrong part of Boston was enough to be attacked. Between 1974 and 1976, the white student population in the Boston Public Schools declined by 17 percent.

In January of 1976, Federal Judge John W. Reynolds issued a decision that the Milwaukee Public Schools (MPS) had been segregated as the cumulative result of school officials' actions for two decades. His ruling required the school district to desegregate one-third of its schools for each of the school years 1977–1978, 1978–1979, and 1979–1980. In July 1975, Lee McMurrin was hired as superintendent of the Milwaukee Public Schools, largely because of his experience in desegregating the Toledo Public Schools. In September of the same year, he proposed a statement to the Milwaukee School Board on Education and Human Rights which stated, in part, "Our multi-ethnic population is potentially one of the richest resources available in our schools" and that "All school districts have the responsibility to overcome any barriers that may exist and to maximize the achievement potential of the children under their care."

I thought he was the right person for the job. He genuinely liked people. Some who disagreed with his leadership called him "Mr. Smiley Face." I had invited him to my motivation seminar and to my surprise, he came. Desegregation was controversial in Milwaukee. Some thought it would provoke another Boston. Most of the students in the course were doctoral students. They peppered him with difficult questions ranging from the potential in the city for violence and how MPS would handle it, to how he would manage his own children in a school system desegregated through busing. He was thoughtful. He didn't give cliché answers.

By chance, that summer I ran into him at a Milwaukee Brewers baseball game. He invited me to sit with him. When I did, I proceeded to watch him talk almost non-stop to seemingly everyone who said hello to him. Because his desegregation plan and its implementation were daily front page news, he was the most recognizable person in the city. There seemed to be no pretense in him, a trait not frequently found among high-powered administrators. Even though the school board was appealing the Reynold's decision, he had publicly declared he would proceed with a desegregation plan to meet the judge's stipulations beginning in September 1976. In October, I received a call from him inviting me to be the human relations specialist for the Milwaukee Public Schools.

My responsibilities would be to provide human relations programming for the entire school system. This included writing grants, establishing a human relations team of seventeen professionals, enhancing safe and peaceful relations within schools, developing a resource center, publishing a newsletter, advising teachers, parents, principals, and the superintendent and his staff, and organizing and delivering in-service programs in the areas of race relations and school-community relations.

Whether to accept this job was one of the most troubling decisions of my life. Professionally, at 34 years of age, I had not jumped off such a cliff before. A month earlier, there had been some violence at Hamilton High School, a magnet school on the far south side of the city and a black student had suffered minor injuries. There were numerous rumors about violence to come because of the yearly increase of black students in predominantly white schools. Our office would be responsible for maintaining peaceful relations across the system. I didn't know who specifically would make up the human relations team other than that they would be school psychologists, counselors, and social workers.

I knew most busing would be black students going to white schools because that was the pattern in other cities such as San Diego, Cincinnati, and Toledo. There were black activists who had made this obvious trend a strong objection to the desegregation process because blacks would carry the burden and suffer the consequences for their efforts. I agreed. Robert L. Green, dean of the College of Urban Development at Michigan State University and an expert on desegregation, in a speech to Milwaukee teachers, had stated that white students would not attend black schools, no matter how good they were: "Black magnet schools ... could have Beethoven teaching music and Einstein teaching math, and they still aren't going to attract whites."

There was initial evidence that black students' achievement levels had increased as a result of desegregation. The desegregation plan was designed to improve schools throughout the city by adding specializations to their curricula—a high school devoted to the arts, another high school specializing in computer technology, and another in college preparatory courses. I knew from experience that implementation on such a major scale took time. McMurrin's staff had written in educational improvements in their desegregation plan. Magnet schools were a key element.[64] Career specialty programs were to be placed in each high school, three middle schools, and fifteen magnet elementary schools. It was anticipated in 1977 that 28,000 of the 100,000 students in the schools system would be bussed. If I had the skills and energy to devote to helping such a massive transformation and I was committed to the value of an integrated society, shouldn't I be a leader in this effort? Some changes to the plan could be made but there was no turning back. A federal court order and a time line had to be implemented.

I went to McMurrin's office for the interview about a week after his call. He greeted me like I was a poker buddy and we were planning a trip to another Brewer's game. "Hey Raymond. Great to see you! How've you been?"

"Pretty good. I've been thinking a lot about your call."

"Good." He came around from behind his desk to shake my hand. He was a big man, thick around the middle, with a quick smile and bright eyes, light on his feet. My hand was completely enveloped in his as we shook, but his grip was easy and warm. He had his trademark grey three-piece suit on. With an almost completely bald head, his look was typically jolly. But he was no clown.

He pointed me to a seat and then sat next to me, "I think being human relations specialist is a job you can do. A lot of people in the schools know you, administrators and teachers, and both groups speak well of you. You've got credibility and we need that in this kind of work. I'm not worried about the academic side. There's grant writing and a newsletter but you should have those skills. What I need most is a peacekeeper."

With this last sentence, his smile vanished. It was replaced by a look that said, "I'm serious about this aspect and if you have any doubts, speak them now."

I let out a deep breath and said, "I know something about conflict resolution. I've worked with angry students and teachers but never on this scale and not under these circumstances."

He leaned toward me, still serious, "Unless you've been in the military or a civil rights activist down South, I don't think many people have. We're all learning as we go along. But I think you have to believe you can learn on the job and be open and committed to it."

"What do you have in mind?"

"If you take the job, and I hope you do, we'll send you to some of the places where desegregation has been going on for a while and where people have some skills with handling conflict and threat, like Louisville and San Diego."

We only talked for about 15 more minutes. I think he wanted to convey that he was approachable, had confidence in me, and was dedicated to desegregating the Milwaukee Public Schools with a carefully designed plan. When I left, he was still upbeat, like a genial guide offering to take me down the Colorado River. Big rapids ahead.

That same afternoon, I met with Gloria Wilson, assistant superintendent for community relations. If I were to take the position, she would be my immediate supervisor. She was thin, and in her mid-fifties with shoulder length hair and wearing a grey tailored suit. She spoke with a soft voice and seemed outwardly calm but with a slight touch of anxiety, like she had a lot of things on her mind and they were crowding her at the moment. I felt the decision already had been made to hire me because most of our time was spent going over the job's details like my contract (one-year), pay scale (same as the university), and office and secretarial help. We were professionally cordial. I had a week to decide.

When I left the MPS administrative offices, I was leaning toward taking the position. Facing a serious challenge, I had learned to ask myself catastrophic questions: What were the worst things that could happen? If there were riots, I might get beaten up. More likely, I might lose my temper and make a fool of myself, embarrass my family and university, and do damage to MPS and its teachers and students. What were my weaknesses? Racial prejudice and ignorance—the structural racism of the school system which I'm complicit with as soon as I take the job. Plus, I didn't know what I didn't know. Political ineptitude—I wasn't familiar with the internal politics of the MPS system and I might make blunders about whom I trusted and which people needed to be involved in the decision-making. Wanting perfection and everything to get done on time—I became impatient, worried, and anxious when I was not accomplishing what I thought I should be accomplishing. I stopped there. I knew I had to talk with friends and look at the other side—strengths and values—before I felt overwhelmed.

My friends had all been schooled in Rogerian counseling. That meant the last thing they would do would be to give me advice. I had to come to a decision through "my own process." That meant voicing my own emotions, my understanding of these feelings, and my critique of them to arrive at a self-determined decision. I trusted Dick Larson the most because he had been a principal in a desegregated school in Racine, Wisconsin. He was even tempered, a published poet, and committed to integration. Athletic, proud of his Swedish heritage, with a thick mustache and a mellifluent voice, he had done community theatre. After a few drinks, if we were lucky, we might get him to do the River City Soliloquy from The Music Man. When I called him and said I needed to talk, he suggested meeting him in the evening at his house. We sat down in his kitchen.

"Dick, I need someone to help me make a decision about this human relations job. There's no doubt I have some fear. Like I might get in over my head. Blunder. I'm not sure if I have the strengths to counter those challenges. Do you think you could ask me some questions to help me sort through this?"

"Sure. I appreciate your trust." He put on a pot of coffee and brought over a bottle of red wine with two cups and two glasses. I pointed to the wine. He gave me a full pour and said, "Now we're ready to begin. Let's start with what you think is your biggest fear."

"I expect an earthquake. I'm just not sure how big it's going to be. It could be a small one and then again, it could be a big one. Look what happened in Boston."

"So let's go with Boston. What do you think happens if it's like Boston?"

"I'd be afraid. I'm not sure what I'd do. Except, I think I'd want to make sure the kids and teachers were safe."

Dick looked off, "Who's going to help you to do that?"

"McMurrin says he'll send me to a couple of cities that have had better success than Boston so I can learn from them."

"Do you trust him?"

"Yes."

"Can you get to him if real trouble starts?"

"I think so. He's hands on and he's everywhere. I don't know if he even sleeps."

Dick thought for a moment. "Let's ask how Milwaukee is different from Boston."

"It's more a German city, less Irish. Historically, less rebellious against government edicts. The school system seems better organized. The plan seems to initially desegregate the schools more gradually with black kids being bussed the most. There's more choice with the development of the magnet schools."

"Okay, what do you bring to the table?"

"I think I'm earnest about desegregation. It's one of the few things that might work. Make schools better for everyone. Get integration going for real. I'm good at compartmentalizing. I don't lose my temper in professional situations."

"What else?' What are the strengths that would make you effective? More than someone else."

"I'm organized. If I care about something, I plan for it. Most of the time I can think on my feet. So far, I still have a sense of humor. I'm Polish-American. On the South side, that will make a difference. That's where they expect the most trouble."

We kept at it until about midnight. Then he asked the final question, "Do you still want the job?"

"You know, Dick, after all this discussion, it's still mostly intuition, but the answer is yes."

When I told Norm about my decision he said, "Somebody's got to do it. It's a funny thing about us professors. We'll fight like hell inside these walls but there aren't many of us who'll take it outside. If you have trouble, want to talk, need a place to rest or settle down, count on me. But nothing in the streets. I want to make the sordid beautiful. I don't want to get beat up."

Finley was protective, "Raymond, you amaze me. You sure you want to do this? People are crazy when they get angry. All the so-called civilizations had riots. Many times. In Rome, the emperors were afraid of the mobs. Including Augustus. Be careful."

When I went to my department to ask for a leave of absence, they granted it easily. The mood was somber. They wished me luck. Two colleagues later stopped by my office to warn me against taking the position. They would understand if I changed my mind.

∴

Going to Louisville was a bust. I didn't think the administrators who spoke with me were candid. It was clear they would not have had anything to do with desegregation by busing had there not been a court order. With a crooked smile the last one I met said, "Good luck. Try not to have a mess."

San Diego had not had any significant violence. The scale of their integration effort was much smaller than Milwaukee's would be. The thrust of their efforts was in building community relations so that families felt safe about busing. They also seemed well organized, thorough in their communications throughout their schools, and committed to peaceful desegregation. San Diego was a large military center and integration via the armed forces was a more common past experience for many of its residents.

When I came back from my trips, I was firmly aware of two things. First, the cultural history and political climate of each individual city has a profound effect on how school desegregation occurs. In this regard, there was little that was transferrable from Louisville or San Diego to Milwaukee. While Milwaukee was a Midwest industrial manufacturing city, Louisville and San Diego were not. The largest minority population in San Diego was Mexican-American. Unions were more powerful in Milwaukee and could do much to facilitate or disrupt peaceful desegregation. Magnet schools and academic improvement were a large part of Milwaukee's plan while this seemed far less so for Louisville. And second, we would have to learn how to safely conduct school desegregation on our own and as we did it.

Being responsible for safe and peaceful relations within schools during the desegregation of the Milwaukee Public Schools was like living in the path of a tornado that never touched down. There were constant sightings of potential violence: parents storming out of meetings, black student busing schedules in disarray and overwhelmed by new routes to avoid the backlash from hostile white communities, and frequent rumors that "trouble was ahead" when kids from different racial groups antagonized each other with insults. "N____rs aren't wanted here!" "Honkies go to hell!" And, like a vast dark cloud rising from the east, the shadow of Boston's debacle.

Yet nothing severe materialized. The avoidance of physical harm to students was a praiseworthy accomplishment, but of the sort that comes from dodging a bullet rather than achieving a higher level of understanding and respect. Much of the pressure toward violence was relieved by blacks bearing the burden of being bussed and whites having the means to leave the city. There was no significant shift in racial attitudes. Between 1975 and 1985, Milwaukee lost 115,000 of its white population,[65] most of whom moved to nearly all-white suburbs. No one from the Milwaukee school administration admitted it at the time, but as research later concluded, the fundamental strategy for busing was to bus only black students and to leave white students where they were.[66] School administrators believed that would integrate the schools as the court order required but significantly lessen white flight. Deputy Superintendent Dave Bennett was the chief architect of the Milwaukee busing plan and admitted this strategy in 1999 when he mentioned it twice at a forum on race issues. Anthony Busalacchi, school board president from 1978 until 1979 agreed, saying, "It was an issue of how do we least disrupt the white community."

The most disturbing transgressions during my year with MPS occurred during a teachers' strike that began on April 7, 1977.[67] There were numerous issues at stake. Foremost among them were the pay scale for teachers, the length of the school day, and the right of the administration to fill the 69 vacancies in the specialty schools according to skill levels of teachers. The union wanted seniority to determine who filled those vacancies regardless of teaching expertise. Parent groups largely opposed the strike and saw it as an illegal action.

The majority of the 800 black teachers in the Milwaukee Teachers Education Association (MTEA) did not strike.[68] A power struggle between the Black Teachers Caucus and the MTEA had developed with accusations of racism being made against the union. The Black Teachers Caucus said that its recommendations to promote desegregation had been ignored by the MTEA in its negotiations with the school board. The MTEA executive director, James Colter, dismissed the caucus as "a minority of a minority"[69] and suggested it was being used by the two black members of the school board to split the union. Among the recommendations the caucus wanted the union to consider were separate seniority lists for white and black teachers, so that black teachers received more equitable treatment when transfers and promotions were considered, and greater representation on the MTEA executive board.

Two weeks into the strike, 921 teachers had crossed the picket lines. That number represented sixteen percent of the union's teachers and most of their black teachers. Some of the non-striking teachers began to write editorials in the Milwaukee papers.[70] Elizabeth Jensen's letter drew sympathy and was widely distributed at various parent meetings. She wrote, "I have in the past crossed picket lines and will do so in the future. First of all, I am a Christian. I was called by God to teach children. That's my job, my purpose. Secondly, strikes by public employees are illegal in Wisconsin. Teachers are public employees. Thirdly, even if there were not a law against strikes by teachers, I would not strike. For when teachers strike, they are not withholding their services from a school board or an administration; they are withholding them from children."

At this point, the strike took an ugly turn. Without backing from the Milwaukee County Labor Council and the AFL-CIO,[71] and facing growing community resentment and media criticism for an illegal strike, in addition to accusations of racist practices, the union feared more teachers might splinter away from their group. The Milwaukee papers and parent groups hammered home the message that the safety of students was eroding. When a survey of MPS students showed that most opposed the strike,[72] that clinched it. The union called for a protest and increased their numbers in the picket lines along the driveway of the School Administration Building,[73] focusing their pressure on central office administrators.[74]

I had never crossed a picket line. My father was a United Auto Worker union member for over 30 years. My brother was a Teamster, and I was a member of the American Federation of Teachers when I taught in Detroit. It wasn't a passage I wanted to make. Yet, I didn't have any qualms. Nearly 10,000 students were going to school and our human relations unit had responsibility for their safety. We had talked it over as a team of twenty people and we were bonded in our purpose.

When I saw the group I had to walk through, my legs began to tremble. They were about six deep, largely white males, looking like an angry mob from a newsreel of what black students faced when they desegregated lunch counters in the South. As some cars drove up the building's driveway, they would slowly move aside and at the same time slap at the windows and bang their hands on the fenders. They were shouting, "Here come the fucking scabs! Smell their stink! Traitors!"

I didn't want to put my head down as I walked past them. No one jostled me, but I felt menaced by their signs, like one might slam against me at any moment. The shouting was unnerving me and I quickened my pace. That's when I felt it: the collision of the warm slime of someone's spit on my cheek. I quickly looked and saw it came from a teacher, one of my former students.

He yelled, "How's that feel, Mr. Human Relations?"

My first thought was, "I gave him an A." I must have shown my disbelief.

He didn't hesitate. He glared at me. "You're just a jerk! Another phony."

I didn't respond. Although I felt it oozing down the side of my face, I didn't wipe it away. I didn't want to give him any satisfaction. I felt scared though. I could feel a desire to run. I hated recognizing that feeling in me. I had hoped for defiance.

Once inside the doors of the building, I started breathing again. I went to the men's room and washed my face repeatedly. Then I slammed my hands on the sink top. I looked in the mirror. My face was crimson and my eyes narrow, a growl rising from my throat. I hoped I would see that student again. Away from the crowd. It wasn't that I wanted vengeance. I just didn't want it to end the way it did. I thought, "You got to spit on me and I couldn't do a damn thing about it."

For those of us who came in that day, our morning, between assignments, was spent answering the question, "What happened to you when you went through the line?" Although some may have felt differently, no one publicly gave the strikers in the picket line any empathy. At best, we were silent. I was glad I could turn my attention toward work. Making friends takes time, enemies only moments.

Though there was nothing serious in the way of physical violence, many staff and administrators had their cars vandalized by strikers in the parking lot. There was an assortment of slashed tires, broken windows, scratched doors, dented fenders, and glued door locks. Some of the faculty who continued to teach during the strike had their homes assaulted with most of the damage due to broken windows, paint splattered sidings, and "scab" tattooed across their garages. The strike lasted 17 days, bitterly ending when teachers returned to work on May 10th. With six arrests for disorderly conduct,[75] documentation of over $13,000 in damages against non-striking teachers, and members of other unions crossing their picket lines, the MTEA may have been its own worst enemy.

∴

One of the wisest elements in the desegregation plan was establishing human relations councils in the high schools.[76] These groups were made up of local students, teachers, community members, and administrators. Our central office team helped to establish their presence in the schools and offered guidance for their operation. Most were effective. They offered each school a means to investigate and quell rumors, which took on an insidious life of their own when they weren't abated. The councils met weekly or on demand as situations merited. They could respond to "hot spots" that emerged among students such as threats and fights. They used their personal understanding of the students and teachers to make the councils' reactions more sensitive and influential. They were a continual force for peaceful interactions, creating these opportunities based on the local norms of their community and school: everything from multicultural materials for teachers to "harmony dances" for opposing ethnic and racial groups. Much of our team's work was to meet the councils' needs and support them. I felt most present and useful doing this work.

Our human relations team worked well together. We were united in our mission to keep the peace. The adversity in the schools strengthened our solidarity. Clearly, we needed each other. Away from work, it was easy to have a drink and dance together. The person whose advice I most trusted was Clem Magner. He had the look of an aging hippy with black rimmed glasses, a wide face, and shoulder length dark hair. He was peaceful. His girlfriend was a black teacher and he was knowledgeable as well as comfortable in the black community, at home in mixed-race bars and parties. He was a good listener and offered his opinions with restraint. Outside of meetings, in the case of potential violence, I went to him first. We usually talked in in person. It was so much easier to understand each other face-to-face. Worry and fear often can't be detected through words and intonations over a phone. Most of the time our meetings were in my office, a small windowless compartment with typical school furniture: a steel green enamel desk and two wooden slatted chairs wrapped around by ivory painted walls with a translucent glass and metal door.

"Clem, I've gotten a couple of calls about a looming fight between white and black students at Bay View High School."

Like the psychologist he was, he stayed calm and analytical, "How do you know it's more than a rumor?"

"One of the calls was from a teacher and the other from the co-chair of the human relations council there. They both said pretty much the same thing. They don't know when it's going to happen but both sides are planning for it. And kids all over the school are buzzing with it."

"Does anyone know who the leaders are?"

"I didn't get that deep into it. I was hoping you might go over to the school and check it out in person."

"Okay. If it's for real and I can find out which kids are planning the fight, what do you think about me doing a little conflict resolution with the leaders privately on school grounds?"

"Heck, I'd appreciate it, but check it out with the human relations co-chair before suggesting it."

This conversation reflects a lot of the work our team did, keeping our ears to the ground and heading off racial conflicts before they gained momentum. We were all versed in the conflict resolution methods popular at the time. We role-played them among ourselves to gain experience before working with students and teachers.

Initially, school desegregation in Milwaukee was considered by many to be successful because it desegregated the sixteenth largest urban school system in the United States without the type of violence characterized in cities such as Boston and Louisville. In 1977, the federal court-appointed monitor of school desegregation in Milwaukee, John Gronouski, said Milwaukee's desegregation plan was "the model of human relations for the nation, not just human relations but desegregation and quality education as well." In 1981, *Newsweek* reported "Milwaukee has managed to achieve what bigger cities no longer even dream of.[77] It has desegregated most of its schools through largely voluntary means, and avoided the white flight that usually follows on the heels of forced bussing." Many of us closer to the school system knew that these appraisals were too contemporary, narrow, and wishful.

An evaluation reported by Ian Harris in 1983 indicated some of the serious shortcomings of school desegregation in Milwaukee.[78] Many black students continued to attend sixteen schools where at least 95 percent of the students were black and whose average achievement rates were lower than for students in other schools in the city. Black children bore the burden of desegregating the schools, making up over 80 percent of the students transported. Only five percent of these students had access to the educational improvements in the specialty programs of the magnet schools.

Today, Milwaukee is seen as a primary example of the "boomerang trend toward re-segregation."[79] From being one of the most integrated school systems in the country during the 1980s, it is now intensely segregated. Of all the large cities in the United States, Chicago and Milwaukee are tied for having the highest percentage of black students attending schools where the enrollment is at least 90 percent one race. Following a nation-wide trend for black students in public schools, test scores have declined, disciplinary actions and drop-out rates have increased, and racial attitudes have polarized. As a federal policy, desegregation did not overcome a racially biased beginning, housing discrimination, diminishing job opportunities, economic deterioration, and institutional racism. Nevertheless, national studies continue to show that black students experience lifelong benefits from attending desegregated schools which include academic achievement, success in college, and more job opportunities. Racial separation in schools contributes to unequal opportunities in life.

Upon ending my contract in December of 1977, I returned to the University of Wisconsin-Milwaukee. I had been welcomed to stay with MPS for at least another year. However, the appeal of a life where teaching, writing, research, and community service were possible was greater than being part of a large school system where my duties were circumscribed by a hierarchy of administrators who expected close adherence to their mandates. I preferred my far more independent life of study to one of activism within a large bureaucracy. This may seem a small confinement, but as human relations specialist, I could never show even an ounce of anger. Early on in this role, I did once and it got back to central office within moments: "The human relations guy got mad! He's not supposed to do that if he wants the rest of us to remain calm." Right, no argument there. I left with some uncomfortable realizations. Abandoning confrontation was a professional price I was reluctant to pay for more than a year.

I had far less power to change my local community than I had realized before my work with MPS. A school board action, an assistant superintendent's whim, a sudden lack of funding were all potentially huge barriers to what I thought should be done. Political realities frequently overcame personal motivation, communal unity, and creative planning. If I wanted change, I had to be active and persevering for years, not months. I would have to remain a school leader for the length of time necessary for transformation, willing to engage the hostility of people who opposed my ideas whether they were school administrators and teachers or parents.

As a university professor in a school of education, I was far less effective in how schools operated than what I thought I was. Getting a class of students to think had far less of an impact than the power of legislation or law. I came back to UWM more humble. I had been enlisted in a bold policy of social change for equity. I hadn't been pulverized or vanquished. But I hadn't been on the indisputable side of social justice either. Busing in Milwaukee had flaws, the largest of which, in my mind, was its deceit of having black students bear the weight of busing so the entire enterprise had a chance for success. This fact was recognized early on, so much so that the plan became recognized locally, not as one of choice, but of forced choice.[80] I was complicit in that plan. Ends and means are not separate. Human relations work, which I had loved to learn and do, being intrinsically motivated throughout this endeavor, was not beyond being stained. I left MPS with a number of questions to contemplate, the most troubling of which was: In a massive undertaking for social transformation, at what point does a moral compromise corrupt the entire action? Upon my return to UWM, I was still trying to sort out a valid response, knowing I wasn't close to an answer.

When I shared these thoughts with Norm, he waved me off. "Hey, there's trash around here too. But the flies are different. Welcome back."

CHAPTER 13

Therapy Lessons

My work in school desegregation at MPS had instilled within me greater faith in the importance of understanding human motivation to learn. Aware of my limited effectiveness, I asked myself: From what I have experienced in the last year, what do I believe is worth pursuing—dedicating myself to understanding and taking the next step to more fully realize? I was 35 and the world still seemed ahead of me. What I thought I could trust as essential beyond professional success or failure was: *When we support a love of learning in students, we equip them with a powerful lifelong tool: the means, the drive to delve deeper than their ancestors could to solve the unresolved problems of their generation.* Youth who found learning itself to be a triumph might persevere toward solutions beyond their predecessors' imagination. In this way, the failures of myself and my peers to leave adequate knowledge to meet the great challenges of our own time, such as unequal educational opportunity, did not remain static because the energy and hope of the next generation had been well nurtured and safeguarded. To this purpose, I could dedicate myself. It offered the potential to continue learning, to further my chances for discovery, and to avoid reifying my beliefs.

However, life is often far less lofty in its design and reality. To this point, the way for me to begin realizing this purpose was preceded by a poker game in Houston. This was the night before I was to give a small presentation (one of more than 250 such sessions) on Saturday morning at the national conference of the Association for Supervision and Curriculum Development. Dick Larson held the game in his hotel room starting at 9:00pm. As was customary, anyone leaving before midnight had to announce the time of their departure before we started playing so that no one suddenly left early with major winnings.

As we sat down and the cards were being shuffled, I said, "Sorry guys, I'll have to leave at 11:00."

Dick frowned, "Why so early?"

"I'm presenting a session tomorrow morning at 8:00am. I'll need a little time for breakfast and reviewing my notes."

He laughed, "At 8:00am? On Saturday, the last day of the conference when it ends at noon, most people are partying Friday night. They're not going to get up for an early session. You could be B. F. Skinner teaching pigeons to play ping-pong and they wouldn't come. They're going to sleep in and catch a flight home. Sorry, but that's how it goes."

I looked around the table and saw the heads of my colleagues nodding along with him. I felt disappointed, "You sure?"

"So sure, I'll bet you twenty dollars you don't have ten people at your session at 8:00am tomorrow."

I hesitated and let out a sigh, "Okay, twenty dollars says it eleven or more."

Dick shook my hand, "Good. So you won't be alone, I'll be there to collect my money but you can't count me as one of the participants. Alright?"

"Alright."

When I woke up the next morning, I felt calm, partly because of Dick's certainty about the small attendance at my session. Even though it was my first national presentation on the topic of teaching and motivation, I didn't envision a large group and my excitement had diminished.

I had prepared a hundred handouts. When I entered the session room at 7:45am, there was seating for sixty people and no one was there. At 7:55am, Dick came in along with three others, joining five people who had preceded them. Dick took a back seat and grinning, signaled the number eight with his fingers. At 7:59am, three more people came in. Dick rose from his seat at 8:00am waving a twenty dollar bill which he handed to the person sitting in front of him to give to me. He left to catch his plane silently mouthing, "You lucky son-of-a-gun!"

By the time I started the session at 8:05am, twenty-five more people had arrived. I began by telling them how I had just won twenty dollars and, "Because luck is infatuated with effort, this was going to be one darn good session. We'll all be glad we came." By the time I finished my story, there were over a hundred people in the room, many of whom stood the length of the presentation, an entire hour. My handouts were gone. I had to borrow one from a participant to lead the program.

Two "big hits" during the session were the practicality of the motivational strategies and the realism of my stories, such as how easy it was to become a menacing teacher, "Children did pay attention when I raised my voice but that kind of reinforcement led me to shouting at them most of the time: an action that made me feel powerful and hate myself in the same moment."

Afterwards, a number of people came up to me to ask questions. The man who waited until the very end was Gordon Felton, director of publications for the National Education Association.

His directness surprised me, "How would you like to do a book for the NEA on the topic you just presented?"

I was so naïve and inexperienced, I didn't quite know how to answer. I hesitated. Then I stumbled out a reply. "Well, it's certainly something I'd enjoy talking about with you."

Three weeks later, I was in Gordon's office in Washington, D. C. He had invited me to plan the book and negotiate a publishing contract. There was a considerable amount of security in the building. I had to briefly interact with three people as I was led to his office. All pronounced my name perfectly. They had obviously been schooled and practiced. Gordon had been an executive with Look Magazine and vice-president of The Cambridge Book Company. He looked East Coast: black double breasted, pin-striped suit, long black hair combed straight back ala Kirk Douglas in "Wall Street," elegant shoes, and a squire's bearing with perfect enunciation and lots of four syllable words like the "sumptuousness" of good writing. Not surprisingly, he was a charmer. When with little scrutiny, I said yes to the proffered contract, Gordon's reaction was, "Golden! This is just golden."

The book that resulted from this array of good fortune was *Motivation and Teaching: A Practical Guide.* It was my first single authorship and the quickest book I've ever written. In nine months, the ideas that had been percolating in my mind for two years emerged easily, and remarkably, in a well-organized manner. It was a book I could speak as well as write, much of it constructed as a flow experience. As I wrote in the preface, "I've written a book that I've wanted and needed—but could not find—ever since I started teaching 15 years ago. What I sought then—and what I've tried to create now—is a straightforward, useful, and realistic book about motivation and teaching."[81] For me, writing the manuscript was a work in which knowledge, experience, values, and inspiration seemed to blend seamlessly. Looking back, it's what all my books have ever been about: how to think motivationally. The book went through double digit printings and was translated into Japanese. Best of all, teachers found what I shared to be helpful. I now had a voice to begin to put motivation on the same plane as learning.

When I sent a copy to Finley, he called to congratulate me, "Raymond, I like this book. It's optimistic. However, I'm afraid you trust teachers much more than I do. All these methods. How do you know they won't screw them up?"

"I don't, but my bigger fear is they'll never use them. Only read about them."

"That's true. The world is filled with *aboutism*. I heard about that. I read about that. Don't go any further. You might bore me. Understanding takes a lot more, including practice. But historians are all about aboutism. We write about things that happened in the past that we've never seen."

"How can you stand yourself?"

"That's why I take five years to write a book. I cover my tracks well."

∴

With the potential for new learning opportunities that a well-received book allows, I wanted to expand my understanding of motivation beyond *Motivation and Teaching*. Although the study and practice might be demanding, the choice was effortless. Because I was a psychologist and trained extensively as a graduate student in therapeutic work, I believed that the most creative and fertile direction for developing a deeper comprehension of motivation to learn was in the craft of therapy. Much of such clinical work is about creating interventions with people who want to change their lives in some significant way: a transformational pursuit of the highest order and a fertile intersection for new ways to understand motivation.

I had been easing into beginning a small practice as a therapist for a couple of years: passing the Wisconsin Psychology Licensing Exam, finding out the areas in which I was competent to practice, and talking with other psychologists who were doing therapy about receiving supervision for clinical work. One of the psychologists I seemed to naturally gravitate toward was David Oliensis. He was thoughtful, adventurous, and arguably the best play therapist in Milwaukee. He had studied with Virginia Axline,[82] the author of *Dibs in Search of Self*, a classic text in non-directive play therapy and required reading in family counseling programs everywhere. He spoke with a gravelly, high pitched voice, had a robust sense of humor, and looked the part of a 1950s' film noir gangster with a thick mustache and a fire hydrant body build. Although eighteen years my senior, I found that I could talk with him across a range of topics from classical music to cult films. He had lived in Uganda and we were both avid Monty Python fans.

David introduced me to the Milwaukee Gestalt Training Group. This small avant-garde group of psychiatrists, psychologists, and clinical social workers conducted self-directed training at the frontiers of Gestalt Therapy. With about twenty members, we pooled our money to invite leading gestalt therapists such as Laura Perls, Erving Polster, and Joseph Zinker to conduct weekend seminars where we committed to their teaching. Some of this work was phenomenal. Much of it was experimental. We were a Midwest Esalen Institute without the Pacific Ocean, the Eden-like surroundings, or the media pizzazz. We were dedicated and, at times, bizarre. My lasting image is twenty of us standing in a circle around a large mattress while a Cleveland Gestalt Institute therapist tells us to strip to our underwear for "complete absorption in the process of returning to infantile conflicts with our parents." Without the camouflage of everyday clothing, our bodies looked clammy, pale and irregularly slumped, about as sexy as week-old cheese on a dinner table. I noticed two buckets at diagonal corners of the mattress and asked, "What are the buckets for?"

To which the therapist blandly responded, "That's in case anyone needs to throw up while we're doing this exercise."

"Sounds like fun," David smirked while raising his pastel blue shorts to his belly button.

For the five years I participated, the Milwaukee Gestalt Training Group became one of the most important learning experiences of my life. It was totally safe. We cared for each other professionally and personally. We worked on difficult issues such as deep scars from childhood traumas, unresolved issues of sexual intimacy and identity, and searing family conflicts. We had real problems to work on and among us, some of the best therapists in the city to practice their skills. Role playing was often the real thing. We knew this and took the risks to heal and learn.

The essence of Gestalt Therapy is enhancing one's awareness of sensation, perception, bodily feelings, emotion, and behavior in the present moment—similar in purpose to what is known as *mindfulness* today. As Gestalt therapists, we focused on the patient's relationship between the self, its environment, and others. Motivationally speaking, there is a tension that develops within us when we split off from our experience: those thoughts, sensations, and emotions that make us uncomfortable. The role of the therapist is to help the patient stay in the present and make meaning of such sentient impressions in order to resolve them to develop a healthy gestalt or wholeness of oneself. For example:

> A patient might say, "I have a dull headache."
> Therapist, "Who comes to mind while you feel the pain from the headache?"
> Patient, "No one."
> Therapist, "Do you mind if you stay with that pain a bit longer?"
> Patient, "No."
> Therapist, "Good. Focus on the discomfort and tell me when a person comes to mind."
> Patient, "Okay ... now I'm starting to think about my father."
> Therapist, "Let's stay with that ..." (The therapist begins to probe the patient's relationship to her father for clues about unresolved issues.)

What Gestalt Therapy taught me that I might apply to the classroom was to accept students' perceptions as real,[83] no matter what I might think or what the objective reality might be. In a culturally diverse world, this is especially true. It's also important to stay in the present with students. Even the past has to be connected through the present: Memories happen now. Imagining past failures and their projections happen in the moment. As an example, a question that I learned in my Gestalt training, that I frequently used as a therapist with "unmotivated" students for greater insight was: Imagine your teacher sitting in that chair. What would you tell him if you knew you could be honest and it wouldn't be held against you?

To use principles of Gestalt Therapy as a teacher means to remember that practicing inclusion entails accepting how the student chooses to be present, whether defensive and obnoxious or superficially cooperative. Genuine inclusion is openness to a student's resistance, not as a gimmick, but in full realization that this is how that person is actually present and is the best he or she can do at this time. Such acceptance avoids resentment and may provide a way through resistance for both the student and the teacher, such as spontaneous humor and growing respect and trust. Aggressive resistance is often a mask for fear of being misunderstood, becoming too vulnerable, or revealing unmanageable anger. Though the ways vary, most human beings self-protect against what they believe will cause them to lose control.

∴

I began a small clinical practice under David's supervision. My specialization was working with families whose children had motivational challenges at school. Most of the young people I saw were adolescents between 12 and 17. It was work that informed all of my teaching and writing after 1978. I made it part of my practice whenever possible to visit each client's classroom in order to observe the reluctant student as well as the teacher in their authentic environments.

The first thing I noticed was that in most instances, the student whom I was counseling acted in ways that were not very likable or extremely passive. What I had learned about resistance made immediate sense. But there was more, much more. The teachers were often not very motivating. They lectured far too long, often were nearly humorless, and didn't use activities that were engaging. In addition, a good number of those who were not very motivating teachers were obvious in their dislike of my clients: calling on them without using their names, cutting them off when they didn't know answers to their questions, and not smiling in the direction of these students as they normally did toward other students. They were like rude bosses. Whether realizing it or not, what parents were asking of me as a psychologist was to make their children *compliant.* To take their medicine on a regular basis no matter what it tasted like.

There was another aspect to this work as well. Most of the families were two parent families. However, in many of the families the parents disagreed between themselves about how to discipline or manage their child. Punishment and limits were often a matter of argument with fathers tending toward pragmatic punishment (taking away privileges such as use of the car, grounding, and similar consequences for poor grades or homework not done) and mothers being more psychologically strategic (advocating family meetings, checklists for homework, or seeing someone such as a psychologist).

I knew immediately I was not going to change how teachers taught. I had some influence on how they might build a better relationship with my clients, but I wasn't going to influence them to stop using worksheets or to not grade on a curve. I knew systems theory, a tenet of which is: One significant change changes everything. I also knew surrender to a disliked teacher was a major conflict for many "normal" adolescents. I didn't want to be complicit with teachers who were hostile toward my clients. However, one of the influential lessons from my clinical training at Wayne was: *If you were going to be an ethical and effective psychologist, you couldn't afford not to see the humanity of the people you serve, even rapists and murderers. That's where the work is to be done. Your job is to help in ways that deepen or broaden that humanity.*

I had to find interventions that respected all parties. I had worked out a cooperative parent-teacher process (with the student participating) based on the idea that all of them were concerned and making their best efforts for the good of the student. It was often successful and eventually made into a nationally distributed video workshop,[84] *Motivation to Learn*. It was also very difficult to practice outside of school. Getting both parents, the teacher, and the student to meet with me for an hour seemed nearly impossible. For two hours, impossible. Scheduling became a Gordian knot.

This dilemma led to the creation of three therapeutic mediations practiced simultaneously. The first was teaching the teacher the *Two-By-Ten Strategy*:[85] Giving my client two minutes of undivided attention for ten consecutive days, each day using positive light conversation (about sports, TV shows, and so forth), making one sincere compliment (nice shirt, well done chore or assignment, and so forth), and moving from talking to listening to the student as the days proceeded. The strategy is simple and often effective because most adolescents, especially the challenging ones, want that positive connection with a teacher who respectfully likes them.

With the parents, I worked on uniting their hierarchy of authority, attempting to have them see how their differences in disciplining and managing their child led to his abdication of responsibility due to their mixed messages. "Why have the homework done when Mom says I should, but Dad says he never did his homework when he was my age?" "Dad says to have the car home by ten but

Mom will be okay with it if I bring it by eleven." Most parents understood that boundaries aren't kept by any of us when they're not clear or consistently sanctioned. We may get away with something but the situation remains confusing and anxiety provoking.

I had the most fun with the kids. Frequently, they were boys and they didn't like seeing a psychologist. Initially, their primary motivation was, "What can I do so I can stop coming here?" At their age, I think I would've felt the same way, especially about school work. I respected their attitude and worked to gain their trust. Sometimes, I would not try for any immediate change on their part because it only affirmed what they thought I was after: getting them to "give in." There were times I might only play cards with them, talking and listening to understand their perspective. If the teachers and parents were following through on the interventions I taught them, it made it easier for me to establish a relationship because the student could see things were changing for the better. When the moment felt right, I would usually use Gestalt techniques, like talking to an empty chair as though it was occupied by a significant other, to lessen their resistance, to allow them to generate and to own their new behavior.

"Derek, even though your parents aren't here, let's imagine they might be. I think it would be helpful to get their perspective so I'm going to ask you to do something that might seem strange. To talk to them as though they were here. To figure out what they might want and how you see it. Is that okay?"

Hesitating, Derek responds, "Yeah ... okay. How are we going to do this?"

"First I need to ask who you think worries more about you, your Mom or your Dad?"

"My Mom."

"Then let's imagine she's in this chair and you're having a conversation."

I pull a chair so it's across from Derek and sit off to the side to coach him.

"What's a question you'd like to ask your Mom?"

Derek sits up in his chair. His face becomes more animated.

"I think you hit it earlier. Mom, why do you worry so much about me?"

"Now, Derek, I'd like you to sit in that chair and answer your question just how you think your Mom would answer it."

"Okay." Derek sits in the chair. "I worry about you because you do so poorly in school. You're smarter than the grades you get. It's going to catch up with you. The terrible report cards. Bad habits. And there's no end in sight."

I signal Derek to switch seats. "Could you answer your Mom?"

"School doesn't work for me. It's so boring."

I say, "And your Mom answers ..."

"Derek, I've worked so hard. When you talk like that, it seems selfish. I know your teacher's talking to you more and trying to be friendly. You told me so yourself. Right?"

"Yeah, but that doesn't change how she teaches."

As his Mom, Derek replies, "You know this school thing is poison. There's always tension about it. We can't enjoy small stuff like watching TV or taking a drive. Derek, if only you'd try, we could be so much happier as a family."

I can see Derek's eyes starting to tear up. We stop and talk about what has just happened.

More often than not, kids were excellent at using Gestalt techniques. When there was trust, their emotions were quickly present and they were creative constructors of conversations and scenarios. Possibly because I identified strongly with them, I felt drawn in and could authentically respond to them. I was only in my 30s. I was rooting for them, wanting them to find an honorable way to emerge healthier and whole.

In terms of successful therapeutic outcomes, where children improved their learning and adjustment to school and families became more cohesive and peaceful, the fathers were my biggest challenge. Dads were sometimes more resistant to changing than their children were. Too often, gains in the direction of improving family relations were stymied by the fathers' inability to learn behaviors such as to talk reasonably rather than yelling, or to keep their agreements about not being critical of their wives in front of their children. After one particularly grueling session, where the husband outright refused to consider a request from his wife to stop threatening their child with a raised fist, I remembered writing in the back of my appointment schedule, "Stubborn is a stereotype we males come by honestly." I had to take some responsibility for this pattern, if only by how many times I said in my mind, "Come on, now!" to men who had reneged on their commitments or seemingly sabotaged momentum toward a change they had endorsed. A review of my clinical notes indicated that statistically the most frequent disruptions of the therapeutic process were associated with the fathers' behavior. I regarded it as the Achilles heel in my practice.

When I talked with David about this finding, he seemed wistful, "I think if you gathered all the family therapists in Milwaukee and shared with them what you're realizing in your practice, they wouldn't be surprised. Therapy goes against the grain of how many men solve their problems. Patriarchal dominance. Power. Deception. At best, charm, which is really deception with a seductive twist. Look at the *Godfather* films. Immensely popular. A family saga but not much therapy going on there. When Al Pacino's wife tries to get him to soften up, he only becomes more murderous. Men love those films."

"Okay. So what do you do with macho men in your practice?"

David smiled, "I invite them to play guns ... No, just kidding. That's play therapy. Obviously inappropriate ... Sometimes I ask them to remember conflict with their fathers. What would they have changed? Was there a conflict their father handled more peacefully? How did it turn out? What if I asked you that question?"

"You know the first thing that comes to my mind isn't a conflict. More like an unsettled frustration that he couldn't resolve. When my father was in his 60s, he went to a lawyer to do his will. I think he knew his time left in this life wasn't going to last that long. He asked me to come with him. It was a small office. Nothing fancy, just a local guy on Seven Mile Road. Toward the end of the meeting, he asked the lawyer to put in the will that my brother should let him live in the basement of my brother's home, if my mother died before my father did. He was so deferent with the question. Actually gentle. The lawyer told him no, that he couldn't put that in a will. He needed to talk with my brother about that kind of an arrangement. My Dad looked down and made a small sound like a sigh. Watching him, seeing his worry and fear, I started to cry. I felt so much love for him at that moment."

We sat silent for about a minute. Then David said, "Amazing how much we hide our vulnerability. Just a peek at it, can make such a difference to those who care about us. It's a shame, isn't it?"

Still quiet, I nodded.

"Has what we've been talking about given you any ideas?"

"No, not immediately."

It hadn't, but I told David I planned to go to the library at UWM and look at what's been written or researched about adult motivation. Maybe there were some concepts or strategies I could apply to my practice. An angle or idea I hadn't considered.

∴

After the better part of an afternoon in the Golda Meir Library, I felt disappointment bordering on defeat. There was minimal information about adult motivation. And, what existed was tertiary, not about what directly motivated adults to learn, but how their beliefs and perceptions toward their education related to socioeconomic status or how their age influenced the topics they might find inherently interesting, like being between ages 23 and 28 and viewing the subject of getting married as appealing. What to do when face-to-face with adults to evoke their motivation to learn, whether to read a book or to change their behavior toward their children had hardly been addressed in adult education.

Sitting on the floor between library shelves with stacks of books surrounding my splayed legs, I was dismayed. I hadn't anticipated such an academic vacuum. Then it hit me. I was well prepared to investigate adult motivation, to develop an expertise in understanding it. Like an athlete who was conditioned to run the hundred yard dash could likely sprint the two hundred yard dash. The musculature, the stride, and the burst of energy were primed for such an event. I was well versed in motivational theory and research. I had successfully taught adults for over a decade: educators, parents, and clinicians. I had experience with responsibility for adults in unstable motivational circumstances such as desegregating schools, family crises, and the outer edges of Gestalt Therapy. And, I loved to learn about motivation. I stood up with a rush of adrenaline. I wasn't sure where to go. Home? Call David? A drink with Norm? I walked out of the library and started running.

CHAPTER 14

Adult Learning

Although we were close, my mother and I didn't talk that much. From the time I was six, I helped my mother dry the dishes. I did that every evening until I left home at twenty-one. Even with only two of us in a small, mustard yellow tile kitchen, we would say very little beyond how certain meals left the plates difficult to clean, how it felt for her to prepare dinner, the effort it took to grind potatoes or season meat, or how the dinner reminded us of other family meals. She always wore a fresh apron and she usually was calm—the washing being a kind of slow, light music, like a veil falling over the evening. Being with her at such times was one of the things I missed when I left. There was no drama or heavy insights, just a kind of proximity of love for each other without ever having to say it. Looking back, "doing the dishes together" reflects so much of our life—the gentleness of her affectionate presence, a candle that never went out until death took it away.

When my mother died, it was like losing my heartbeat, something faint but vital, the constant that took me through everything. She displayed a courage I always want to remember. The doctors had found she had a cancerous brain tumor. Surgery was an option, but the odds for a full recovery were not very good. After the surgeon provided his prognosis, he left my mother, my brother, and me alone in the hospital room to talk.

Richard began, "What do you think, Mom?"

"I don't think surgery is a good idea."

I was surprised by how quick and firm her reaction was, "Why so sure, Mom?"

"Look, this is cancer. I'm 74. At my age, it's likely to come back. I don't want to go through operations that only keep me living but not alive."

For a moment we didn't say anything. I think my brother and I agreed with her but to affirm her thinking quickly was too sudden for such a serious decision. As she approached her mid-seventies, I had seen her strength diminish: first in how she walked, more slowly with less of an upright posture and with more uncertainty in her step. What had brought us to the doctor in the first place was her inability to stand up from sitting on the couch after posing for a family Thanksgiving photo. Her hair, once full and thick, a trait of personal pride, had become thin and lost its luster.

"Are you sure, Mom?" Richard asked.

"Pretty sure. I've lived a long life. I don't need to hang on. It's been good. It's been enough. You think so?"

Our agreement was in our eyes. Richard and I took her hand. We didn't say much more and we didn't cry. It wasn't stoicism. I think we wanted our mother to feel good about her decision and to feel firmly it was the right one.

She only lived about a year longer, the last six months heavily sedated, immobile, and unable to communicate. A corpse before her death at 75, my mother would have greatly benefited from palliative care, a multidiscipline approach to medical care that provides relief from the physical and mental stress of a terminal illness. A part of the hospice movement, it was not widely available in the United States until the mid-90s. She did not deserve such an end.

After my mother's passing, I felt less tied to conventional society, less bound by others' opinions, and less anchored to anything resembling a human afterlife. I couldn't see her in a heaven as fabricated by traditional religion, not that she didn't deserve it. I just couldn't muster such a fantasy. Her suffering and debilitation at the end intensified my distance from church orthodoxy and its fostered guidance, a system I saw as abetting her prolonged distress. Nearing 40, I felt more alone, dependent on myself to determine what is singularly important. This perspective left me with a firmer resolve for learning on this earth, right now. If we have anything approaching a perpetual legacy, it is the next life. For our children and the lives of those who follow them on this earth, for those generations, what we learn matters.

∴

My mother's death made plain how little formal learning was available to working adult women as they aged. My mother and her six sisters never went to school beyond high school. As I began to seriously study adults as learners, the first thing that caught my attention was that the discipline was also an advocacy. Adults were underserved learners who needed colleges to adjust to their needs and realities. Due to how courses were scheduled and programs were organized, college was out of reach for most adults working full time in the 1980s. The higher education system was oriented to 18 to 22 year-olds who could attend classes during the day and arrange their attendance to classes conveniently offered at times, often more for the benefit of the faculty who taught them than for the students who took them. This awareness had hit home much earlier in my life while visiting with friends in Detroit.

I had known Bob since we were children. He had become a pipe fitter with General Motors, a skilled and well-paying job. As we were talking, Bob mentioned some physical trouble he was having with his back. He thought working another twenty years in his occupation might be impossible given the wear and tear on his body.

I suggested, "Why don't you go back to school? You're only in your late 30s."

He looked at me and I couldn't mistake the hostility in his eyes, "Are you kidding?"

"No. I'm serious. If you wanted to go back, you'd do well in college. You have work experience. You could easily enter a business or management program."

Now, Bob was angry, "Christ, Raymond! You know how long it would take me to get a degree? It's still a hundred and twenty credits, isn't it?"

"Yeah, in most programs. Could be a little longer in some."

"Damn right it could be. You do the math. If I take one course a semester, that's three credits. With summer school, that's nine credits a year. My division might be off, but I think that's at least thirteen years. And, that's counting on all the courses being offered when I can take them. I'd finish in my 50s when all the companies are beating the bushes for new managers who are geezers," he said sarcastically.

I apologized and changed the subject.

When I began reading the adult education literature in 1981, I realized Bob was one of millions of people who wanted a college education, but couldn't find a way to adjust their work to take classes or were discouraged by the amount of time it would take to complete a degree. Adult educators wanted to change the college system: to make it more available, doable, and quicker for everyone.

They also wanted to make society aware that adults learned differently than children, and, therefore, should be taught differently. The person probably most responsible for this shift of perspective was Malcolm Knowles who popularized the distinction between *andragogy* and *pedagogy*.[86] The idea of andragogy was that adults preferred to be self-directed learners whom teachers "facilitated," based on their innate need to be self-determined. As opposed to pedagogy, which applied to children who needed content presented to them with far less need for their previous experience to validate its usefulness. When I found this distinction doing research on adult learning in the UWM Library to better serve parents as a psychotherapist, I became excited because these ideas *were harmonious with intrinsic motivation*, the most promising theory I had found for how *all* people *could be motivated* to learn, understanding that as children mature into adults, they seek greater self-determination based on their cultural values. When a person is 6, learning can simply be fun, but as that individual grows older, and certainly by 21, learning has to mean something and have a relevant purpose.

∴

For the next year, I spent my time researching the question: What motivates adults to learn? The most concise and applicable answer I found was:

As learners, adults strive for understanding and competence, and tend to be motivated when they are effectively learning something they value. This idea covers everything from learning how to gamble to learning the most advanced theories in physics. It's an idea I've never had to back away from. Much more difficult to answer is the question: What motivates *all* adults to learn across *all* subject areas? This question has many answers and has propelled the rest of my professional life. It's analogous to the question: How do you make all nutritious food appealing for all adults?

I was also deeply interested in another question: How does one make motivating learning an inherently rewarding process for *both* adult learners and their instructors? I knew from experience that motivating teaching takes more work than conventional instruction and that without this consideration, the ideas I would suggest might be doomed to obsolescence.

After two years of research and experimentation with ideas and motivational strategies in my courses and workshops, I was ready to write a useful book about adult motivation. I had ventured out into the field of adult education and I liked what I found.[87] Most of the teachers were what I would describe as a game and experienced crew, people who taught in prisons, factories, the military, community colleges, G.E.D. programs, migrant camps, federal and state institutions, religious organizations, unions, and Indian reservations. They were serious about their work, liked their students, and were open to innovation. They were looking for help and willing to change.

∴

The first time I went to Alaska was for an adult education conference. I remember landing in a small plane in Fairbanks and seeing a large bear standing upright on the runway, watching the plane coast to a stop. I was elated. What's next? A moose in the baggage area? It seemed possible. When I started my presentation, I told the audience about how thrilled I was by such a novel experience. Down time for me during the rest of the conference was drinks and bear stories with the participants. I never tired of them and hoped I would remember at least a few, like the fellow who met a bear in his outhouse.

Since good examples were obviously needed for any guide for teaching adults, I began a journal of their responses to motivationally challenging situations. One of the questions that drew numerous insights was,

> Consider a course you've taken where, at the moment it began, your attitude was negative. You didn't want to be there. You thought the subject was boring or unimportant. If you had been free to leave, you would have.

But by the end of that course, your attitude had shifted 180 degrees. You were now glad you had taken the course, grateful for the knowledge you'd gained, and sorry it was coming to an end. What did that instructor do or what happened that turned your attitude completely around, from negative to positive?

I based this question on what might be called a university "urban legend" that most students in a college course who begin a course with a negative attitude never change their disposition. What begins darkly is doomed as it's born. Roughly half of the learners I asked couldn't remember a single course where their initial negative attitude had changed.

Most of the students who did change struck upon one or both of these characteristics: connection and relevance.

"The teacher had a great sense of humor. I just couldn't stop smiling. Eventually, I started smiling at what she was teaching."

"The guy was friendly. He never backed off. Didn't matter if we liked what he was teaching or not. I started to identify with him and all of a sudden my attitude shifted."

"Statistics. Are you kidding me? BORING! But she made it matter from how bridges are built to how airplanes withstand terrible weather. When I could see how statistics tied into my own health, I got the message and I was on board."

"Research was a requirement. Otherwise, I would never have taken it. Those journal articles kill you with a dull knife. But once we started doing research on personal issues like cancer rates according to ethnicity and race, predictability of regional disasters, and income stratification by education and occupation, I bought in. Knowing how to understand research connected to my future and the choices I made."

With a surplus of relevant examples and scholarship I trusted to be realistically helpful to instructors of adults, I began writing *Enhancing Adult Motivation to Learn: A Comprehensive Guide for Teaching All Adults* in the early 80s.[88] Unlike my first book, *Motivation and Teaching: A Practical Guide,* this book did not pour out of me. It required more of a focus on theory and research. Although practical, the book had to establish a conceptual framework on which all its strategies could be based. I was finding the pieces that made this puzzle of a book fit. Yet, the search for them and their configuration took much more time than I anticipated. I needed a leave of absence from UWM to complete writing it.

Again, my colleagues came to my support, voting to grant me a year's time away to complete the book. However, there was another disturbing problem. I didn't have a publisher. Faith in its promise made a difference because

I continued to write as though I did. I was also bolstered by the writing, by this time in my life a vitally engaging process.

After a year and a half, the book was finished, but I still had no publisher. Finley had had such an experience himself. Having dinner together at Carl's Chop House in downtown Detroit, in a darkened booth nursing a stinger, I could see his mood shift to a sadder tone as he began his story.

"I had no publisher for *Greek Realities*. It took me nearly six years to write it ... It's a painful memory ... two publishers turned it down before Scribner's picked it up. I lost confidence. I came close to having a nervous breakdown. No, I think I had a nervous breakdown. Anyway, who wants to remember something like that? You just can't give up. The fact that the book is complete is in your favor. Book conferences or those publishers selling texts at your professional meetings are worth visiting. Often editors are at their own exhibits and will talk to authors if the material seems relevant to their market. Meeting you in person makes a big difference. I'm with you all the way, Raymond. You'll find one."

Following Finley's advice, I found out the American Booksellers Association was having its national conference in Chicago later that month. The day the conference opened, I drove to Chicago with twenty summaries and the initial two chapters of my book. When I arrived and went to register for the conference, I was denied admission. The registrar explained, "You have to have a sponsor, preferably a publishing company. Otherwise, you can't be admitted." Then he added, "If we didn't have this rule, McCormick Place would be crawling with desperate, untalented writers. Frankly, they're a nuisance and a pain in the ass."

Who? Me? I wasn't going to give up. Faith, exhilaration, and nothing to lose make for bold choices. I parked myself just outside the registration area. Then I scrutinized the badges of the people entering the main gallery. Red badges were booksellers. Lots of those. Blue badges were sponsored authors. Lots of those too. Gold badges were publishers. Not too many of those. I had to talk one of them into sponsoring me on the spot for the conference without seeming maniacal, amateurish, or prehensile—not an easy sell. I had to be able to make my request in less than twenty seconds. Anything longer would seem overbearing. It took me a half an hour to tighten up a reasonable plea. Now, I had to find the right person. I didn't think I could ask more than three people. If it didn't work by then, I feared I would lose my confidence. Not a chance after that.

It took me an hour to find the right person. Women were out of the question because I thought that being a man would make the whole thing seem too forward. That was a loss of nearly fifty percent of the publishers. It couldn't be a young guy. They're too competitive. At least, that's what I told myself. Middle-aged was best. Young enough to remember how hard it is to break into the writing business and old enough to have the empathy for supporting a new writer. Also, no one too stylish. My problem. I tend to l have less confidence with people who are better dressed than I am. I was down to one out of ten publishers who passed my way. Then I saw him. About 50, a little portly, full grey hair down to his collar, turtle shell glasses, and casually dressed in a brown tweed jacket and olive green slacks.

I took a breath and began walking beside him. "I'm sorry to interrupt you. My name is Raymond Wlodkowski. I'm at the University of Wisconsin in Milwaukee and I've just written a book that I think is strongly needed. It's how to work with adults in ways to help them to stay motivated while they learn. I know it's a good book. I was hoping to show it to some publishers, but I can't get into the conference without a sponsor. Any chance you might help me?"

He stopped and looked at me. It seemed like he was making up his mind how to feel about me. I tried to look back in a way that held his gaze and seemed more poised than scary. Then he said, "What's that name?"

"Raymond. Raymond Wlodkowski."

"Good to meet you Raymond. I'm Eric Kohl. You're what this conference is all about. Let's go over and get you registered."

∴

It was difficult for me to walk down the aisles of the gallery. I was so excited I felt like skipping and clicking my heels in mid-air. I gave myself a chance to walk about and take it all in. It felt like the first time I played college football in a regular game with people in the stands. I was only on special teams, maybe four or five chances to get in the game, but it was the real thing. Luminous authors were everywhere, an arm's length away: Margaret Atwood, Ken Follet, Mario Puzo, Erica Jong, and many more. But most important, I had a legitimate chance to find a publisher.

On my first run through, I searched for displays where professional books and how-to books were being advertised or available for perusal. That narrowed the options to less than twenty percent of all the exhibits at the conference. Among those, I eliminated all the publishers of highly technical books because mine was clearly outside of their market. That left me with only fifteen publishers. I talked to every one of them. Most were polite and listened. About half said, "I don't think so," after my first few sentences. The rest peppered me with marketing questions. Only one, Prentice-Hall, asked me for the two chapters I had brought with me. Their representative was the acquisition editor, a woman about my age, very smartly dressed in a tailored blue suit with long brown hair and a distinct New Jersey accent. She wore little make-up and was poised and confident. There were few pleasantries.

"Why do you think your book would sell?"

"Because it's the first of its kind in Adult Education. It's needed. Most teachers face many students who aren't motivated and they aren't sure what to do."

"Adult Education?" she frowned. "Isn't that a backwater in most universities?"

"Well it's not as prestigious as medical or law school, but it's a burgeoning field. Many adults are going to community colleges or the military or being trained in various businesses."

"You said the military?"

Now, I had her attention. "All those soldiers have to be trained and the military is very interested in how adults learn."

"You said you brought a couple chapters from your book. Right?"

"Right."

"Why don't you leave those with me? If we're interested, you should hear from me in about two weeks. If not, our policy is not to send back material which we don't contract for. Is that alright?"

"Sure."

One nibble. That's what I told myself as I drove back to Milwaukee. I felt discouraged and determined, a combination of feelings that often prompted my memory of a painful scene in the film, "The L-Shaped Room," when Anthony Booth, a writer, rages and wrecks his London apartment. His lover, Leslie Caron, upon her return to their flat, is horrified and pleads with him, "What's the matter? What happened?"

He shouts, "They rejected my novel!"

She reaches out to him, "That's okay. A lot of writers have their book rejected. You'll write another one."

He screams, "That was my sixth novel!" Then whimpers, "Not a single one published," sobbing and sliding, his back against the wall, swooning into a heap on the floor.

∴

With a month passing, I had not heard from Prentice-Hall. My only other hope was a small publisher, Jossey-Bass, located in San Francisco that specialized in therapy-oriented books and adult learning. At times, when a book is proposed which is not on their publishing list, publishers will show interest in a manuscript that might be marketable for them. It's a long shot for the writer. At their field editor's request, I had been sending them individual chapters as I continued to write the book. But I had heard very little beyond acknowledgement that they had received each chapter as it arrived. I was having ruminations about how to save face and entertaining ideas for fibbing to my colleagues about why my book had not yet been published.

If asked, I thought I might say, "You know, it sounds crazy. No one in the United States has picked it up but there's a small South Korean publisher that's possibly going to begin translating it next year."

Or possibly, "The book didn't seem to draw an interested publisher. So I think I'll serialize the chapters and maybe get some journal articles out of it."

Or, I might creatively use a rumor, "A few publishers suggested that the times are not right now. Once the field of Adult Education expands, I should bring it out again when there may be greater interest. I think I'll give it a couple of years on the shelf and try that."

When the letter from Prentice-Hall arrived, *I had one of those moments*. I put the envelope on the kitchen table and sat and stared at it for about ten minutes. I thought maybe I should call a friend and have him with me when I opened it. Better yet, I could call Finley and have him on the line as I read it to him. But what if it was a rejection? Then I didn't know if I'd cry or howl. I tried holding it up to the light to see if I could make out whether it held a contract or not. No luck. Then I ripped it open.

I savored the sweet words most authors want to see over and over again, "It gives me great pleasure to send you this publishing agreement ..." The contract was brief and I read it thoroughly. It indicated an initial print run of 3000 copies with standard royalties. While I was thinking about how I was going to tell my friends about this grand great news, the phone rang. It was Allen Jossey-Bass, founder and president of Jossey-Bass publishing. He asked me if I had a moment to talk. His first question was, "Could you please tell me about your name? It's so interesting." He asked me about my parents, about Poland, and then quite deferentially told me about his own history. He was a direct descendent of William Bass, founder of Bass Brewery and Bass Ale in 1776. He was a conversationalist, using language and stories as a fly fisherman might use a rod and reel to catch a brook trout, a symmetry of line and lure. He was intrigued with how motivational strategies could make learning for the sake of learning possible and what made a lesson stimulating or dull. He never once mentioned marketing. He had an anthropological curiosity about how a class of strangers could become a caring community. His knowledge of the book was detailed and specific. He had had the manuscript reviewed by Malcolm Knowles, casually remarking that Malcolm was "wildly enthusiastic" about it. We didn't talk about a book agreement until at least a half an hour had passed. Just after telling me some of his favorite places to walk in San Francisco, he offered a contract with an initial print run of 1500 copies. I liked him. I accepted his offer as we spoke.

CHAPTER 15

Perspectives and Connections

When I told Finley my good news about Jossey-Bass, he shouted, "Alcibiades returns!" his jubilant exclamation adapted from how the Athenians welcomed back their prodigal son and foremost commander from Sparta during the Peloponnesian War. He relished the story about Allen Jossey-Bass. It reminded him of his relationship with Charles Scribner's Sons publishing where he had a personal bond beyond how many units of *Greek Realities* had been sold.[89]

"In years to come, you'll be glad about this decision. In that kind of publishing house, you become part of an extended family of sorts—one of *their* authors. They'll work with you to birth other fine books. Money matters, but in such companies excellent books come first. Their editors won't let you release a poor one. They have a tradition and a legacy to continue."

Most authors only have a few chances to dedicate a book in their lifetime. It's a precious and rare opportunity. It was a privilege I didn't allow myself to think about until I was sure the book was going to press and my editor, Lynn Luckow, had asked for it. After wrestling with different expressions and more angst than I ever anticipated, I settled on: *To my friend and teacher, Finley Hooper.*

Without announcing the book was published, I sent Finley a copy. A few days later, I received his letter which began:

Dear Raymond,
The book arrived Friday afternoon. I am deeply moved by the dedication and I thank you for this very special honor. As always, of course, I am very proud of you. What I so admire about your work, and this book in particular, is that it is for the purpose of helping other people. That is of course what the higher religions are all about. To turn away from what is selfish and to use our abilities to serve a greater cause. While, as you know, I do not share your optimism about how many can be helped, it is the basic intention to serve which is crucial and this surely brings in return much happiness ...

Beyond the feelings of fulfillment upon receiving such words from someone I loved and admired, I continued to wonder about the role I wanted in the world. After my year with the Milwaukee Public Schools, I had deliberately immersed myself in deeper learning about motivation. But in a life of study and teaching, how much could I expect my writing to influence how adults were taught? How much had I been changed by reading what others wrote? The short answer was always because learning is change from the microscopic to the majestic. Significant moments had arrived out of seemingly nowhere as when, a decade prior, I read *Catch 22* and was riveted with new awareness by Yossarian's discernment that in certain situations, only the person himself can judge his own sanity, a timely insight after my mother's death and the growing distance I felt from my life in Detroit.

It's why I've loved reading. Piling books into my suitcase for a vacation was half the fun of taking one. Letting my imagination mix with someone else's has been exhilarating—for decades. These excursions into streams of stories and reflection seldom led to dramatic personal change, but they've kept my thinking alive and open, from something as serious as how I vote and participate in local politics, to something as nebulous as the formation of an idea.

Published in 1985, the content of *Enhancing Adult Motivation to Learn:*[90] *A Comprehensive Guide for Teaching All Adults* brought new invitations for professional work and a more international network of opportunities. Adult learning was globally recognized as an important means to improving a country's human capital and economic productivity. One of the invitations that changed the direction of my life came in 1985 from the British Columbia Institute of Technology (BCIT). While living in Milwaukee, I travelled on a regular basis to Vancouver to work with a caring and diligent band of professional educators and faculty. They took their learning seriously and knew how to have fun.

Because I was new to the United States Northwest and Canadian Southwest, they went out of their way to introduce me to the wondrous beauty of this part of the world: salmon fishing in English Bay, sailing in the Strait of Georgia, hiking Black Mountain, and pubbing in the city. Lots of that. I was unprepared for how spectacular Vancouver would be: seeing bald eagles in the city's beautiful Stanley Park, precipitous mountains that came down to the edge of the metropolis, and pristine forests minutes away with giant Douglas Firs and Sequoias as common as Maple trees in the Midwest.

While sitting on a ferry to Vancouver Island, in the mist I saw a pod of six orcas come alongside the boat. They were at eye level as they silently began their rhythmic swimming, dipping in and out of the cobalt blue water, the black sheen of their arcing bodies all grace and power. They looked more like spirits than animals. I was stunned. I had to grip a table and remind myself not to shout. The woman next to me was so moved by this extraordinary sighting that without any words she began crying, tears flowing down her cheeks, her eyes filled with awe. I knew after that moment I would live the Northwest.

∴

The work with the BCIT faculty was a splendid, five-year experience. The faculty were a mixture of people from the trades such as welding and carpentry, and general education instructors. Their student population was rapidly shifting. Nearly half their students were immigrants or children of immigrants, most of whom were from China and Southeast Asia. The vast majority of the instructors were men from Euro-Canadian ethnic groups. The first participants were faculty volunteers who would eventually teach their peers. We worked together to learn a peer coaching process to improve the use of culturally responsive teaching practices. Every member of this group went through a cycle of teaching, receiving coaching, practicing coaching, and receiving feedback on their coaching. We used role-playing and video to refine their learning and to offer supportive feedback. Using video to watch themselves teach and coach was a new experience. There was a constant flow of banter and self-deprecating humor.

Lewis watching himself on video for the first time remarked, "Well, I knew I wasn't that good looking but don't you think the video makes me look worse?"

Samuel from the group around the monitor responded, "No Lewis. I think that's how you really look. Maybe we should have makeup. I think more than a few of us need it. That's what they do on real TV."

Joshua joined the conversation. "Remember Nixon. He was dripping like a faucet, all sweaty above his lip. Refused the makeup and lost the election. Our peers are going to see these tapes. Right? It's peer coaching. Right? If we're making fun of ourselves, think of what they're going to say?"

Lewis, eyeing the rest of the group, offered, "Yep, and no one's mentioned weight yet. Let's see a show of hands for those who are going on diets starting tomorrow." Lewis raised his hand and looked for others to join him. Most of the instructors were smiling but no one else raised their hand.

Lewis shook his head, "You guys are living in a fantasy."

Once we got past the novelty of using video, the faculty, while still playful, took seriously the learning ahead of us. Many of their students were English learners who tended to be passive in their classrooms during discussions for varied reasons, including insecurity about their listening comprehension, pronunciation, word choice, and culturally appropriate interactions such as when to interrupt or ask a question. Consequently, we worked initially on a host of teaching methods to assist language and facilitate active participation for English learners. Some were:

- *Make corrections indirectly by mirroring in correct form what the student has said.* For example, suppose a student says, "Majority immigrants Vancouver from Pacific Rim." The teacher can repeat, "That is correct. A majority of the immigrants in Vancouver come from the Pacific Rim."
- *Use clarification requests.* For example, "Will you explain your point so that I can be sure I understand?"
- *Use confirmation checks.* For example, "Is this what you're saying?"

Practicing these methods, using them in their classroom, and being coached to do them well had immediate results the faculty appreciated and endorsed. English learners in their classrooms became more active participants with greater confidence and more positive attitudes toward learning. As with most teachers, when what they are learning is obviously relevant and their professional competence increases, they are highly motivated. The BCIT professional development team began an extended program which became the BCIT Faculty Coaching Association. Surveys in later years indicated that more than two thirds of the instructors who had participated in the program reported an improved attitude toward their role as teacher as well as toward their students and colleagues.[91]

∴

In 1987, two years after I began my work at BCIT, I moved to Seattle and became a faculty member at Antioch University. In that year, Microsoft introduced Windows 2.0. It was not the behemoth it is now and Amazon was only a dream. As they said then in downtown Seattle, "We roll up the sidewalks at 6 o'clock." Yet, the environs were as beautiful as Vancouver. On a clear day (and there are more than Seattleites want to admit), Mt. Rainier beckoned with its massive snow-capped peak, the Olympic Mountains cast a sunset profile, and Puget Sound offered ferries to island homes less than half an hour away. But moment-to-moment, what I noticed most, no matter what the weather, was that no one blew their car horns. It seemed to be considered gauche, reflecting a calmer, egalitarian mood, a sense that no one ought to dare to invade the peace of others with their need to hurry or paw ahead. Coming from Detroit and Milwaukee, I was enthralled by such a civil urban gestalt.

In similar fashion, Antioch University in Seattle was far different than the University of Wisconsin-Milwaukee and most colleges and universities across the United States. How different? It didn't give grades. At that time, there were only five other higher education institutions that could make this claim. That's a structural difference that has the power to change the dynamic of learning from extrinsically motivated (grade driven) to intrinsically motivated (interest/value driven). As faculty, we wrote an essay on the progress, performance, personal characteristics, and quality of learning displayed by each student in our class. I was elated with this opportunity because it offered a chance to write with nuance and depth about another person's learning. It convened a true dialogue between a student and myself.

Another difference was that Antioch took its mission far more seriously than most schools with which I was familiar. Founded in 1852 in Yellow Springs,

Ohio by Horace Mann,[92] a social reformer and abolitionist, it was created to be a university that was nonsectarian, coeducational, and open to all races. The school made a genuine attempt, not always successful or consistent, to carry out Mann's famous quote, "Be ashamed to die until you have won some victory for humanity." Many of its students and graduates were civil rights, gay rights, and anti-war activists, Coretta King being among those most famous. When I arrived, I felt immediately at home and grateful to be part of the faculty.

One of the qualities of the school with which I grew less enamored was like a high pitched sound, one that I might barely notice, but once I had, seemed to grow louder and more strident. It was the constant psychological analysis of most matters deemed important by faculty and students. It was as though a clinical psychology program had morphed into a university in Seattle. It wasn't a malevolent quality or a form of arrogance. The language used and the continual personal dissection gave the feeling that the people there were in therapy or had been. At less than a thousand students, the psychology and counseling programs had the highest enrollment and the largest faculty, dominating the school academically. As the most popular programs, they drew students oriented toward a psychological perspective.

At times, this atmosphere grew problematic for me when I became aware that some faculty tended to "process" conflict with other faculty as a result of some underlying personal issue. Rather than seeing it as a matter of political or rational argument—a "normal" occurrence among faculty at most universities—with the disagreeing faculty member, they would attribute the reason for the disagreement to a personal problem such as a recent divorce or having a middle-age crisis.

This dense psychological climate sometimes leached into coursework with unpredictable results. In all courses I taught, I knew the importance of building a community of learners as rapidly as possible. Once students felt respected and connected to one another, they were more motivated to cooperate and support each other's learning, which increased achievement and camaraderie, making the entire course more enjoyable and fruitful. To contribute to a sense of community, I tried to find ways for people to creatively introduce themselves, adding some possibilities for humor and insight. For the first class of the first course I taught at Antioch, Introduction to Research, I asked students to introduce themselves as their mother might do so. Having used this exercise once before at UWM, I had found it both stimulating and endearing. At Antioch the following scenario developed:

I went first, emulating the shyness of my mother, using a quieter voice and some uncertainty and saying, "This is my son, Raymond. I'm not quite sure what he does for a living although I know some people call him a Doctor.

I've asked him directly about this and I'm sure he's not a medical one. He's pretty good with numbers, always has been. So, I think he'll be okay at research. He likes to teach. I've heard from a few of his friends he's pretty good. Thank you and good luck."

Now came the first student, a man about forty, rather distinguished looking, "This is my son, Lee. I love his older brother more than I love him. In fact, Lee has a younger brother and I love him more than Lee, too. I can't figure out why Lee's going to college past the age of forty. He doesn't need it. He's a successful manager at Nordstrom's. Plus, why research? Must be a required course. He'll do fine. He's a workaholic."

At this point, I started to feel the moisture in my armpits.

The second student was a woman about thirty in jeans and a sweatshirt, "This is my daughter Sara. I abandoned her when she was about fifteen. I didn't physically leave her, I just didn't have much to do with her. She was so rebellious and with a terrible mouth. Cursing and swearing. I hope God forgives me for the times I thought it might be better for all of us if she ran away. (Sara begins to cry.) I think she'll do fine in research. She's interested in the past and why things happened the way they did."

When I saw the next student was already crying, I stopped the exercise and apologized to the class for my choice of an introduction process that was obviously too penetrating and sensitive for the beginning of our course. We took a break and continued with straightforward introductions and any expectations students had for the course. Remarkably, and as I found out in the time I was there, quite typical of Antioch students, they forgave my mistake and the course went very well.

∴

In July of 1990, I received an invitation to participate in the International Conference on Continuing Education in Central Europe. I was elated. The purpose of the conference was to share ideas and methods about how most effectively to help adults learn in settings that ranged from the industrial workplace to the university classroom. The conference was held in order to bring together a small group of adult educators from England and the United States with a cadre of educational leaders from the countries of Poland, Hungary, Czechoslovakia, Lithuania, Latvia, and Estonia. With the recent political shifts in these countries as a result of the ongoing dissolution of the Soviet Union, there was a dire need to find, as quickly as possible, optimal ways to educate massive groups of adults who were facing new systems of economy, work, and expectation.

The location of the conference was Budapest, Hungary. The statement I remember with my first experience in this part of the world was uttered by Andra Akers, the director of the International Synergy Institute during our initial briefing, "Living in Eastern Europe today is like living in a 150 mile-per-hour wind." Like objects bound too tightly and then released by a single blow, these countries could not help but flay themselves open. Almost every conversation on any topic, including food, had a political context. If Mikhail Gorbachev's name came up, I could hear him described as saint, devil, peacemaker, hypocrite, despot, visionary, and victim within a space of moments.

We found out these countries did not have vocational-technical schools, community colleges, and the professional learning networks available in Western Europe and the United States. There was no money to publish their own books. Probably the most coveted skill we could provide was the knowledge necessary to submit a grant proposal to a Western institution for educational funding. In pursuit of this goal, the Eastern European educational leaders sought collaborative educational partnerships with the universities we represented or with which we had trusted contacts.

Although personal friendships and professional relationships had been nurtured throughout the conference, the ending of the conference was not free of anxiety. The potential for future resources seemed promising but no concrete agreements of funding had been established. Listening to the Eastern European educators and the challenges they faced provided testimony about how governments can malign the spirit of their citizens, substantially weakening their will to work and learn. No one anywhere is immune to this catastrophe.

Another unforgettable remembrance was the closing of the conference and the person sitting next to me. A heavy man with large eyes and wavy white hair combed straight back, he was a medical doctor, 68 years old, the associate director of the Institute of Health Education in Prague. His name was Ldenek Kucera.

As we awaited the final speaker, he kept talking to himself. I could tell he was agitated, but I was afraid to look at him for fear of his or my embarrassment. Finally, I could not resist, and as he caught my glance he gripped my arm and pulling me toward him, said, "Do you believe this? Only four months ago, if I spoke to a stranger in English I had to report myself to the authorities. And now, this." And then he looked about the room once more and whispered, "Amazing."

∴

After a few years, *Enhancing Adult Motivation to Learn* became a professional book used in many adult learning programs across the United States. With its popularity also came requests for workshops and presentations. Many of those requests came from organizations and institutions that knew they needed to improve their effectiveness with adult learners. At the time, sixty percent or more of adult students who began postsecondary education, had exited two-year and four-year colleges without certificates or degrees.[93]

Unsurprisingly, programs of this sort often served populations of students who were low-income, traditionally marginalized, or English language learners such as immigrants. What was common to all such programs was the fact that the faculty was usually from a considerably different background than their students. The instructors were generally European-American, working or middle class, and with college or advanced degrees. This was true of myself as well. With the exception of Antioch, where a strong norm of civil rights, gay rights, and women's rights had been established in the fabric of the university's culture, there was little direct or programmatic attention from these colleges on how to teach in ways that prevented discrimination and affirmed the low-income learners and students of color. I rarely heard faculty ask the question, "What can I learn from these students from whom I am so different?"

What I offered were ways to design teaching for adults with motivation in mind, and an array of effective motivational strategies to use while teaching them. I didn't directly enhance the cultural connection between faculty and their students. I wasn't altering the widespread norm among faculty that expected student behavior to be normed to middle-class, European-American values.[94] More faculty than I expected assumed students of any background should:

– Look them in the eye. (In some Asian and Latin American cultures this is considered rude.)
– Listen without interrupting. (In some Jewish-American, African-American, and Arab-American cultures *interrupting* is how you show you are listening.)
– Smile only when pleased or humored. (In some Asian cultures, continual smiling is an expression of anxiety.)
– Do not invade their personal space; stay an arm's length away. (In many cultures throughout the world, personal space is a much shorter distance.)

Worse yet, I would see behaviors in small cooperative learning groups (a strategy I taught and generally an excellent means to enhance motivation and learning) that were oppressive and discriminating such as a male faculty member joking to another, "Hey, don't act like a faggot." Or, one or two men dominate a group, taking up most of the air space in a discussion without including women or students of color in the conversation—not even aware that they were doing so. When I would make a comment, "You know using an expression like faggot is insulting to many people. I'm uncomfortable when

I hear that word." The reaction on the part of the speaker, and usually the rest of group, was dead silence. Often, following such occasions, the motivation of the workshop participants diminished. And, I would have to resist feeling alienated from these faculty.

Antioch was changing me. I was becoming more sensitive to subtle and systemic forms of discrimination but learning the hard way. Once, during a class, I used the word *primitive* to describe "a society that would not be advanced enough to use conflict resolution."

A student about my age raised her hand, "And, what society would that be?"

I hesitated, "I'm not sure."

She responded, "You must have had some society in mind to use that word—primitive."

I remained silent, but I was starting to feel defensive.

"You weren't thinking of a tribe in the Amazon rainforest or some such place, were you?"

"No, but that's a possibility."

She responded angrily, "That's terrible. That you would even think that. I doubt you know anything about those tribes."

"You're ... you're right."

"Primitive is a terrible word. White privileged people use it all the time about people they don't even know. People they think less of." She paused. "Hey, remember. This is Antioch. We don't let that crap go by."

I nodded. I appreciated the lesson but not the moment. I knew I had much to learn, starting with better ways to talk about cultural differences and issues as they emerged in a course, so the conversations led to insight and better communication, rather than resentment and withdrawal. I knew enough to know that if a person's perspective was not considered—did not matter enough to be regarded as a possible opinion in a class. That person would be likely not to feel respected. And, therefore, not motivated to learn with that group or the teacher who led it, no matter what strategies were used. I knew this experience was happening to low-income students and students of color in colleges everywhere. But where should I begin? And, who would teach me?

CHAPTER 16

Conversations of Respect

In 1990, after I gave a class on motivation to trainers from a heavy equipment construction company at Fort McMurray, Alberta, I knew I had arrived at a crossroads—the realization that what I knew psychologically was no longer adequate, and that to continue offering my ideas, as they were, would be hypocritical. Fort McMurray was the location of the Athabasca Oil Sands. As the price for oil increased in the beginning of this decade, the extraction of oil from these deposits became profitable, drawing workers from across Canada. The University of Alberta had established adult education courses in the vicinity and requested my services. I relished the experience. Oil workers had no commerce with "fancy-dandy" psychology. Training adults in their milieu with earthmovers that could be as large as two stories high with tires as big as a small house was dangerous and demanding.

The trainers and I got along well. I went into the field to visit their work setting and attempted to make the course as relevant as possible. After I had a better idea of what their work day entailed and the kind of environment it was, I immediately added two elements to the course. The first was to meet in small groups and to brainstorm what authentic, work-related challenges they hoped a course on motivation would help them resolve. I posted these and used them for exemplifying motivational strategies for the rest of the course.

The second was to ask them to think of a lesson they had taught "in the field" which they would definitely want to revise if they had a second chance. Then I asked them report out and the whole class as a group to vote on which lesson seemed to have the most common ground among them. After choosing two of the reported lessons, I asked them to reassemble into small groups to make revisions based on what they were learning in our course and to share these in another whole group format. I posted the lessons on large worksheets so other trainers could make written comments and ask questions as they assessed them for potential personal use. In this manner, the self-generated knowledge of the entire class was available and more obvious.

Enthusiasm increased. The trainers appreciated my adjustments and at the end, when we closed the course with a small party, feelings of gratitude flowed in both directions. I knew I had had a singular experience in "the bush" I might never have again. As I was sipping a Molson's Ale and taking in my surroundings—the empty white interior space of a Quonset hut, with no other building in sight, surrounded by a maple-blond meadow against a blue sky—a woman from the Cree tribe approached me. She was a supervisor dressed in jeans, ankle high work boots, and a tan multi-pocketed vest over a purple t-shirt. She wore her dark black hair in a single braid that reached down to middle of her back.

She smiled, "I enjoyed the course. Thank you."

"I did too. Thanks for being part of it."

"Is it okay if I tell you some things to consider if you teach another one here?"

"Sure. Please do."

"Many of the workers are First Nations People. Your exercises and examples might not fit for us. We don't like to draw attention to ourselves, especially as individuals. We feel uncomfortable talking that way. If you could offer strategies that let us talk without always having to say 'me' or 'I', that would be helpful."

"Thank you. I'd like to hear anything else you might suggest."

"A lot of the questions you ask are about how we feel. To speak publicly or to strangers about our feelings is very difficult. Not something we normally do. I think you want to be good at what you do, Please take what I'm saying in that regard."

She smiled and left. I knew everything she said was true. And, it wasn't the first time I'd heard it. I had a Japanese student who told me something quite similar. There was now no doubt, I needed to shift my thinking about motivation with culture as a central aspect of it.

∴

At Antioch, in 1991, I met Margery Ginsberg. Teaching with her changed the course of my life personally and professionally. What appealed to me most about Margery as an instructor was how she answered difficult questions about race and inequity: with respect for the questioner, with humility about her response, without becoming defensive, and without rushing either to an answer or an end. As a matter of practice, she tried to learn from people who had perspectives that were different from her own. Margery did not back away from the dilemmas students faced. I remember the following encounter because it happened early in our course, Diversity and Motivation, when we were first getting to know each other as co-instructors. Our students often felt frustrated by how difficult it was to address multiple perspectives in situations where students were from many different backgrounds. One person asked:

"I teach at a community college. I have English language learners from Southeast Asia, Latin America, Eastern Europe, and many students of color and white students. In a class of thirty people, there might be members of twenty different ethnic groups. How am I going to be able to know and plan for the diverse perspectives students may have on any number of issues?

Without seeming perplexed or certain, Margery answered, "That sounds like a fascinating challenge and I respect that you want to be pragmatic and inclusive. What makes you think you have to know all your students differently *from the start* to plan inclusive learning experiences?" The student replied, "As faculty, we're supposed to be sensitive to different cultures."

"Then maybe the question could be 'How could you be sensitive and respectful as a teacher to students from a broad range of backgrounds without yet knowing the students personally?'"

"Okay. How?"

"There's probably a number of different ways to consider. I can begin by offering one possible approach and then I'll ask our class if anyone else has another method that works well in this kind of situation. I'll record these ideas on the board. My suggestion is to provide some draft norms for the class to deliberate with the goal of making the environment unthreatening for all students to express their ideas and perspectives. Here are a few norms that students in multicultural and more homogenous classes have appreciated: (1) *Share airtime, so that everyone has a chance to speak,* (2) *When someone has the floor, give them the time and space they need to express themselves without fear of interruption,* (3) *maintain a problem-solving orientation so that when problems arise, we assume we can work together to solve them,* (4) *Respect the absence of others, so that if someone is not in the room to speak for themselves, they can return to class without worrying that others talked about them in a negative or misleading way.*

"Now who else would like to make a suggestion from their own teaching experience?"

Pretty simple stuff. But without making a big deal, Margery engaged a white, European-American student who seemed frustrated, and she listened carefully, was empathic, offered practical suggestions, and brought in the experience of the rest of the students, making the entire process a constructive and inclusive learning activity.

I knew I had much to learn from her. She had been a teacher with United Cerebral Palsy in Denver and on the Menominee Indian Reservation in Keshena, Wisconsin and the Southern Ute Reservation in Ignacio, Colorado. Her recent dissertation from the University of Colorado-Boulder was a study for a non-profit program that worked to support college completion among Native Americans. The lens she brought to her discussion of anything was that of a learner who cared about inclusive and nuanced teaching, and who was political and feminist. Was I intimidated by her? Yes.

Part of what struck me about Margery was that she operated from a set of assumptions that often seemed ethically and philosophically superior to my own. She also had a range of experiences that authentically validated what she said. She wasn't talking from a textbook. One of the main reasons I asked her if she would like to co-teach a course was because I knew I could learn so much from her in the process.

She openly challenged the dominance of psychology in education.

"You know, Raymond, psychology can be seen as a pseudoscience based on the work of a bunch of white men in Europe who were followed by a bunch of white men in the United States. Who are the famous women psychologists? How many women have been presidents of the American Psychological Association? How many men? What's with always blaming mothers for the sins of their sons? Until just a few years ago, being gay or lesbian was identified as having a psychological disorder. Who are the psychologists in the civil rights movement? Why do psychologists assist schools in labeling and excluding children from learning with others? And, by what standards? How have schools been made better because of psychology? And please, don't tell me you can separate motivation from culture. If all people are motivated, then why aren't psychologists more concerned with all of the ways that schools suppress motivation, especially among lower-income black and brown families, who are tracked into lower-level courses.

I felt like waving a white flag. But I also knew it's fairly easy to critique psychology. What answers did she have and what did she do about them? Her way of living in the world based on what she knew is what convinced me I needed to learn with her.

Margery particularly loved working in under-resourced schools. She sat alongside students, cared about their opinions, probed their insights for deeper understanding, and remembered their names and stories. She always hated to leave the schools she worked in when kids were around.

She asked tough questions of people in authority without hostility. Whether a superintendent or a principal, she might query, "Beyond test scores, how have you been able to show the public how smart your students are?" "What data do you look at on a regular basis?" What are some of the enduring challenges that puzzle you?" Margery also thought quite a bit about power and power relationships. It was not unusual for us to discuss how a person or group or a decision might influence the power imbalances or power relationships in a system.

Yet, Margery was open to better teaching methods from psychology when they could promote learning or change. She loved learning and wanted everyone else to love learning too: students, teachers, parents, administrators. That was her first priority. It was what bonded us as colleagues. She appreciated the idea of intrinsic motivation, learning for the sake of learning where the process was as valued as the outcome. Her question was, "How can we teach in ways that help make schools and colleges places where everyone is excited to learn?" "How can we make formal education a relevant and integrity-rich experience for students?"

∴

When do you realize you're in love with someone? As Margery and I spent more time together—planning our course, reviewing each class, and discussing motivation and culture, as well as the politics of our campus—we grew closer and closer. I realized how deep our relationship had become when I began imagining a life with Margery and her children. (Margery has told me the turning point for her was my reassurance and assistance in delivering a large order of pizzas for a workshop she was giving. A small act of mundane kindness that she saw as tender and caring.)

Not long afterwards, over dinner, I said, "I think we're in love." Margery looked at me, with a pensive stare. She knew what I said was true. We didn't kiss or touch hands, the moment was sobering, a suggestion of years to come. She said, "I know ... I know."

Margery's sons, Matthew and Danny, were a treasure I did not expect. At 8 and 6 respectively, they were trusting, gentle, and filled with wonder. When we were together in the Northwest forests, they were curious and playful. They walked across the trunks of fallen trees as large as the pillars of the Parthenon, chased each other down leaf laden paths surrounded in a panorama of iridescent green ferns, and marveled at the family of raccoons that appeared every morning for food at our cottage's screen door. Their delight, imagination and easy affection were beautiful. They even found my fourteen year old cat, Cannidles, to be everything from a panther to a sleep mate. I respected and loved them.

∴

As Margery and I continued to teach, we began to envision a book based on our course: *Diversity and Motivation: Culturally Responsive Teaching*. We believed higher education had a moral obligation to accommodate diversity and to transform itself as the society it serves is transformed by the vast array of cultures that compose it. We believed colleges could be the agents of genuine social and economic improvement. However, without changing how they taught students, they would achieve little more than the pretense of equity in an increasingly unequal world.

Our contribution to this mission would be a useful culturally responsive pedagogy. The essentials of this approach to teaching were that it (1) respected diversity, (2) engaged the intrinsic motivation of *all* learners, (3) created a safe, inclusive, and respectful learning environment, (4) derived teaching practices from across cultures, and (5) promoted justice and equity in society.

When I called Lynn Luckow, my former editor who was now the president of Jossey-Bass, he was ecstatic about the idea. "That's really a needed book. It will be a contribution. When you can, write a detailed outline and marketing plan and please send it along. I see no difficulty in drawing up a contract for this work. Full speed ahead!" I was thrilled. I knew what we proposed to write would be for me the most difficult book I had ever authored. But I had Margery writing with me and thinking with me. I knew there would be an immense amount of learning ahead for us. I also knew it would be painful. We wanted to live together but where would we live? And, how would we afford it? And, perhaps, most difficult of all, because teaching is permeated by ethical considerations that influence bias, racism, homophobia, sexism, and much more, writing about motivation and culturally diversity would be emotionally wrought. Ideas about entrenched problems made writers vulnerable, exposing their own ignorance and prejudice.

∴

In early 1992, Finley's health took a steep turn downward. I hadn't seen him in about nine months and when I did, I felt the sadness that overcomes me when I see someone I love, and know with certainty that they are seriously ill; the vitality they've had before seems crushed and hollow with their eyes much deeper set and their bodies arched and thinner. He answered the door using a walker, which I knew troubled him greatly. Yet, I laughed heartily when, as only Finley could, he stood back after kissing me and, with his right hand in a palm upward gesture toward the walker, said with a mock expression of exasperation, "Well, how do you like it? This old age bit is not for sissies."

As was our habit, we drank scotch and talked. He refused to say anything about his illness other than that it was cancer and when and if it really got bad, he would tell me more. He wanted to talk about the book he was writing. It was a history of 1919. He said it was a much more interesting year than most people realized, partly because of the huge immigration to the United States from Central and Southern Europe. He remembered that my father had migrated here in 1919. He told me he had never been to Poland and wondered what it would be like to visit there.

That gave me an idea. I told him that I knew how much he loved to travel and that if there were a trip he'd like to take, I'd love to be his companion.

"I like that proposition, Raymond. There is a place I've always wanted to go but for one reason or another I haven't made it yet. That's the Grand Canyon."

"Terrific. I took a float trip down the Colorado River for ten days when I was still living in Milwaukee. We went with two geologists. It was fabulous."

"You know, I'd probably have to go in a wheelchair. How do you feel about that?"

"Hey, there were people in wheel chairs at the rim of the canyon the last time I was there. They seemed to be having a great time. There are excellent accommodations nearby. And, the vistas, even if you can't go to the bottom of the canyon, are unforgettable. Let's do it. I'll get some brochures and send them your way. We can plan the trip together. It'll be fun."

He smiled and nodded, "Okay, Raymond. You can be my tour guide."

When I left, I wondered if I would see him again. I knew he didn't like anything morbid and might be holding back on how serious things really were. I wrote this letter to him upon my return to Seattle.

Dear Finley,

I recently read somewhere that it is not the living of life that helps one to escape the vain and trivial but what one realizes from that living that makes life transcendent. You have helped me to realize so much.

When I first knew you as a student I saw you as someone who lived in another reality, as otherworldly to me, from my background, as some of the figures from ancient history you so eloquently described. As our relationship moved into friendship through our conversations and times together, I was able to see a more promising life for myself, one in which the different friendships I could have and the different work I could do was so far greater than I had imagined.

You opened a larger door to a deeper world for me. You wrote "real" books, and that is probably why I still try today to write them myself. You were the first person who spoke intimately with me about places like Rome and London, and I know some of my lust for travel has its genesis in those conversations. Yet, I could also appreciate within myself the established earthly pursuits of food, drink, and sport. Seeing your excitement and beer spilling when Gordie Howe got that hat trick was one of the highlights of the good fun we could always freely have together.

You have also been my anchor. Through the rough tumble of ended relationships, academia's neurotic systems, and the passing on of my father, my mother, and my loving Aunt Ann, I could come to you for a viewpoint, a scotch, and the warmth of my dear friend. And a laugh. Always and evermore I will hear the raspy wheeze of the many hoots we have had together.

In some ways one of your greatest gifts to me has been a question, "What will Finley think?" You are my horizon for decency, for dignity, for wit in the face of disaster, and for obstinacy in the path of fops and bullies.

I realize as you face cancer, I will face it also. I have been graced with you as part of my life. And, the most honor I can give you is to share with others the gifts I have received through you and from you.

To this end I will be true.

Love,

Raymond

Finley died in early 1993. He had colon cancer. We never made it to the Grand Canyon. By the time I called the travel agents and put the brochures together, his condition worsened and the trip wasn't possible. "Don't be disappointed, Raymond. We'll save it for the next life. That will give us something to look forward to."

∴

In close proximity to Finley's passing, Margery decided she would return to Colorado. We made plans to live together in Boulder where she and Matthew and Danny's father could share family responsibility for the boys. Neither of us had jobs, but with two Ph.D.'s between us and a great deal of teaching experience, we both felt we would find meaningful work.

Where to live? was the most vexing question. We wanted to find a small house, not too far from their father's home to make sharing the boys and having them remain at their local school possible. In late summer, we drove to Colorado and began house hunting immediately.

We took the boys with us to look at residences and to make sure it was a family decision. They were great house hunters: polite and discerning, taking pride in spotting chipping paint, bad roofs, and broken stairs. Yet our choices were meager. Everything seemed either in ill repair or too expensive. After three days of looking, on our way back to the hotel, we were feeling pretty dismal.

As we drove along Jay Road, a southern boundary to Boulder, we spotted an owner-made house-for-sale sign on a fence post. When we looked beyond it, we saw a small blue house sitting about 60 yards away. Crossing a flowing irrigation ditch, we pulled into the gravel laden driveway. However, no one answered the door, so we thought to look behind the house. When we did, we saw a woman watering a large colorful flower garden.

She was a local florist. She greeted us warmly and took us into the house to get a better look. It was funky: half built in 1954 and half built in 1970 with an old fireplace with a large, cast iron, dark wood stove inside of it, a beamed barn-timbered ceiling in the kitchen, and dark pine slabbed floors. Nothing fancy, but homey feeling with wooden and brick walls throughout. The most appealing features were outside of the house. It lay on an acre of land, the south and west sides of which were open space, rented as a cattle pasture with about forty head grazing and all facing in the same direction north. The east side was bound by a larger irrigation ditch and farm land with mature cottonwood trees lining the ribbon of water from the road to about a quarter mile beyond. Directly behind the house, between it and the flower garden, was an expansive wooden deck, ideal for summer meals.

But what quickly drew the earnest money out of my pocket beyond Margery and the boys' approval was the view west of the Rocky Mountain Continental Divide and the nest of great horned owls at the southern edge of the property. We had found a home in a setting beautiful beyond my expectations. We would learn our way through the rest.

∴

Margery continued to evolve our ideas about motivation, culturally responsive teaching, and strengthening public education. She went on to serve in several State Educational Agencies and regional migrant education programs, led two higher education programs, and now consults directly with schools and colleges.

I consulted and wrote for four years before accepting a position in 1996 as a Professor at Regis University in Denver, eventually becoming the founding Director of the Center for the Study of Accelerated Learning.

After three years of research and writing, we completed the first edition of *Diversity and Motivation: Culturally Responsive Teaching*,[95] published by Jossey-Bass in 1995.

PART 2

Activities

CHAPTER 17

An Overview of Intrinsic Motivation, Flow, and Vital Engagement

What makes motivation compelling is our common understanding that without it, most performance, whether in play, work, or learning, is diminished. Throughout our lives we have seen the motivated person surpass the less motivated person, though both may have the same opportunities and very similar capabilities. We also know that when people are not motivated to do what they are required to do, their behavior is often accompanied by boredom, frustration, distraction, and hostility. Four hours for a teacher with a group of unmotivated adult learners? As a colleague once said, "That's like trying to feed hamburger to a humming bird."

Realizing how challenging and unstable motivation, including our own, can be makes most instructors aware of the need to consider it as an important part of the instructional process. From a biological perspective, John Ratey writes that motivation is a process that "determines how much energy and attention the brain and body assign to a given stimulus—whether it's a thought coming in or a situation that confronts one."[96] Simply put, it is the natural human process for directing energy to accomplish a goal.[97] Being motivated means being purposeful. We use attention, concentration, imagination, effort, and passion to pursue such goals as learning a subject or completing a degree. But because motivation is a process that occurs within a person, and we cannot see or touch it, we have to infer it from what people say or do. We look for signs of interest, perseverance, and completion, or for such words as "I want to ...," "I will ...," and so forth. Motivation is why people do what they do, a persistent mystery that has provoked human beings for thousands of years.

People motivated to learn are more likely to do things they believe will help them learn.[98] They pay attention more carefully to instruction. They rehearse material in order to remember it. They take notes to improve their studying. They are more likely to ask for help when they are uncertain. Motivation improves learning because it is a part of learning, the energy within the learning process. When we want to learn—to change what we know or can do through studying, practicing, or reflecting—it is motivation that gets us to pick up a book, surf the internet, and so forth. Motivation also mediates learning, focusing our attention, deepening our concentration, and providing the effort necessary to learn. Finally, motivation is a consequence of learning. When we have a wonderful experience reading a particular book, we are often likely to be more interested in other books on a similar topic or books written by the same author.

Intrinsic Motivation: Along with Fire and the Blind Future a Gift from the Gods

The brain has an inherent propensity for knowing what it wants. Relevance guides our inclinations.[99] We have to pay attention to things that matter to us. What matters to us is understood through our cultural perspectives, which carry language, values, norms, and frameworks to interpret the world we live in.

Intrinsic motivation occurs when people act or respond for the satisfaction inherent in the behavior itself.[100] For example, we read a novel for the interest it generates while we read it. We solve a problem because we enjoy encountering the puzzle itself. We conduct an experiment because of how each step engages our curiosity. When people see that what they are learning makes sense and is important according to their own perspectives, their motivation emerges as a physical energy, an emotional state to support learning. What is culturally relevant to adult learners evokes their intrinsic motivation. We want to be effective at what we value. When we are intrinsically motivated to learn, we usually care about what we are learning and we feel such emotions as interest, concentration, and satisfaction.

In 2015, an alliance of psychologists, The Coalition for Psychology in Schools and Education, supported by the American Psychological Association, presented the twenty most important principles based on psychological science for preK-12 teaching and learning. First among the four motivation principles was, "Students tend to enjoy learning and do better when they are more intrinsically rather than extrinsically motivated to achieve."[101] I believe this principle is equally applicable to adults.[102]

As the coalition explains and has been demonstrated in this memoir, as learners become more competent and learning becomes more easily accomplished and enjoyable, "learning often becomes its own intrinsic reward." People who find reading, writing, calculating, and expanding their stores of knowledge compelling and satisfying are likely to be lifelong learners.[103] The tendency to find such processes worthwhile is considered to be the *trait of motivation to learn*:[104] a propensity for learning that develops over time. That's a magnificent human characteristic.

Flow

Intrinsic motivation has several qualitative variations. One of its most exhilarating forms is *flow*. According to Mihaly Csikszentmihalyi, when we're in flow, "living becomes its own justification."[105] I agree. I love the feeling of flow: the deeply satisfying experience of an intrinsically motivating activity. We have all had *flow experiences* outside an educational context: the feeling and concentration that sometimes emerge in a closely contested athletic contest, in a challenging board game such as chess, or more simply, in reading a book that seems as if it were written just for us or in the spontaneous exhilaration that accompanies a long, deep conversation with an old friend.

In such activities, we feel totally absorbed, with no time to worry about what might happen next and with a sense that we are fully participating with all the skills necessary at the moment. There is often a loss of self-awareness that sometimes results in a feeling of transcendence or a merging with the activity and the environment. Writers, dancers, therapists, surgeons, lawyers, pilots, and instructors report feelings of flow during engrossing tasks in their repertoire of activities. In fact, when interviewed, they report that flow experiences are among the major reasons why they enjoy and continue to do the work they do.

Learners can have flow experiences as well. If we think of our best courses and finest instructors, we often can remember being captivated by the learning events we shared with them: challenging and creative activities in which we participated at a level where a new depth and extension of our capabilities emerged. Time passed quickly during such experiences, and our desire to return to them was self-evident. They were also not trivial. Effort and concentration on our part were necessary to gain what we did accomplish.

Because flow can be found across cultures, it may be a sense that humans have developed in order to recognize patterns of action that are worth preserving.[106] Whether we are inspired in a course or in ecstasy in a spiritual ritual, our flow experiences have remarkably similar characteristics.[107]

Goals are clear and compatible. That's why playing games like chess, tennis, and poker induce flow, but so can playing a musical piece or designing computer software. As long as our intentions are clear and our emotions support them, we can concentrate even when the task is difficult. We absorb ourselves in those vivid dreams to which we commit. In such matters, cultural relevance is an inescapable necessity.

Feedback is immediate, continuous, and relevant as the activity unfolds. We are clear about how well we are doing. Each move of a game usually tells us whether we are advancing or retreating from our goal; as we read we *flow* across lines and paragraphs and pages. In a good conversation, words, facial expressions, and gestures give immediate feedback. In learning situations, there should be distinct information or signals that let us assess our work.

The challenge is in balance with our skills or knowledge but stretches existing capacities. The challenge is manageable but pulls us toward further development of our knowledge or skill. Flow experiences usually occur when our ability to act and the available opportunity for action correspond closely. If challenges get significantly beyond our skills, we usually begin to worry; and if they get too far away from what we're capable of doing, real anxiety or fear can emerge. To use a cliché, we're in over our heads, whether it's a project, a job, or a sport. Conversely, when the challenge is minimal, even if we have the skills we feel apathetic. (Busywork comes to mind.) When the challenge is reasonable but our skills still exceed it, we are likely to become bored. However, if the activity is a *valued* hobby such as crossword puzzles or cooking we might actually feel relaxed. In general, when desired challenges and personal skills approach harmony, we become energized and stop worrying about control. We're acting instinctively with full concentration, and deep involvement and exhilaration lie ahead. For example, just think of the last time you've had a great match in any game, sport, project, or job-related activity. When I'm in a course and we're really "cooking," I still get goose bumps when it's over and need to find a quiet place afterwards just to settle in and absorb the feelings I have. Remarkable.

Vital Engagement

As indicated in studies by Jeanne Nakamura, at its highest qualitative level, intrinsic motivation is vital engagement: the experience of learning "characterized by both felt meaning (subjective significance) and ... enjoyed absorption (flow)."[108] This kind of motivation occurs in the immediate experience of learning and over time as an enduring relationship. Just think of a most cherished subject, book, technology, sport, hobby, or vocation. Whatever our choice, it's a pretty good bet that we love to get involved with what we selected. While immersed within it, we experience flow, but we take what we're learning seriously as well, possibly for years, or at least months, realizing it has inherent worth to sustain our concentration and energy. This felt meaning allows for a range of commitments from marathon sports to programming video games to teaching, sculpting, and activism—anything in which our action personally matters to us. As my memoir reveals, I became vitally engaged in the study of motivation to learn which I followed as a teacher through professions that included becoming a psychologist, a human relations specialist, a psychotherapist, and finally, an adult educator.

Although inseparable, the reason I think vital engagement is as important as learning itself is because it is one of the few things that makes life worth living beyond survival. It is integral to our well-being. Vital engagement constitutes the meaningful relationships we have as we live whether with people, beliefs, concerns, causes, interests, or any aspect of the world that we deeply value.[109] Because it offers the experience of enjoyment and significance, we are more likely to become persistently involved, honing our skills, deepening our knowledge, and, consequently having more opportunities for flow and meaning to develop.[110] Through vital engagement we come to realize what we care about. Once we feel the emotion of caring about what we do, we are more likely to pay attention to those things that enhance this particular experience. We talk about it, read about it, search the Internet to know more about it, and go to conferences and workshops to meet people who care about it too. As Nakamura writes, "... vital engagement with some aspect of the world can become an organizing principle in a person's life."[111]

Because vital engagement leads to knowing what is worthwhile and provides such deep joy, we remember these elements of life as important from our past and valued for our future.[112] They beckon us with dreams, hopes, goals, and desires, giving meaning to our lives and supporting us through the strenuous and difficult phases of our existence. From this perspective, happiness and a deep sense of meaning in one's life, essentials for human well-being, are not directly attained, but are consequences of vital-engagement.[113]

Education, as a means for inculcating a higher purpose in life, should cultivate a disposition, an enduring trait among adult learners, to seek vital engagement, to see their lives as oriented toward learning filled with meaning and challenge as they work toward the fulfillment of what matters to them. This need is especially relevant as our society develops greater capacity for enrolling adults in two and four-year colleges. From the standpoint of purpose, emotion, and social impact, developing an aptitude for vital engagement, elevates and illuminates the greater part of one's entire life.

A person in sustained vital engagement with some aspect of the world is likely to transform it and be transformed by it. Adults involved in such learning are intense and cherish what they are doing. They want to improve their knowledge and enhance the work with which they are engaged. They are involved in what John Dewey described as a *double change*,[114] being self-realized and simultaneously changing the world. These are not only artists, inventors, and innovators, they are parents, environmentalists, activists, lawyers, and leaders of every stripe. At their very best, they want to make things better as well as ensure the common good. Vital engagement is not a value free process because motivation is always purposeful and involves an individual's will.

Culture, as transmitted through teachers, mentors, friends, and family plays an integral role in shaping the arc of its development. The foundation for vital engagement was laid by my family, my father's indomitable will, Finley's invigorating and devoted friendship, and the trials and challenges of trying to be a fine teacher. Once I turned toward psychology in graduate school, vital engagement set its anchor resulting in my decision at 31 to lead an intrinsically motivated, professional life. I've followed it ever since with transformative learning often being the means for personal and professional change. Let's take a look in the next chapter at how vital engagement and transformative learning can form a powerful kinship to advance our lives toward fulfillment.

CHAPTER 18

Transformative Learning: A Partner to Intrinsic Motivation throughout Life

Once, when I was in my in my late 30s, sitting at the kitchen table in her home, my mother without any forewarning, plaintively said to me, "Raymond, I don't understand you. So many changes." I knew immediately what she meant: another move, a different job, another residence, and more. Probably due to the look of dismay on my face, she quickly added, "But I still love you." I gave her a hug and she asked me to walk with her to see her flower garden, a casual diversion we both could enjoy.

Although transformation can be difficult and challenging, it is usually quite motivating. When I read my memoir, I was struck by how many major changes I had gone through. It seemed to be a rather continual process, not constant, but emerging seemingly spontaneously every few years, especially when I was a younger adult. What I discovered was the frequent intersection of vital engagement and transformative learning. One seemed to beget the other, working together in concert and dynamically composing my life in the moment. Having discussed vital engagement in the previous chapter, let's take a closer look at transformative learning.

According to Jack Mezirow who developed the concept, transformative learning refers to learning that results in a deep change in our beliefs, assumptions, or perspectives, making them more discriminating and able to construct opinions that will prove more truthful to guide our actions.[115] There are other theories of transformative learning which are less rational,[116] placing imagination, intuition, and emotion at the core of transformation. Today, there are scholars who are attempting to unify these theories. They have broadened and made its definition more explicit. Michael Kroth and Patricia Cranton write, "Transformative learning is a process by which individuals engage in the cognitive processes of critical reflection and self-reflection, intuitive and imaginative explorations of the psyche and spirituality, and developmental changes leading to a deep shift in perspective and habits of mind that are more open, permeable, discriminating, and better justified. Individual change may lead to social change, and social change may promote individual change."[117]

By this definition, transformative learning may not always be an *enjoyable* action, but it is usually absorbing and filled with felt significance, qualities integral to vital engagement. When I review one of the most profound transformations in my life, pursuing the study of motivation as I became a psychologist, I see a vitally engaged learning period with Jack Mezirow's ten phases of learning leading to a perspective transformation embedded throughout my experience:[118]

1. Encountering a disorienting dilemma (realizing as a teacher I was far too dependent on discipline with little knowledge of motivation, a much greater force for learning, Chapter 9).
2. Experiencing a self-examination (having mononucleosis and using the time to reflect on insights from the book, *Mental Hygiene in Teaching*, Chapter 9).
3. Posing critical assessment of assumptions (understanding my teaching problems and anxiety resulting from my need for perfection, Chapter 9).
4. Recognizing a connection between one's discontent and the process of transformation (seeing the wisdom of *not withholding affection and positive regard* toward my students and the error of holding expectations that were too high and controlling for behavior among fourth and fifth graders, Chapter 9).
5. Exploring options for new roles, relationships and actions (seeking out psychology as a means to learn more about motivation to learn, Chapter 10).
6. Planning a course of action (enrolling in the School Psychology program at Wayne State University and following its curriculum for certification, Chapter 10).
7. Acquiring knowledge and skills for implementing one's plan (completing coursework in the School Psychology program, Chapter 10).
8. Provisional trying of new roles (realizing as I did the work of a school psychologist that I wanted to get a doctorate in either educational psychology or clinical psychology, Chapter 10).
9. Building competence and self-confidence in new roles and relationships (applying to doctoral programs, being accepted at Wayne State University, and using new knowledge and skills from doctoral coursework to improve my instruction as a substitute teacher, Chapter 10).
10. Reintegrating new roles and relationships into one's life on the basis of conditions dictated by one's new perspective (completing a dissertation and acquiring a position as an assistant professor of educational psychology at the University of Wisconsin-Milwaukee, Chapters 10 & 11).

Reviewing these ten phases in my life offers a number of insights. Transformative learning is a subjective and labile process. Self-constructed, it depends on how one chunks it. In my case it covers five years, but there are also more minor periods of transformative learning such as when I gained new knowledge in graduate school, changed my perspective on how to teach, and practiced school psychology. Then I came to believe I wanted to pursue a doctoral degree and

I developed more changes of perspective as I completed my doctoral studies. During this time, I was often intrinsically motivated in my coursework and vitally engaged as I taught in Detroit and conducted my dissertation research.

However, for me, the leading motivational force was vital engagement, which stimulated my transformations, processes that emerged organically as part of my professional learning throughout this five year period. It seems both vital engagement and transformative learning were working in concert, significantly altering my life. Also, John Dirkx's view that transformation is often a result of unconscious processes experienced as intuition and spontaneous awareness certainly holds true for my personal evolution in graduate school.[119]

If I use Paulo Friere's lens to understand transformative learning, it seems to be a strong fit for my experience as a human relations specialist.[120] His theory advocates instructors of adults to be cultural activists who promote agency among learners through reflective discourse and action to initiate constructive social change. As a form of *self-directed learning*, my work in the Milwaukee Public Schools is a dynamic example of his four pedagogical principles in action:

1. Become involved in a *relevant experience* that solicits the learner's desire (in this case mine) to make meaning because the learner finds it dissonant. (After much discussion with friends and colleagues as well as personal doubt, I took the position of human relations specialist because of a belief in the eventual benefits of school desegregation for the common good of society and the city of Milwaukee in particular.)
2. Collaborate with learners and use *critical self-reflection* to consider the information and ideas generated. (Our human relations team reviewed our actions and feedback from the teachers, administrators, and human relations councils. With colleagues such as Clem Magner, I recognized and had to acknowledge the degree of burden the black community carried to desegregate the Milwaukee Public Schools.)
3. Facilitate *reflective discourse*, a discussion in which learners are able to redefine meaning for themselves based on reciprocal sharing of information and insights with peers. (This insightful dialogue was most evident personally and for our team as the Milwaukee teachers union called for a strike during the desegregation effort. We discussed its merits, its critique by the Black Teachers Caucus, and the decision of other Milwaukee unions not to join the Milwaukee Teacher Education Association strike. Our decision to cross the picket line, a first for me as a member of a union supportive family, was a choice upheld as a result of reflecting on the purpose of this particular strike and its negative effects on race relations and students.)

4. Initiate *effective actions,* determined in collaboration with learners. (The human relations team offered guidance to the Milwaukee high schools but also significantly benefited from ongoing collaborative learning with the human relations councils in those high schools. This cooperation contributed to new learning for us and reciprocally helped the councils to make their reactions more sensitive and influential for race relations in their schools. The councils were a continual force for better understanding and peaceful interactions.)

Other major transformations in the memoir are deciding to become a psychotherapist and committing to adult education. From my perspective, the former follows more closely Mezirow's series of phases and the latter a more Freirean model of transformation. Each has incidents of strong intuitive reckoning. When I make my initial stride toward adult education, I have the realization that I have the capacity and desire to write a book offering a comprehensive understanding of adult motivation to learn. I'm so exhilarated by this spontaneous awareness that I begin to run to release my excitement about this possibility. Again, my propensity toward vital engagement leads me to take a year and a half leave of absence to write the manuscript without a publishing contract. Taking this risk is part of the process of transformative learning (reflective discourse and effective action à la Freire).

There are other parts of this memoir where the leading edges for transformation were more strongly imbedded in such human qualities as admiration and aspiration. My friendship with Finley Hooper (Chapter 7) was deeply immersed in my respect for his ideas and his warmth as a person. As a middle-aged adult, I continued to hold wonder for his unique way of thinking and his wisdom. I did not need to be unsettled by his perspective to alter my own. Many times critical reflection arose within me as part of our conversations and evolved into another way of understanding topics that ranged from government policies to local political action.

When I began to work at Antioch University in Seattle (Chapter 15), the cultural norms of the college and a radical student viewpoint challenged me to think differently about how I taught and related to students. Being "surrounded" by these differences from my previous college experiences stimulated me to rethink (à la Freire) my approach to adult motivation and learning. When I did become consciously aware of the effects of this new milieu, I can remember saying to myself, "I have something to learn here." And, I began to vitally engage in reflective discourse with students and colleagues about their views of the purposes of higher education and in particular how they learned and taught at Antioch.

As a result of writing this memoir, I'm convinced that adult educators and learners benefit from knowing about the satisfying consequences of vital engagement as an individual pursuit and as an agency for the common good. Adult educators are traditionally more likely to be aware of transformative learning and more prepared to enact it. However, as a tandem vital engagement and transformative learning nurture each other. As such, these two processes work in concert to propel people to construct a world view with which they can create social change and enhance their personal fulfillment.

Stories and Non-fiction, as Passageways to Intrinsic Motivation and Transformative Learning

Telling a good story is usually intrinsically motivating. It provides enjoyment and creativity for the teller as well as the told. The narrative form allows for conflict, insight, discovery, challenge, surprise, redemption, and inspiration: emotionally appealing interests throughout its delivery. For those who want to, creating a fine story is often vitally engaging—filled with transcendent absorption and significant meaning. A story of deep and authentic personal change can be a portal to transformative learning for the writer and reader.

In recent years scholars in adult education have advocated and illustrated the use of stories to foster transformative learning.[121] Jerold Apps' *Teaching from the Heart* has been well received by adult educators as a means to changing the way they think about teaching.[122] Stories allow teachers to consider instruction at a more emotional and deeper level; how it has changed their lives and the lives of learners. In *Effective Teaching and Mentoring*, Laurent Daloz relates how teachers and mentors use stories to understand the meaning of life's changes, because they can "reconnect things for us, place our fears in context, help us to see new forms of meaning."[123] Michael Kroth and Patricia Cranton in *Stories of Transformative Learning* use storytelling "to encourage people to explore the potential for transformative learning in their own lives, practices, and communities."[124] The personal nature of stories allows people to readily know how others have "reconsidered hidden assumptions" releasing the constrained aspects of their lives, offering hope for making changes to reach greater fulfillment.

Writing a memoir has allowed me to take the ideas of these scholars, and now, in retrospect apply them to what I've written. For understanding vital engagement and transformative learning it's the most powerful thing I've ever done. Reliving the transformations through writing and reflection took me from tears to elation. But it also deepened at a visceral level how these largely cognitive processes were a reality of immense emotional magnitude.

Because the memoir covered forty years and numerous transformations large and small, it provided a subtle and nuanced experience of how dynamic human change is, how unpredictably it occurs for the person who lives it, and how necessary it is to not look away from those things that deeply affect us but which we don't immediately understand. Stay with it. Talk about it with friends and colleagues. Be a relentless sleuth to understand what an irrevocable gut level call for new learning can bring.

From writing this book, I realize I was fortunate to fall in love with learning and to never let it go. In the next chapter I share some of my ideas about how to use memoir and creative non-fiction to encourage vital engagement and transformative learning among adult learners.

CHAPTER 19

Learning to Evoke and Sustain Intrinsic Motivation with Transformative Learning

The benefits of developing intrinsic motivation for learning as a lifelong trait are exceptional. Just being in the presence of someone who loves what they're doing is a sentient pleasure, even when we're not the recipient of their favor—a cook, a mechanic, a parent, a crossing guard, a physician, a teacher. Name it. The person gives off the scent of energy arising with purpose and abundance, an intensity contagious and life affirming. I've felt it in cancer treatment centers and high school locker rooms. Like seeing an infant smile, I know I'm better for it. To be continuously with someone joyfully absorbed in learning with the purpose of sharing its graces with others—like a friend says, "It's oxygen from the angels. Take a deep breath."

This book was written so that its readers might find, affirm, and follow the intrinsic pleasure of learning in their own lives and share it with others. "Vital engagement with learning" isn't meant as a romantic notion. Just as loving another person isn't all fanciful pleasure. For most of us it's as hard as it is easy. Realizing we deeply care about something means paying attention to it, nurturing it, placing it above gratifications sometimes more tempting, simpler, and near.

This chapter is about discerning vital engagement in learning and appreciating how it can guide us in our work, in our vocational aspirations, and in community with others. There is also the chance that some of the exercises[1] that follow may inspire alternative routes to deepening our intrinsic motivation. We begin with some awareness processes to acknowledge intrinsic motivation in our lives. Then we explore its personal link to transformative learning through storytelling and end with an emphasis on writing creative non-fiction to understand how vital engagement has occurred in our lives and where it may take us in the future.

Acknowledging Intrinsic Motivation in Our Lives

Although there are qualities of brainstorming and list making to this exercise, it should be carried out in a manner that encourages participants to know each other as evolving human beings with mutual needs, emotions, and experiences. At its best, it allows people the possibility to see themselves in each other's worlds.

Three of the emotions that people often feel when they are intrinsically motivated are *creative, capable,* and *joyful.*[125] Not surprisingly, they often feel these three emotions at the same time. Culturally and individually, the definitions of these emotions may take on many different meanings for participants. The following are proposed as broad interpretations of their meaning: Creative—acting in ways personally spontaneous and original. Capable—feeling confident and knowledgeable about what you are doing. Joyful—ranging from feeling playful to subtle or exuberant happiness.

Part 1: (Allow yourself to think deeply about these activities.)
1. Begin by making a list of those things you do that allow you to feel creative, capable, and joyful (all three emotions at the same time) while you do them. Allow at least 10 minutes to compose your list. Consider activities at work, with family and friends, and individually. Recall current as well as past activities.
2. Which of these activities involve flow—total absorption without self-consciousness or concern about time passing?
3. Which of these activities are vitally engaging, characterized by flow as well as having personal significance and felt meaning?
4. Reflect on your activities. Are there any patterns, insights, surprises, or emotional reactions? Are there any activities you would like to extend or deepen? For both of these questions, please write down your thoughts. Take some time to share these with other participants. This discussion should be allowed to move along easily with opportunities for dialogue, gentle questions and probing, and development of further insights individually and as a group.

Part 2: (Allow at least 15 minutes or more for people to reflect as they compose their answers. Encourage people to write down their thoughts. Please allow time for discussion.)
5. Have any of these activities promoted transformative learning for you? How so? Have any of these activities increased or resulted from transformative learning? Again, how so?
6. After reflecting on your inspired actions and transformative learning related to intrinsic motivation, are there any patterns, insights, surprises, or emotional reactions? In these actions and episodes of transformative learning, what specific part did *intrinsically motivated learning* play? As a leading edge? As a compelling consequence?
7. Having reflected upon and discussed questions 1 through 6, are there any further generalizations or inspirations? What about possible actions or goals as a result of this activity? Please discuss.

Linking Intrinsic Motivation and Transformative Learning through Storytelling

As Michael Kroth and Patricia Cranton affirm, "Transformative learning stories can be filled with hope and optimism rather than being a negative disorienting dilemma."[126] We can as easily be unsettled by inspiration and anxious about our keen desire to strive in a more justified direction, as we might be by guilt over our faulty assumptions and recognized mistakes. Physiologically, emotions flow into and out of each other like the tide in a fast moving sea.[127] Psychologists are still confounded by how they generate and change.

In the case of intrinsic motivation as a stimulant or an antecedent of personal disorientation leading to a shift in perspective or a more encompassing world view, is that not how wonder, insight, and discovery work when harnessed in purposeful learning? Such experiences are often accompanied by feelings of vitality, elation, joy, and satisfaction. I've seen more than a few young adults and at least a good number of mature adults jump up and down, slap high-fives, or shout out "Bravo!" upon their reckoning of an unexpected question for their research, a new strategy in a team effort, or at the end of the exclamation, "Why didn't I think of that before!"

Storytelling about past events where flow and vital engagement were the precursors or results of transformative learning can sensitize us to the fortunate possibilities of strengthening intrinsic motivation in our personal lives, work, and communities. These stories may follow at least three themes: (1) Intrinsically motivated learning that led to transformative learning; (2) transformative learning that led to intrinsically motivated learning; and (3) a personal relationship that catalyzed intrinsically motivated learning and/or transformative learning.

Because transformative learning itself can be a form of vital engagement (intensely absorbing and significantly meaningful) and because each can act in concert with the other, it may be difficult at times to separate them out as individual processes. That's as it should be. Recognizing how one may facilitate the other is important but doesn't have to be exact. This isn't a science. It's a human life, where essences such as hope, fear, love, virtue and honor dominate the terrain.

The stories may be written, read, or told depending on the group's preference. Again, discussion of them should be allowed to move along easily with opportunities for dialogue, gentle questions and probing, and development of further insights individually and as a group. Accentuating vital engagement within the stories may help participants to realize its benefits and presence as a personal trait. For transformative learning, emphasis on shifts in perspective, greater self-awareness and openness, and more justified actions offer consideration of how important a process it is during adult development.

Prior to writing or telling stories consider what kind of commentary you may want from the facilitator or participants and what some of the goals of discussion might be. The following prompts are suggestions for possible ideas and examples[2] to elicit and shape the themes of your stories:

1. The role of inspiration as an impulse to vital engagement and/or transformative learning. (Examples: Chapter 2, Sister Mary Desiderata, a lifetime memory of the power of an enthusiastic and vitally engaged teacher; Chapter 10, the teaching, modeling, and writings of Fritz Redl and Jack Kounin at Wayne State University offer a means to respectful and empathic student discipline.)
2. Transformative learning personally or professionally as a result of flow or vital engagement while learning. (Examples: Chapter 6, vital engagement in Finley Hooper's course sparks transformative learning unsettling my religious faith; Chapter 14, absorption in learning about adult motivation shifts my professional commitment to the field of adult education.)
3. Vital engagement personally or professionally as a result of transformative learning. (Examples: Chapter 9, unsettling experiences as an elementary school teacher lead to graduate study in psychology; Chapters 12/13, tumult and reflection as the human relations specialist during Milwaukee school desegregation heightens my desire to renew my study of motivation and therapy.)
4. A personal or professional path followed because of vital engagement without transformative learning as part of the experience. (Examples: Chapter 3, learning the joy of participating in sports as well as mischief; Chapter 11, the excitement of study and teaching as a new assistant professor.)
5. A personal relationship that led to vital engagement and transformative learning as ongoing processes. (Examples: Chapter 7, friendship with Finley Hooper continuously involves flow experiences and critical thinking leading to an evolution of new perspectives; Chapter 16, collaboration with Margery Ginsberg evolves toward re-evaluation of my teaching and the development of an approach to culturally responsive teaching.)

Using Techniques of Memoir and Creative Non-Fiction to Enhance the Awareness and Potential of Intrinsically Motivated Learning and Transformative Learning

In recent years, I have immersed myself in writing creative non-fiction and memoir. Authors of these literary forms suggest they have the potential to lead to a more "truthful"[128, 129] understanding of one's life and circumstances because the writing process provides greater access to intuitive and unconscious insights as well as conflict and vulnerability. Memoirists have described arriving at a deeper meaning of their past decisions and actions that is less inhibited by personal and professional judgments. I have found it to be storytelling with a sharper edge, more revealing of what I actually experienced. Memoirs require serious engagement with personal and social untruthfulness such as denial of personal or structural racism, rationalizing covert sexism, and disclaiming the harm of unfettered consumerism. When I reconsidered my work as a human relations specialist in the Milwaukee Public Schools, I had to acknowledge my complicity with racist education policies and the failure of the desegregation effort.

I think the characteristics of creative non-fiction and memoir require a consciousness and writing that for some of us tugs deeper at what happened in our lives and how to honestly understand its consequences. Creative non-fiction includes memoir, biography, personal essay, travel writing, and anecdote, all of which must be factually accurate but can combine literary devices such as reconstructed dialogue, ethical judgments, and a compelling narrative. Two strong goals of creative non-fiction are to share an entertaining story and to create interest about how the writer looking back understands the tale.

Memoir is a literary form as well as an art form. A memoir is a story "from life."[130] It actually happened and the author is relating it in the first person, composing something of private interest into something of personal meaning to the reader. Memoir has a much narrower focus than an autobiography, usually converging on a singular theme or exploring an aspect of the memoirist's life in depth. In Part 1 of *Living a Motivated Life: A Memoir and Activities*, I consistently spotlight how intrinsic motivation for learning became a valued trait and interacted with transformative learning to influence my personal development. Today, memoir writing is a fairly wide open form of prose with few conventions beyond those just described.

In order to encourage participant use of memoir methods of storytelling, its prevalent characteristics are exemplified and further described below. Please keep in mind it's *the combination* of these elements that makes a story memoir-like. The examples that follow are taken from the memoir in this book. However examples from other memoirs may be relevant and useful as well.

Characteristics and Examples of Memoir Writing
– Thematic—There is focus on a singular topic or subject. For this memoir it has been how intrinsic motivation became the lifelong personal trait of vital engagement for me, often initiating or resulting from transformative learning.

- Story from life—It's not about one's life, it's what actually happened, unflinchingly reliable with vivid details. Some examples: BB golf in Chapter 3, my encounter with Pauline in Chapter 9, crossing the union picket line in Chapter 12.
- Use of dialogue—Accurate-as-can-be reconstruction of conversations. Some examples: talking with my father about my report card in Chapter 4, talking with Finley Hooper throughout Chapter 7, reporting Margery Ginsberg's conversation with a frustrated student in Chapter 16.
- A questioning, ethical frame of mind—Musings, opinions, and judgments in an attempt to arrive at a more truthful understanding. Some examples: teachers inflicting motivational injuries in Chapter 4, my use of discipline methods in Chapter 9, desegregation policies and practices in Chapter 12.
- A candid vulnerable perspective—Relaying descriptions openly and truthfully which may at times place the writer in an exposed and less than complimentary stance. Some examples: Being fired as a bus boy in Chapter 6, inept teaching at Winterhalter Elementary in Chapter 9, complicity with racist school system policies in chapter 12, cultural bias and insensitivities in my work in Canada and at Antioch University-Seattle in Chapter 15.
- An individual voice: a distinct recognizable quality of writing or speaking that in some way captures the author's personality and engages the reader or listener. Often it's some combination of linguistic quirks, sentence rhythms, and imagery.[131] Some examples: the stories about my family in Chapter 1, the series of scenes narrating how it felt to be a first generation college student at Wayne State University in Chapter 5, the gauntlet I travelled to find a publisher in Chapter 14.

When participants compose their story with these characteristics in mind, they may need more time than it takes to simply tell a story. It's helpful to understand that writing with methods that memoirists use is an exploratory and experimental process. It's not the way many of us normally relate as storytellers. It may call upon us to reveal qualities and actions we're reluctant to admit. Yet such revelations serve the purpose of engendering greater self-acceptance and acceptance of others.

(Facilitators of groups using memoir methods of storytelling can gain insights into this process by writing a personal story of vital engagement and/or transformative learning that occurred in their lives as they normally would. Then shortly following this story with writing a story that is the same in theme and occurrence but now written with memoir methods such as dialogue, a questioning ethical frame of mind, and a more candid vulnerable perspective. Reflecting upon and comparing these two stories, what are some insights that emerge? Are

there advantages or disadvantages to either form of storytelling? Which memoir characteristics, singularly or in combination, seemed to (1) make the biggest difference? (2) Influenced your authenticity? or (3) Stimulated your critical thinking? After making these considerations, how might you adapt memoirist characteristics of storytelling to your own teaching or training?)

The prompts and examples found earlier in this chapter can be used with memoirist methods of storytelling. Some further prompts to consider for using this approach to explore how much you may want to seek, affirm, or deepen vital engagement and transformative learning in your life and work are:

- Compose the story using seven words or less. Before writing my memoir, I wrote "Finding light, sharing the path to it." This kind of condensation encourages both conscious and unconscious awareness of the essential truth in your story.
- Tell a story of a hard-won truth you've discovered and held on to.
- Tell a story of accomplishing something you are proud of to this day.
- Tell a story of when you became aware of a personal flaw, the recognition of which led to vital engagement or transformative learning. (For me throughout the writing of this memoir: too white, too male, too analytic, too controlling, too naïve, and a tendency to place personal success above compassion.)
- Tell the story of when you became aware you had become vitally engaged with learning as a lifelong learner.

Suggested Questions and Activities for Closure

Rather than view these suggested ideas as an ending point, please consider them as opportunities to explore new learning and emerging thoughts and feelings: ways to discern themes and make meaning from your stories of vital engagement and transformative learning.

Possible Questions:
- What's emerging for you? What new connections are you making?
- From our storytelling: What had real meaning for you? What surprised you? What challenged you?
- What's been your major insight or discovery so far?
- How can we support each other in taking next steps? How can we each contribute to our leaning as a group?
- If you were to follow vital engagement in your work, where do you think it would take you? What could you accomplish that you would value for yourself and others? What are some concrete actions you can take to begin or continue this exploration?

- What if you lived the rest of your career as a professional devoted to helping the people you serve love learning? If you were to do so, what are the possibilities? Who would care? Who would help? How would you begin? Perhaps, how do you continue?

Possible Activities:
- *Moments of Vital Engagement:* Participants reflect and share times when they were vitally engaged during the span of the course or workshop. These moments might have come while they were writing or telling their stories, reading or listening to stories from their peers, or as part of the discussions that followed or preceded such activities. If the group has had numerous periods of vital engagement, they're welcome to find those that had a special quality or heightened resonance and meaning for them.
- *Acknowledgements and Appreciations:* Participants reflect and offer statements of recognition and gratitude for noteworthy peer and instructor contributions during the workshop or course. Without probing, this activity is an opportunity to offer thanks for those acts which brought or deepened care, sensitivity, courage, and humanity among the learning group.
- *Head, Heart, and Hand:* Participants reflect to integrate different dimensions of their learning during the workshop or course. They are asked to report out to the rest of the group *one or more* of the following possibilities. For "Head," each identifies something they will continue to think about as a consequence of the learning experience. For "Heart," each identifies a feeling that has strongly emerged as a result of the learning experience. For "Hand," each identifies a desired action they will take that has been prompted by the learning experience.

Notes

1 Although written for use by a small group, these exercises may be carried out individually as well.
2 Although taken from this memoir, examples from other stories as well as nonfiction may be relevant and useful. Please consider them as well.

Notes and References

Introduction

1 Howard Gardner, Mihaly Csikszentmihalyi, and William Damon, *Good Work: When Excellence and Ethics Meet* (New York: Basic Books, 2002).

Chapter 2: Sister Mary Desiderata

2 Donald R. Cruickshank et al., *Teaching Is Tough* (Upper Saddle River, NJ: Prentice Hall, 1980).
3 For a comprehensive review of the embodiment process, see Paula M. Niedenthal et al., "Embodiment in the Acquisition and Use of Emotion Knowledge," in *Emotion and Consciousness*, eds. Lisa Feldman Barrett, Paula M. Niedenthal, and Piotr Winkielman (New York: Guilford Press, 2005), 21–50.
4 Giacomo Rizzolatti, Leonardo Fogassi, and Vittorio Gallese, "Mirrors in the Mind," *Scientific American*, 295 (2006), 54–61.
5 A. Guy Larkins et al., *Teacher Enthusiasm: A Critical Review* (Hattiesburg, MS: University of Southern Mississippi, 1985). Although behavioral indicators vary across cultures, in this study learners interpreted the teacher's value for the subject through these five actions:
   1. Speaking with some variation in tone, pitch, volume, and speed
   2. Gesturing with arms and hands
   3. Moving around the room to illustrate points and respond to questions
   4. Making varied emotive facial expressions where appropriate
   5. Displaying energy and vitality

Chapter 3: Having a Ball

6 Sigmund Freud, "Interpretation of Dreams", in *The Basic Writings of Sigmund Freud*, ed. and trans. Abraham A. Brill (New York: Random House, 1938). Although *The Interpretation of Dreams* was originally published in 1900, Freud was prescient when he wrote that the processes that give energy to behavior are complex and varied, including multiple influences from the preconscious, unconscious, and conscious. Years later he identified instincts which represent the somatic demands on mental life in Sigmund Freud, *An Outline of Psychoanalysis* (New York: W. W. Norton, 1949) (Originally published in 1938).
7 Harry F. Harlow, Margaret Kuenne Harlow, and Donald R. Meyer, "Learning Motivated by a Manipulation Drive," *Journal of Experimental Psychology*, 40 (1950),

228–234. Harry Harlow and his colleagues found that monkeys solved puzzles for the gratification of manipulating them. A generation later, Edward Deci found that children enjoy putting together a three dimensional puzzle similar to a Rubik's cube for the satisfaction of the task itself. Many of these experiments are reported in Edward L. Deci, *Intrinsic Motivation* (New York: Plenum, 1975).

8   This idea is documented and discussed at length in Raymond J. Wlodkowski and Margery B. Ginsberg, *Enhancing Adult Motivation to Learn: A Comprehensive Guide for Teaching All Adults*, 4th ed. (San Francisco: Jossey-Bass, 2017).

9   This quote is found on page 32 of Mihaly Csikszentmihalyi, *Finding Flow: The Psychology of Engagement with Everyday Life* (New York: Basic Books, 1997), a book that documents flow experiences across cultures and describes why a cherished engrossing interest is worth learning and lasting over time.

10 Fausto Massimini, Mihaly Csikszentmihalyi, and Antonella Delle Fave, "Flow and Biocultural Evolution," in *Optimal Experience: Psychological Studies of Flow in Consciousness*, eds. Mihaly Csikszentmihalyi and Isabella Selega Csikszentmihalyi (New York: Cambridge University Press, 1988), 60–84. This article documents how flow may contribute across cultures to behavior that develops into an evolutionary trend or norm. Similar to a meme, it may be a sense that humans have developed in order to recognize patterns of action that are worth preserving.

11 Jeanne Nakamura and Mihaly Csikszentmihalyi, "The Construction of Meaning through Vital Engagement," in *Flourishing: Positive Psychology and The Life Well-Lived*, eds. Corey Keyes and Jonathan Haidt (Washington, DC: American Psychological Association, 2003), 83–104. This article describes the similar characteristics of a variety of flow experiences.

12 For a detailed description of how to deepen engagement and challenge through flow experiences with adult learners see: Wlodkowski and Ginsberg, *Enhancing Adult Motivation to Learn*, 260–263.

13 The more people meet their needs for autonomy, connectedness, and competence through valued challenging work, the more likely they are to contribute to compassionate and caring societies. This idea is discussed at length in Richard M. Ryan and Edward L. Deci, *Self-Determination Theory: Basic Psychological Needs in Motivation, Development, and Wellness* (New York: The Guilford Press, 2017).

Chapter 4: Doing Duty

14 Emmy E. Werner, "Resilience in Development," *Current Directions in Psychological Science* 4 (1995), 81–85. Children and youth who are better able to appraise stressful life events more accurately are also better able to figure out strategies for coping with adversity.

NOTES AND REFERENCES   181

15 Edwin A. Locke and Gary Latham, "Building a Practically Useful Theory of Goal Setting and Task Motivation," *American Psychologist* 57 (2005), 705–717. When expectancy for learning is high, learners more easily commit to given learning goals, resulting in an increase in their performance and motivation.

16 Bernard Weiner, "Interpersonal and Intrapersonal Theories of Motivation from an Attributional Perspective," *Educational Psychology Review* 12 (2000), 1–14. There is considerable research indicating that *to what* learners attribute their success affects their motivation while learning. Effort is an aspect of behavior over which most learners feel some degree of control. It makes sense that exerting more effort would lead to higher achievement.

17 Victoria C. Plaut and Hazel R. Markus, "The Inside Story: A Cultural-Historical Analysis of Being Smart and Motivated, American Style," in *Handbook of Competence and Motivation,* eds. Andrew J. Elliot and Carol S. Dweck (New York: Guilford Press, 2005), 457–488. When learners realize they are the ones most responsible for their learning, they build self-efficacy and the capacity to bring energy and direction to their learning.

18 Linda Nilson, *Creating Self-Regulated Learners: Strategies to Strengthen Students' Self-Awareness and Learning Skills* (Sterling, VA: Stylus, 2013). An introduction to self-regulated learning and a compendium of learning strategies for faculty to use with students.

19 *Motivation and Teaching: A Practical Guide* which I wrote in in 1978 was one of the first books directly written for teachers on the topic of how to encourage student motivation through the use of teaching strategies in the classroom. It was published by the National Education Association.

20 Richard A. Depue, "A Neurobiological Framework for the Structure of Personality and Emotions: Implications for Personality Disorder," in *Major Theories of Personality*, eds. John Clarkin and Mark Lenzenweger (New York: Guilford Press, 1996), 347–390. This chapter describes how behavioral inhibition systems function.

21 Mihaly Csikszentmihalyi and Barbara Schneider, *Becoming Adult: How Teenagers Prepare for the World of Work* (New York: Basic Books, 2000). Mental discipline and persistence appear to be forms of motivation that are a mix of habit and attitude that have been developed within adults through practice and the modeling of important others. The story of Charles Darwin and the beetles is cited on p. 18.

Chapter 5: Lucking Out

22 Holly S. Hodgins and C. Raymond Knee, "The Integrating Self and Conscious Experience," in *Handbook of Self-Determination Research*, eds. Edward L. Deci and Richard M. Ryan (Rochester, NY: University of Rochester Press, 2002), 87–100. Relevance is intrinsically motivating because it stimulates natural curiosity. We want

to make sense of things that matter to us, and we are prone to seek out challenges to further our understanding.

Chapter 6: Learning to Flow

23 Barry J. Zimmerman and Manuel Martinez-Pons, "Construct Validation of a Strategy Model of Student Self-Regulated Learning," *Journal of Educational Psychology* 80 (1988), 284–290. What I had learned through trial and error were metacognitive skills that are part of a set of self-regulation strategies learners use to maintain engagement and learning through their own agency.

24 Many examples of strategies for deepening engagement and challenge through flow experiences using the characteristics of clear goals, feedback, and challenge are described in Wlodkowski and Ginsberg, *Enhancing Adult Motivation to Learn*, 260–299. For a full discussion of flow see *Living a Motivated Life* see Part 2, Chapter 17. For activities for understanding and feeling the value of flow for adults in courses and professional development see Part 2, Chapter 19.

25 We were immersed in *vital engagement*, a form of flow which is characterized both by experiences of flow (enjoyed absorption) and by meaning (subjective significance). Nakamura and Csikszentmihalyi, "The Construction of Meaning through Vital Engagement," 87. Vital engagement is an ideal state of learning that involves *challenge;* it creates a valued relationship to learning that stretches learners' capacities while completely occupying their interest and participation. For a full discussion of vital engagement in *Living a Motivated Life* see Part 2, Chapter 17.

26 Jack Mezirow, "Learning to Think like an Adult: Core Concepts of Transformation Theory," in *Learning as Transformation: Critical Perspectives on a Theory in Progress*, eds. Jack Mezirow and Associates (San Francisco: Jossey-Bass, 2000), 3–33. Transformative learning refers to learning that results in a deep change in our beliefs, assumptions, or perspectives, making them more discriminating and able to construct opinions that will prove more true to guide our actions. For a full discussion of transformative learning and activities for understanding and feeling its emotional value for adults in courses and professional development see Part 2, Chapters 18 and 19 in *Living a Motivated Life*.

27 Jack Mezirow, "Transformative Learning Theory," in *Transformative Learning in Practice: Insights from Community, Workplace, and Higher Education*, eds. Jack Mezirow and Edward W. Taylor (San Francisco: Jossey-Bass, 2009), 18–31. A more recent discussion of transformative learning by the scholar most responsible for developing transformative theory and its phases of learning.

28 Sharan B. Merriam and Laura L. Bierema, *Adult Learning: Linking Theory and Practice* (San Francisco: Jossey-Bass, 2014), 82–103. This section offers an overview and

critique of transformation theory that contains both a cultural perspective as well as accounts of educators trying to implement and assess transformative learning.

Chapter 7: Transformative Friendship

29 For a discussion of the influence of a transformative friendship or relationship see Edward W. Taylor and Melissa J. Snyder, "A Critical Review of Research on Transformative Learning Theory, 2006–2010," in *The Handbook of Transformative Learning: Theory, Research, and Practice*, eds. Edward W. Taylor and Patricia Cranton (San Francisco: Jossey-Bass, 2012), 37–55.

30 According to Jack Mezirow, this often is a necessary step for the establishment of a perspective transformation in a person's development. Jack Mezirow, *Education for Perspectives of Transformation: Women's Re-Entry Programs in Community Colleges* (New York: Center for Adult Education, Teachers College, Columbia University, 1975).

31 One transformative experience can connect to the next one building a succession of integrated ideas that give adults the motivation to try new roles and risk developing new relationships. Mezirow, "Learning to Think Like an Adult."

32 Finley's regard for me helped me to look further and more deeply to understand with whom I might be intimate and where I might live. Ibid.

33 I didn't tell anyone using this expression because to me such words seemed pretentious. I was 21 years old. It gave my life direction to retain that feeling. I think for most people who love learning it's a quiet certainty, more so than some passionate romance. It's a feeling that gives a peaceful vitality and steady confidence. Wlodkowski and Ginsberg, *Enhancing Adult Motivation to Learn*, 94–96; 262–263.

Chapter 8: Teacher Newbie

34 This rudimentary empathy is essential for people to be effective in the helping professions and can be found among nurses and teachers across various cultures. Marsha Rossiter, "Radical Mutuality and Self-Other Relationship in Adult Education," in *Global Issues and Adult Education: Perspectives from Latin America, Southern Africa, and the United States*, eds. Sharan B. Merriam, Bradley C. Courtenay, and Ronald M. Cervero (San Francisco: Jossey-Bass, 2006), 387–398. Some degree of compassion is an essential ingredient for any excellent teacher. There seems to be universal agreement in the field of education concerning the importance of compassion in teaching adult learners. For centuries, religious and spiritual leaders have used words like "understanding" and "compassion" to describe how fundamental these qualities are for human life on earth.

35 Another transformative learning experience is underway.

36 Fritz Redl and William W. Wattenberg, *Mental Hygiene in Teaching* (New York: Harcourt, Brace & Company, 1951). Fritz Redl and William Wattenberg, professors at Wayne State University, were specialists in human behavior and educational psychology. They presented the first theory-based approach to humane classroom discipline and are considered twentieth century pioneers for their approach to supporting mental health in educational settings.
37 Using the goal of student self-discipline as a means to enhance their character development became a popular idea across education with numerous books and programs leading to the initiation of *The Journal for Social Responsibility and Character Education* in 2004.
38 I didn't personally use this expression or know its meaning yet, but I felt it.

Chapter 9: Teaching Troubles

39 Again, I am going through some of the transformative learning phases as described by Jack Mezirow in "Learning to Think like an Adult": A disorienting dilemma; self-examination with feelings of shame; exploration of options for new actions; and a reintegration into a life based on a new perspective.
40 Redl, *Mental Hygiene in Teaching*, 12.

Chapter 10: There Are Ways

41 M. Suzanne Donovan, John D. Bransford, and James W. Pellegrino, *How People Learn: Bridging Research and Practice.* (Washington, DC: National Academy Press, 1999). Evidence for when learners have a deep understanding of a subject, they are more able to transform mere information into useable knowledge.
42 Mimi Bong and Einar Skaalvik, "Academic Self-Concept and Self-Efficacy: How Different Are They Really?" *Educational Psychology Review* 15 (2003), 1–40. Self-efficacy is a personal assessment of one's capability to perform a specific task. For example the confidence and high self-efficacy one might have for solving algebraic equations among classmates could vary widely from one's lack of confidence and low self-efficacy for playing tennis well among peers. Self-efficacy beliefs are stronger predictors of adult behavior than self-perceptions such as self-concept and self-esteem which have more global meaning and are more powerful predicators for children's behavior.,
43 Jonathan Kozol, *Death at an Early Age: The Destruction of the Hearts and Minds of Negro Children in the Boston Public Schools* (Boston: Houghton Mifflin, 1967). It won the U.S. National Book Award in the Science, Philosophy and Religion category.
44 Bruno Bettelheim, *Love Is Not Enough: The Treatment of Emotionally Disturbed Children* (New York: The Free Press, 1950). Today Bruno Bettelheim is a controversial

figure. His theories on the causes of autism have been largely discredited, and his reporting rates of cure at the Sonia Shankman Orthogenic School have been questioned.

45 Karl Halvor Teigen, "Luck: The Art of a Near Miss," *Scandinavian Journal of Psychology* 37 (1996), 156–171. Since there was no way to determine how much the other doctoral candidates deserved admittance to the program and clearly the reason given for my rejection was "merit," I attributed my near miss to causes such as insufficient knowledge and experience rather than "bad luck." I could control for these determining factors in the future through greater effort and learning. Thus, I could reasonably expect more success as a psychologist.

46 Jacob S. Kounin, *Discipline and Group Management in Classrooms* (New York: Holt, Rinehart and Winston, Inc., 1970). His most influential book is considered a classic in the analysis of authentic, ongoing classroom teacher and student behavior. It offers concrete, non-punitive techniques to manage students and to increase their motivation to learn.

47 Eveoleen N. Rexford, "The Life Space Interview Workshop, 1957, Strategy and Techniques of the Life Space Interview," *American Journal of Orthopsychiatry* 29 (1959), 1–18. Emotional first aid is one of the basic techniques of the Life Space Interview, an intervention method originally developed by Dr. Redl to provide emotional support using events surrounding a youth's disruptive actions to expand his understanding of the behavior and the responses of others. Emotional first aid is still advocated today among mental health professionals as a means to assist people who are experiencing "floods" of emotion and includes strategies such as having a drink of water, taking a walk, or assisting the person to breath evenly.

48 Wlodkowski and Ginsberg, *Enhancing Adult Motivation to Learn*. This book contains sixty documented motivational strategies for teaching adults.

49 Kounin, *Discipline and Group Management in Classrooms*.

50 Ivan Illich, *Deschooling Society* (New York, Harper and Row, 1971).

51 Neil Postman and Charles Weingartner, *Teaching as a Subversive Activity* (New York: Delta, 1969). With an apple emitting a burning fuse on the cover, it was one of many books advocating, or better yet, shouting for a radical change in how people learned in schools.

52 Robert Rosenthal and Lenore Jacobson, *Pygmalion in the Classroom: Teacher Expectation and Pupils' Intellectual Development* (New York: Holt, Rinehart and Winston, 1968).

53 Raymond J. Wlodkowski, "The Effect of Dissonance and Arousal on Assignment Performance as They Relate to Student Expectancy and Teacher Support Characteristics," *Journal of Educational Research* 67 (1973), 23–28. A refereed journal article that summarizes the findings of my dissertation.

54 Locke and Latham, "Building a Practically Useful Theory of Goal Setting and Task Motivation." This article summarizes the findings from the vast field of expectancy research.

Chapter 11: Entering a Life of Study

55 B. F. Skinner, *Beyond Freedom and Dignity* (New York: Knopf, 1971). In this book, the most influential psychologist of his day and advocate for operant conditioning offers his philosophical treatise that people can achieve a better society and greater well-being by letting go of their pretensions concerning the freedom and dignity of man. He explains why it is necessary for human beings to take total control of their evolution by consciously designing an entire culture that it will shape the behavior needed for survival. On the New York Times best seller's list for twenty-six weeks, it was probably the most debated book in academe for a decade after its publication.

56 The students rewarded me for these efforts by nominating me for the university teaching award which I received in 1973.

Chapter 12: Human Relations

57 Albert Bandura, "Self-Efficacy Mechanism in Human Agency," *American Psychologist* 37 (1982), 122–147. The powerful influence of models whom we observe and with which we identify was originally derived from the research of Albert Bandura.

58 Barry J. Zimmerman and Anastasia Kitsantas, "The Hidden Dimension of Personal Competence: Self-Regulated Learning and Practice," in *Handbook of Competence and Motivation*, eds. Andrew J. Elliot and Carol S. Dweck (New York: Guilford, 2005), 509–526. A compendium of research studies that offers evidence in academics and athletics of the motivation and success of people who learn vicariously from models in their lives. See also Nicole M. Stephens, Andrea G. Dittmann, and Sarah S. M. Townsend, "Social Class and Models of Competence," in *Handbook of Competence and Motivation,* 2nd eds. Andrew J. Elliot, Carol S. Dweck, and David S. Yeager (New York: Guilford, 2017), 512–528.

59 Paulo Freire, *Pedagogy of the Oppressed* (New York: Continuum, 1970).

60 David Benjamin Oppenheimer, "Martin Luther King, Walker v. City of Birmingham, and the Letter from Birmingham Jail." *UC Davis L. Rev.* 26 (1992), 791.

61 Maggi Savin-Baden, *Facilitating Problem-Based Learning* (Berkshire, England: Open University Press, 2003). The book offers a variety of useful problem-based learning methods.

62 Jeannie Brooks-Gunn and Greg J. Duncan, "The Effects of Poverty on Children," *The Future of Children* (1997), July 55–71. This article examines the relationships and the consequences for children who grow up poor.
63 Ian M. Harris, "Criteria for Evaluating School Desegregation in Milwaukee," *Journal of Negro Education* 52 (1983), 423–435.
64 "Magnet School Failures Recited," *Milwaukee Sentinel* (November 5, 1976), Part 1, 6.
65 Erin Richards and Lydia Mulvany, "60 Years after Brown v. Board of Education, Intense Segregation Returns" *Milwaukee Sentinel* (May 17, 2014). http://www.jsonline.com/news/education/60-years-after-brown-v-board-of-education-intense-segregation-returns-b99271365z1-259682171.html
66 Jack Dougherty, *More than One Struggle: The Evolution of Black School Reform in Milwaukee* (Chapel Hill, NC: The University of North Carolina Press, 2004), 161.
67 "Lengthy School Strike Feared," *Milwaukee Sentinel* (April 19, 1977). http://www.mu.edu/cgi-bin/cuap/db.cgi?uid=default&ID=3901&view=Search&mh=1
68 "Black Teachers to Ignore Strike," *Milwaukee Sentinel* (April 4, 1977). Part 1, 5.
69 "Blacks Put Crimp in MTEA Solidarity," *The Milwaukee Journal* (April 21, 1977), 1, 4.
70 "From Teachers' Viewpoints," *The Milwaukee Journal* (April 21, 1977), Editorial Page.
71 "Labor Not an Ally for Teachers," *The Milwaukee Journal* (April 12, 1977), 5.
72 "Pupils Hold Rally, Ask End of Strike," *Milwaukee Sentinel* (April 15, 1977), 1.
73 "Disciplinary Probes Start in Picketing," *Milwaukee Sentinel* (April 25, 1977), Part 1, 1.
74 "Strikers Protest En Masse," *The Milwaukee Journal* (April 28, 1977), 1.
75 "Schools pay Non strikers for Damages," *The Milwaukee Journal* (May 17, 1977), 1.
76 Harris, "Criteria for Evaluating School Desegregation in Milwaukee." 424.
77 "Hope for the Schools," *Newsweek* (May 4, 1981), 69.
78 Harris, "Criteria for Evaluating School Desegregation in Milwaukee," 423–435.
79 Richards and Mulvany, "60 Years after Brown v. Board of Education, Intense Segregation Returns."
80 James K. Nelsen, *From No Choice to Forced Choice to School Choice: A History of Educational Options in Milwaukee Public Schools* (Doctoral Dissertation, University of Wisconsin-Milwaukee, 2012).

Chapter 13: Therapy Lessons

81 Raymond J. Wlodkowski, *Motivation and Teaching: A Practical Guide* (Washington, DC: National Education Association, 1978), 7.
82 Virginia Axline, *Dibs in Search of Self* (New York: Ballantine, 1964).
83 Frederick Perls, Ralph Hefferline, and Paul Goodman, *Gestalt Therapy: Excitement and Growth in the Human Personality* (New York: Julian, 1951). The book that most influenced our initial work in the Milwaukee Gestalt Training Group.

84 Raymond J. Wlodkowski, *Motivation to Learn: How Parents and Teachers Can Help* (Alexandria, VA: Association for Supervision and Curriculum Development, 1990).
85 Rick Smith and Mary Lambert, "The Positive Classroom," *Educational Leadership*, 66 (2008), 16–21. This article describes how to implement the Two-by-Ten Strategy.

Chapter 14: Adult Learning

86 Malcolm S. Knowles, *The Modern Practice of Adult Education: From Pedagogy to Andragogy*, 2nd ed. (New York: Cambridge Books, 1980). A comprehensive treatment of the need, theory, and research that supports andragogy for adult learners. Though highly respected, most adult learning scholars today would consider this book dated and regard adult learning as more complex and culturally influenced.
87 Carol E. Kasworm, Amy D. Rose, and Jovita M. Ross-Gordon, eds. *Handbook of Adult and Continuing Education: 2010 Edition*. (Thousand Oaks, CA: Sage, 2010). For an overview of the depth and expanse of adult education as a discipline, this is a fine book to peruse.
88 Wlodkowski and Ginsberg, *Enhancing Adult Motivation to Learn*. This book is now in its fourth edition.

Chapter 15: Perspectives and Connections

89 Finley Hooper, *Greek Realities: Life and Thought in Ancient Greece* (New York: Charles Scribner's Sons, 1967).
90 Carol Kasworm, "Enhancing Adult Motivation to Learn: A Comprehensive Guide for Teaching All Adults," *The Review of Higher Education* 32 (2009), 280–281. This review contains a concise overview and critique of the contents of the third edition of this book.)
91 Raymond J. Wlodkowski, "An Analysis of the History, Status, and Impact of Peer Coaching at the British Columbia Institute of Technology," *Report to the Learning Skills Center of the British Columbia Institute of Technology* (Vancouver: British Columbia Institute of Technology, 1992).
92 Horace Mann, *Horace Mann on the Crisis in Education* (Antioch, OH: Antioch Press, 1865). His landmark book remains a significant progressive influence on the philosophy of education practiced throughout Antioch University.
93 Wlodkowski and Ginsberg, *Enhancing Adult Motivation to Learn*, 20–28. Degree and certificate completion among underserved and diverse adult learners in postsecondary education is a complex dynamic which has to be seen through the lenses of income, race, gender, ethnicity, age, and disability to more fully understand the troubling disparities and challenges that emerge.

94 Larry A. Samovar, Richard E. Porter, and Edwin R. McDaniel, *Intercultural Communication: A Reader*, 13th ed. (Boston: Wadsworth Publishing, 2012). A useful book to explore how communication, values, and styles can be similar or different for members of various cultures and communities.

Chapter 16: Conversations of Respect

95 Margery B. Ginsberg and Raymond J. Wlodkowski, *Diversity and Motivation: Culturally Responsive Teaching in* College, 2nd ed. (San Francisco: Jossey-Bass, 2009). The current edition of the book we wrote in 1995. Both editions contain the Motivational Framework for Culturally Responsive Teaching, an internationally recognized and researched model to design lessons and create intrinsically motivating learning environments for learners from culturally diverse backgrounds.

Part 2

Chapter 17: An Overview of Intrinsic Motivation, Flow, and Vital Engagement

96 John J. Ratey, *A User's Guide to the Brain: Perception, Attention, and the Four Theatres of the Brain* (New York: Pantheon, 2001), 247.
97 Wlodkowski and Ginsberg, *Enhancing Adult Motivation to Learn.*
98 Paul R. Pintrich, ed. Special Issue: "Current Issues and New Directions in Motivational Theory and Research," *Education Psychologist* 26 (1991), 199–205.
99 Ehud Ahissar et al., "Dependence of Cortical Plasticity on Correlated Activity of Single Neurons and on Behavioral Context," *Science* 257 (1992), 1412–1415.
100 Richard M. Ryan and Edward L. Deci, "When Rewards Compete with Nature: The Undermining of Intrinsic Motivation and Self-Regulation," in *Intrinsic and Extrinsic Motivation: The Search for Optimal Motivation and Performance*, eds. Carol Sansone and Judith M. Harackiewicz (San Diego: Academic Press, 2000), 14–56.
101 Coalition for Psychology in Schools & Education, *Top 20 Principles from Psychology for PreK–12 Teaching and Learning* (Washington, DC: American Psychological Association, 2015), 16.
102 Wlodkowski and Ginsberg, *Enhancing Adult Motivation to Learn.* Ryan and Deci, *Self-Determination Theory.* Daniel H. Pink, *Drive: The Surprising Truth about What Motivates Us* (New York: Riverhead Books, 2009).
103 Sharan B. Merriam, B., Rosemary S. Caffarella, and Lisa M. Baumgartner, *Learning in Adulthood: A Comprehensive Guide* 3rd ed. (Hoboken, NJ: John Wiley & Sons Inc., 2007).

104 Jere Brophy, *Motivating Students to Learn* 2nd ed. (Mahwah, NJ: Erlbaum, 2004).
105 Csikszentmihalyi, *Finding Flow*, 32.
106 Massimini, Csikszentmihalyi, and Delle Fave, "Flow and Biocultural Evolution."
107 Nakamura and Csikszentmihalyi, "The Construction of Meaning through Vital Engagement."
108 Jeanne Nakamura, "The Nature of Vital Engagement in Adulthood," *New Directions for Child and Adolescent Development* 93 (San Francisco: Jossey-Bass, 2001), 8, 5–18.
109 Sharon Daloz Parks et al., *Common Fire: Leading Lives of Commitment in a Complex World* (Boston: Beacon Press, 1996).
110 Nakamura, "The Nature of Vital Engagement in Adulthood."
111 Nakamura, "The Nature of Vital Engagement in Adulthood," 16.
112 Anne Colby and William Damon, *Some Do Care* (New York: Simon and Schuster, 2010).
113 Nakamura, "The Nature of Vital Engagement in Adulthood." Ryan and Deci, *Self-Determination Theory*. Victor E. Frankl, *Man's Search for Meaning* (Boston: Beacon Press, 2006).
114 John Dewey, *Art as Experience* (New York: Perigee Books, 1934).

Chapter 18: Transformative Learning: A Partner to Intrinsic Motivation throughout Life

115 Mezirow, "Learning to think like an adult."
116 John M. Dirkx, "Images, Transformative Learning, and the Work of Soul," *Adult Learning* 12 (2001), 15–16.
117 Michael Kroth and Patricia Cranton, *Stories of Transformative Learning* (Rotterdam, The Netherlands: Sense Publishers, 2014), 9.
118 Mezirow, "Perspective Transformation."
119 Dirkx, "Images, Transformative Learning, and the Work of Soul."
120 Freire, *Pedagogy of the Oppressed*.
121 Christine Jarvis, "Fiction and Film and Transformative Learning," in *The Handbook of Transformative Learning: Theory, Research, and Practice,* eds. Edward W. Taylor and Patricia Cranton San Francisco: Jossey-Bass, 2012), 486–502. Kroth and Cranton, *Stories of Transformative Learning*.
122 Jerold W. Apps, *Teaching from the Heart* (Malabar, FL: Krieger, 1996).
123 Laurent Daloz, *Effective Teaching and Mentoring* (San Francisco: Jossey-Bass, 1986), 24.
124 Kroth and Cranton, *Stories of Transformative Learning*, xv.

Chapter 19: Learning to Evoke and Sustain Intrinsic Motivation with Transformative Learning

125 Csikszentmihalyi and Csikszentmihalyi, *Optimal Experience*.
126 Kroth and Cranton, *Stories of Transformative Learning*, 103.
127 Wlodkowski and Ginsberg, *Enhancing Adult Motivation to Learn*.
128 Judith Barrington, *Writing the Memoir* (Portland, OR: Eighth Mountain Press, 2002).
129 Mary Karr, *The Art of Memoir* (New York: HarperCollins, 2015).
130 Barrington, *Writing the Memoir*.
131 Barrington, *Writing the Memoir*.

www.ingramcontent.com/pod-product-compliance
Lightning Source LLC
Chambersburg PA
CBHW021142230426
43667CB00005B/219